CONTENTS

KV-638-714

Note: All newly introduced countries and PTTs are in **bold** type.

The Stanley Gibbons Catalogue of

Telephone Cards

S.E.R. HISCOCKS

Stanley Gibbons Publications Limited · Ringwood & London

© Dr S.E.R. Hiscocks (1990)

ISBN   0 85259 264 7

Published by

Stanley Gibbons Publications Limited
Parkside
Christchurch Road
Ringwood
Hants. BH24 3SH
England

in association with

Dr S.E.R.Hiscocks
P.O.Box 77
Woking
Surrey, GU22 0HB
England

Printed by

Acorn Litho Colour Printers Ltd
The Foxwood Press,
Old Woking,
Surrey,
GU22 9LH
England.

PREFACE

The hobby of collecting telephone cards has made enormous strides since the first edition of this book was published in the Autumn of 1988. Not only has the availability of information on the many interesting and attractive telephone cards issued around the world over the past ten years brought many enthusiastic new collectors into the field but the telephone companies and the card and telephone manufacturers have also been quick to appreciate the potential of the hobby and to act accordingly. The sixty-two countries listed in the first edition have now grown to around a hundred and yet further new countries and telephone companies are known to be preparing to adopt prepayment telephone card systems in the near future.

A further encouraging development is the emergence of specialists prepared to carry out detailed research into varieties of the more common, usually definitive, cards of those countries where collecting is strong. Scholarly papers are beginning to appear to the amazement of the manufacturers of the cards who are, for the most part, unconscious of the small variations that creep into their manufacturing processes and are astonished that anyone should care. There is, at the time of writing, no journal specifically for telephone card collectors but several major philatelic journals such as Gibbons Stamp Monthly in the UK and Le Monde des Philatélistes in France now carry regular features on the hobby and nearly all album producers have introduced albums for telephone cards over the past year or so. There are now dealers in most European countries. The hobby, after a remarkably short childhood, is coming of age.

Now that the number of cards is growing to the point that the building up of a comprehensive world collection is difficult and expensive, some collectors are beginning to turn to thematic collecting (or topical collecting as it is called in the USA). Satellites and earth stations, automobiles and telephones are some that I have come across but there must be others.

Another development is the collecting of what might be termed peripherals – the envelopes and wallets in which some cards are supplied, the little booklets of instructions that come with some, the advertising material supplied to telephone card outlets by the PTTs and so on. Taiwan for example carries advertising on the plastic envelopes for their cards. There are, I think, four varieties of the sealed sachets in which BT cards are supplied and there were several special types of the earlier open envelopes some of which, for example the Wimbledon envelope, are highly prized. Mercury have for the last two years adopted their favourite design from their Christmas telephone cards for their corporate Christmas card; they used the design for the Aladdin card in 1989 and it is a beautiful and already much sought after item.

Not all developments have been for the better. There is a worrying tendency in a few countries for large numbers of very limited issue cards to appear and immediately to command very high prices. Since the number of ~~~~~~~~~~~~~~~ ~~~~~~~~~~~~~~~~~~~~ ~~~~~~~~~~~~~~~~~~~~~ less than the number of collectors in the country, the result is predictably that ordinary collectors, who can never hope to build up anything like a complete collection, become discouraged. Some are turning to specialisation in the definitives of their countries, some to collecting the cards of other countries and some, unfortunately, are giving up the hobby altogether. 'Responsible issuing policy' is a phrase well known in the stamp world and the postal authorities of the vast majority of countries have learned over many years that, in the long run, such policies are to everyone's advantage. It is perhaps inevitable that history should repeat itself but it is to be hoped that the process can be completed in the telephone card field before too much damage is done.

In this book I have tried to include all cards issued up to the date of sending the manuscript to the printer in all countries of the world except for those of Japan where a recent count of the cards in the Japanese catalogues came up with a total of around 21,500. Clearly it is not possible to include the cards of Japan in such a book as this. It will be noticed that the information I am able to give for some countries, Belgium, France, Netherlands and the UK for example, is much more detailed than for others. Most of the the manufacturers and the PTTs are very helpful but they do not in general understand collecting and are not themselves aware of the differences which are important to us. The more detailed information can only come from enthusiastic collectors and, if your country is not covered as well as it might be, it is probably because no knowledgeable collector from your country has yet contacted me. I am always happy to receive new information (and always reply - eventually) but please note that I can only correspond in English.

Some explanations:

Prices. All prices in the English language edition of this book are in pounds sterling. Where I can, I have reflected market prices at the time of going to press but in many cases I have had to attempt a reasonable guess in the light of the number of cards originally produced, the number likely to have survived, the popularity of that country and so on. I have tried to reflect real prices rather than the somewhat inflated prices sometimes asked, but not necessarily demanded, by some dealers. Where it can be seen, without access to a payphone of that country, whether the card has been used or not, I give different prices for unused (in the left column) and used (in the right column). Where the collector outside the country of issue cannot tell whether a card is used or not, I give a single price which is effectively the price of a used card in good condition. If such cards can be seen to be unused, for example in the case of many French cards still sealed in their plastic sachets, a higher price than that which I give might be justified. Prices have risen rapidly over the past year and it is likely that those here will appear a little low before long. Finally, please note that I am not a dealer and I do not sell cards. Like all collectors, I exchange cards but I have no particular interest in setting high prices.

I separate the cards into several categories. These include: 'Complimentary', which are cards given out by the telephone companies, usually to introduce customers to cardphones when they are installed for the first time. 'Definitive', which are the ordinary day-to-day cards which continue in use for some time and are reprinted as required. 'Special' cards are those issued for a limited period and which may be commemorative or merely decorative but which are in most cases issued in reasonable quantities and are available to the general public through the normal channels of distribution. 'Advertising' cards carry advertisements and are generally available to collectors either through normal channels or to anyone buying the advertised product. 'Private' cards are usually advertising but may be commemorative, official gift cards and so on. They are produced in limited editions, generally of a thousand or so, and are not available to the general public through normal PTT channels or to purchasers of the advertised products but are owned and distributed privately by the sponsor. 'Closed User Group' cards are available only to people in a restricted location such as a prison, hospital, hotel or ship and are often not usable anywhere else.

A French language edition of this book entitled 'Le Guide Mondial de Cartes-Téléphone' with prices in French francs is also available through all good stockists in France or directly from myself or from Stanley Gibbons.

Happy collecting!

P.O. Box 77
WOKING
Steve Hiscocks   Surrey
                                                        GU22 0HB
April, 1990   UK

ACKNOWLEDGEMENTS

In compiling this catalogue I have received generous help from many people and organizations which have provided information and specimens of their cards for illustration. I should particularly mention the following:

Mick Herbert, Chairman of British Telecom's Phonecard Collector Club, for much help with the cards of British Telecom,

Rowena Allen of Mercury Telecommunications Ltd, UK, for keeping me completely up to date on the Mercury and Paytelco cards and for providing illustrations of their cards.

Many friends at Cable and Wireless plc, UK, but especially Clifford Redwood and Dwayne Taylor for help in the Atlantic and Carribean areas and to Mare-Claude Syddall both for help in the middle and far east areas and for proof reading part of the text of the French edition.

Mary Radcliffe of Landis and Gyr, UK, and Bernard Hornung of Landis and Gyr, Switzerland, manufacturers of optical telephone cards for many countries, for generous help with all those countries for which they supply cards.

Jane Windsor and Carole Sweeney at GEC-Plessey Telecommunication Ltd., UK, (GPT), suppliers of magnetic telephone cards and systems for many countries, for much information and many illustrations.

Johannes Kaufmann of the Deutches Bundespost for much information on the cards of Germany and for lending me the 'official' DBP collection to provide illustrations.

Marc Schindler and his colleagues of Schlumberger Industries, France, for information and illustrations for the growing number of countries outside France for which they supply cards and systems.

Rod Galloway and his colleagues at Telecom Australia for much help and support.

Martin Zeh of Autelca, AG/SA/Ltd, Switzerland, for help with Korea and Brunei.

Yves Girardot of Bull CP8, France, for help on the new cards of Spain.

J. Van Eenoo of Bell-Alcatel, Belgium for information on their cards for China.

Janez Zabasu of Muflon, Yugoslavia, for help with that country.

Daniel Jouet of L'Avant Musée in Paris for information on and permission to illustrate those 'art cards' which he publishes.

Representatives of other PTTs have been equally helpful in providing me with information and samples or illustrations and I should also thank Tony Small of Manx Telecom; Mary Leslie of Telecom Eireann; Ian Cowley of Hong Kong Telephone; Valli Christensen of KTAS, Kim Jörstad of Fyns Telefon and P.R.Nielsen of Jydsk Telefon, all of Denmark; Terry Mangos of New Zealand; Peter Goldsmith of Comsat; Geoff Hanlon of the British Virgin Islands; Xian Shao Hua of Shenda in China; Barry Laine of IPL in the UK; Raimo Pöntynen and Juhani Tapiola of P&T, Finland; Eva Bengtssen of Swedish Telecom; David Barden of Grantel (Grenada); R.P.Lawrence of Jersey Telecoms; Eva Lo of CTM, Macau; J.A.Payet of Seychelles Telephones; Trevor Sylvester of Textel (Trinadad and Tobago); and Lee Chow Chye of Telecom Singapore who has, I hope, forgiven me for omitting his country from the first edition.

I am most grateful to all of them.

In addition, I have received generous help from many collectors from around the world. To list them all would take several pages but I must express my especial gratitude to Alex Rendon (USA) and Tony Winter (France) for advice, information and illustrations for many countries, Jelle Sietsma (Netherlands), Carlos Demunter and Ferre De Groote (Belgium), Ciro Marta, Marcello Cecconi and Dr Bombrini for much help on Italy, and to Andrew Goodall, Peter Harradine, Dev Sooranna, Jeff Brook-Smith, Brian Willett, Eric Elias, Alain Maton and many other friends for continuing help in many areas.

Last, but far from least, I must acknowledge my enormous debt of gratitude to Monique Berly who has laboured throughout the past eighteen months to keep me informed of developments in France and, without whose efforts, coverage of France would simply not have been possible

ALGERIA

Optical cards are manufactured by Landis and Gyr in Switzerland. Only definitive cards have been issued specifically for Algeria. General service cards have been issued in several countries for which Landis and Gyr have supplied. That illustrated below, with the number '11' in the arrows, has been used in Algeria, Morocco, Finland, Tunisia, Saudi Arabia, and Senegal. Those with '22' in the arrows have been used in Curaçao and Iceland and also reportedly in Mali, Tchad and the Central African Republic. The unit for Algeria represents 0.5 Dinar. It has been reported that French-made smart cards have been or are about to be issued in Algeria but no further information is available at present.

D1

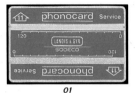

01

First Issue. 1.5mm white band over optical strip.

Nº	Ill.	Units	Date	Description	Value	
D1	(D1)	50	7/85	Green / silver (5567)	75.00 ◻	50.00 ◻

Second Issue. 2mm white band

Nº	Ill.	Units	Date	Description	Value	
D2	(D1)	50	1986	Green / silver, Control: numbers only (1000)	90.00 ◻	75.00 ◻
D3	(D1)	50	1986	·· ·· ·· ·· Control with letter (10,000)	25.00 ◻	15.00 ◻

Note. It is not known whether either D2 or D3 exists with both 3.2mm and 4.5mm gaps in the green background (see under Belgium for further information on these varieties).

Third Issue. 4mm white band

Nº	Ill.	Units	Date	Description	Value	
D4	(D1)	10	6/87	Green / silver (60,000)	10.00 ◻	6.00 ◻
D5	(D1)	50	6/87	·· ·· ·· ·· (21,600)	25.00 ◻	15.00 ◻

Fourth Issue. 3mm white band. Notched.

Nº	Ill.	Units	Date	Description	Value	
D6	D1	50	1988	Green / silver (28,000)	15.00 ◻	10.00 ◻

O - OFFICIAL/SERVICE CARD (see note above)

Nº	Ill.	Units	Date	Description	Value	
O1	O1	240	Various	Blue / silver	--- ◻	30.00 ◻

ANGUILLA

Magnetic cards supplied by GPT (UK) are about to be introduced.

First Issue. Magnetic cards by GPT.

D1

Nº	Ill.	Units	Date	Description	Value
D1	D1	EC$5.40	1989	Multicolour (1000)	20.00 ◻
D2	(D1)	EC$10	1989	Multicolour (25,000)	10.00 ◻
D3	(D1)	EC$20	1989	Multicolour (10,000)	15.00 ◻
D4	(D1)	EC$40	1989	Multicolour (5000)	20.00 ◻

Note. D1 is included in the Cable and Wireless collectors pack of British West Indies cards (see under Promotional Cards at the end of this book).

ANTIGUA AND BARBUDA

Magnetic cards supplied by GPT (UK) are about to be introduced.

First Issue. Magnetic cards by GPT.

D1

Nº	Ill.	Units	Date	Description	Value
D1	*D1*	EC$5.40	1989	Multicolour (1000)	20.00 ☐
D2	*(D1)*	EC$10	1989	Multicolour (15,000)	10.00 ☐
D3	*(D1)*	EC$20	1989	Multicolour (10,000)	15.00 ☐
D4	*(D1)*	EC$40	1989	Multicolour (5000)	20.00 ☐

Note.   D1 is included in the Cable and Wireless collectors pack of British West Indies cards (see under Promotional Cards at the end of this book).

ARUBA

Aruba is, like the group of island comprising Curaçao (q.v.), part of what used to be called the Netherlands Antilles in the Carribean.   It issues seperate cards, also manufactured by Landis and Gyr in Switzerland.   The unit is 0.25 AFL.

D - DEFINITIVE CARDS.

First Issue. 3mm white band over optical strip. Notched.

D1

Nº	Ill.	Units	Date	Description			Value	
D1	*(D1)*	10	9/89	Blue / silver		(4000)	12.00 ☐	4.00 ☐
D2	*D1*	20	9/89	·· ·· ··		(4000)	15.00 ☐	5.00 ☐
D3	*(D1)*	60	9/89	·· ·· ··	(28,000)		6.00 ☐	2.00 ☐
D4	*(D1)*	240	9/89	·· ·· ··		(6000)	15.00 ☐	5.00 ☐

Note.   The Service and Test cards are of the general Landis and Gyr type with the number '22' in the arrows.

ASCENSION ISLAND

Cards have been supplied by Autelca Ltd, Switzerland, to Cable and Wireless for use on Ascension. Control numbers are in black. Magnetic cards supplied by GPT are now being introduced.

AD1

AD1 (reverse)

CONDITIONS OF USE

1. This card is not refundable
2. Do not bend
3. Payphone will not accept damaged cards
4. For time per unit please see display in booth
5. Valid for use in country of purchase only

C1

D1

D2

AD - DEFINITIVE CARDS (Autelca)

Nº	Ill.	Units	Date	Description		Value
AD1	AD1	17	1985	Silver, blue / white	(?0,000)	8.00 ☐
AD2	(AD1)	50	1985	Green, blue / white	(20,000)	10.00 ☐
AD3	(AD1)	100	1985	Light blue, blue / white	(?0,000)	25.00 ☐
AD4	(AD1)	200	1985	Red, blue / white	(?0,000)	30.00 ☐

Note. Most Autelca cards (except for that for Finland, the pictorial cards and the test card types used in Nigeria, Thailand, Sri Lanka, and Yugoslavia) have inscriptions on the reverse and that shown above is typical although usually the country of issue is named.

GPT CARDS

C - COMLIMENTARY CARD

Nº	Ill.	Units	Date	Description		Value
C1	C1	(£?)	1/90	ASCENSION FRIGATE BIRD, Multicolour	(100)	50.00 ☐

D - DEFINITIVE CARDS

Nº	Ill.	Units	Date	Description		Value
D1	D1	£5	1/90	WHITE BOOBY, Multicolour	(3500)	12.00 ☐
D2	D2	£10	1/90	FAIRY TERN, Multicolour	(6000)	15.00 ☐
D3	(C1)	£15	1/90	ASCENSION FRIGATE BIRD, Multicolour	(500)	65.00 ☐

AUSTRALIA

The issue of telephone cards in Australia for engineering trials began on 26 December, 1989, in and around the town of Geelong on the Bellarine peninsular in the state of Victoria. Thirty telephones are being installed. The cards and telephones are manufactured by Anritsu of Japan. As with all Japanese cards, a hole is punched at the end of each call and used cards are thus easily distinguished. These field trials are being followed by market trials of six more cards in Adelaide, South Australia, in March, 1990.

Cards may be bought from Stanley Gibbons in the UK or directly from: Sue Bailey/ Telecom Australia Payphone Services / PO Box 3964 / PARRAMATTA, NSW 2124 / Australia. The set of six costs $A23.50. Cheques or postal orders made out to 'Telecom Australia Payphone Services'. Add $A3.00 postage and handling for the first set and $A2.00 for each additional set. Price from Stanley Gibbons is £11.10 plus £2.50 postage and handling - cheque, postal order or credit card.

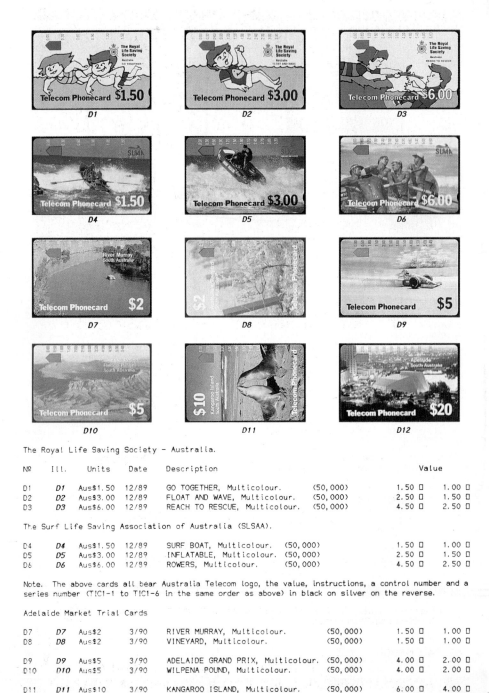

The Royal Life Saving Society - Australia.

Nº	Ill.	Units	Date	Description		Value	
D1	D1	Aus$1.50	12/89	GO TOGETHER, Multicolour.	(50,000)	1.50 ☐	1.00 ☐
D2	D2	Aus$3.00	12/89	FLOAT AND WAVE, Multicolour.	(50,000)	2.50 ☐	1.50 ☐
D3	D3	Aus$6.00	12/89	REACH TO RESCUE, Multicolour.	(50,000)	4.50 ☐	2.50 ☐

The Surf Life Saving Association of Australia (SLSAA).

D4	D4	Aus$1.50	12/89	SURF BOAT, Multicolour.	(50,000)	1.50 ☐	1.00 ☐
D5	D5	Aus$3.00	12/89	INFLATABLE, Multicolour.	(50,000)	2.50 ☐	1.50 ☐
D6	D6	Aus$6.00	12/89	ROWERS, Multicolour.	(50,000)	4.50 ☐	2.50 ☐

Note. The above cards all bear Australia Telecom logo, the value, instructions, a control number and a series number (TIC1-1 to TIC1-6 in the same order as above) in black on silver on the reverse.

Adelaide Market Trial Cards

D7	D7	Aus$2	3/90	RIVER MURRAY, Multicolour.	(50,000)	1.50 ☐	1.00 ☐
D8	D8	Aus$2	3/90	VINEYARD, Multicolour.	(50,000)	1.50 ☐	1.00 ☐
D9	D9	Aus$5	3/90	ADELAIDE GRAND PRIX, Multicolour.	(50,000)	4.00 ☐	2.00 ☐
D10	D10	Aus$5	3/90	WILPENA POUND, Multicolour.	(50,000)	4.00 ☐	2.00 ☐
D11	D11	Aus$10	3/90	KANGAROO ISLAND, Multicolour.	(50,000)	6.00 ☐	4.00 ☐
D12	D12	Aus$20	3/90	ADELAIDE, Multicolour.	(50,000)	12.00 ☐	6.00 ☐

Australia Calling...

All International Telephone Card Collectors

Telephone card collecting, or Cartelegery, is becoming one of the world's fastest growing and most rewarding hobbies. As more and more countries develop their telephone card networks, the number and variety of cards available is rapidly increasing and providing collectors with a wealth of new material to choose from. Now you can keep right up to date with all the latest news and new releases throughout the world by joining
THE INTERNATIONAL TELEPHONE CARD EXCHANGE.
Located at the Australian Telecom Phonecard offices, this club has been established to meet the growing needs of collectors from all parts of the globe.

Consider some of the immediate advantages:
• FREE membership.
• FREE new members starter pack.
• Regular International newsletter.
• Access to advance information on new Australian Telecom Phonecard releases and preferred purchase arrangements.
• One-stop information source for telephone cards from all major world networks.
• A medium through which you can directly communicate with other collectors throughout the world.

To register as a member and receive your free starter pack, simply mail this coupon.

MAIL TO: SUE BAILEY, TELECOM AUSTRALIA PAYPHONE SERVICES,
P.O. BOX 3964, PARRAMATTA,
NSW 2124, AUSTRALIA   **Telecom Australia**

Please enrol me in The International Telephone Card Exchange and send me my free Members Starter Pack.

NAME ....

ADDRESS ....

.... POSTCODE................................... COUNTRY....................

AGE GROUP: UNDER 10 ☐ 11-20 ☐ 21-30 ☐ 31-40 ☐ 41-50 ☐ 51-60 ☐ OVER 60 ☐

OCCUPATION OR BUSINESS ....

Optical cards are manufactured by Landis and Gyr, Switzerland. The earliest issue was as in illustration *D1* below. The white band was introduced later to improve the performance of the system and this band was subsequently widened from 1.5mm to 2mm, then to 4mm and finally reduced to 3mm as in most countries employing the optical system. The laquer over the optical strip is 'thermographic' and shows a black mark at the end of each call thus making it easier for the user to see how many units remain unused. Advertising cards have appeared but not Special or Commemorative cards. The unit equates to 1 Austrian Schilling.

D - DEFINITIVE CARDS

First Issue. No white band.

Nº	Ill.	Units	Date	Description	Value	
D1	*D1*	100	7/81	Yellow / silver (92,337)	15.00 ☐	10.00 ☐

Second Issue. Design changed to omit 'Ihre'.

D2	*D2*	100	9/83	Yellow on silver (318,000)	12.00 ☐	7.50 ☐

Note. Records suggest that, of the above, 16,000 were protected by a layer of laquer.

Third Series - 1.5mm white bar introduced over optical strip.

D3	(D3)	50	9/84	Metallic green, white / silver (350,000)	15.00 ☐	7.00 ☐
D4	*D4*	100	9/84	Metallic gold, white / silver (861,400)	25.00 ☐	10.00 ☐

Fourth Series. 2mm white band in 3.2mm gap (as for third series).

D5	(D4)	20	7/85	Metallic green, white / silver (included below)	25.00 ☐	10.00 ☐
D6	(D4)	105	7/85	Metallic gold, white / silver (included below)	40.00 ☐	15.00 ☐

Fifth Series. 2mm white band in 4.5mm gap (as for sixth series).

D7	(D3)	50	7/85	Metallic green, white / silver (301,600)	6.50 ☐	4.00 ☐
D8	(D4)	100	7/85	Metallic gold, white / silver (1,100,000)	13.00 ☐	6.50 ☐

Sixth Series. 4mm white band.

D9	*D3*	50	1/87	Metallic green, white / silver (200,000)	2.50 ☐	0.75 ☐

Seventh Series. 3mm white band. No notch.

D10	(D3)	50	10/87	Metallic green, white / silver (300,000)	2.50 ☐	1.50 ☐
D10(a)				Control number inverted	3.50 ☐	2.00 ☐
D11	(D4)	100	10/87	Metallic gold, white / silver (200,000)	12.50 ☐	2.50 ☐
D11(a)				Control number inverted	15.00 ☐	3.00 ☐

Eighth Series. 3mm white band. Notched.

D12	(D3)	50	??/88	Metallic green, white / silver (600,000)	1.50 ☐	0.50 ☐
D12(a)				Control number inverted	3.00 ☐	1.00 ☐
D13	(D4)	100	??/88	Metallic gold, white / silver (999,000)	12.50 ☐	2.50 ☐
D13(a)				Control number inverted	15.00 ☐	3.00 ☐

A - ADVERTISING CARDS

A1	*A1*	50	6/88	P.S.K. BANK, Yellow, black, white/silver (10,000)	5.00 ☐	2.50 ☐
A2	*A2*	100	2/89	EMS, Multicolour (240,000)	7.00 ☐	2.00 ☐

Note. A further batch of P.S.K. cards were produced in October, 1989, (A9 below) with changed telephone numbers on the reverse. Precise details are not, unfortunately, available but the control numbers should be helpful.

A3	*A3*	20	2/89	TELENORMA, Red, black, white, silver (10,000)	20.00 ☐	5.00 ☐
A4	(A4)	50	6/89	BLV, Blue, black, white, silver (100,000)	7.50 ☐	2.50 ☐
A5	*A4*	100	6/89	BLV, ... (596,000)	15.00 ☐	2.50 ☐
A6	*A5*	20	7/89	L&G, Multicolour (10,000)	20.00 ☐	7.50 ☐
A7	*A6*	50	10/89	HONEYWELL, Red, black, white, silver (2000)	35.00 ☐	20.00 ☐
A8	*A7*	50	10/89	RZB, Blue, black, white/silver (3300)	18.00 ☐	5.00 ☐
A9	(A1)	50	10/88	P.S.K. BANK, Yellow, black, white/silver (10,000)	8.00 ☐	4.00 ☐

D1 D2 D3

D4 A1 A2

A3 A4 A5

A6 A7 O1

O2

O - OFFICIAL/SERVICE CARDS

№	Ill.	Units	Date	Description		Value
01	*O1*	100	1981	Yellow / silver	--- ▯	45.00 ▯
02	*(O1)*	120	1983	Yellow / silver	--- ▯	45.00 ▯
03	*(O2)*	120	1985	Yellow, white / silver (1.5mm white band)	--- ▯	30.00 ▯
04	*O2*	240	1987	Yellow, white / silver (2mm white band)	--- ▯	25.00 ▯
05	*(O2)*	240	1988	Yellow, white / silver (4mm white band)	--- ▯	20.00 ▯
06	*(O2)*	240	1988	Yellow, white / silver (3mm white band)	--- ▯	20.00 ▯

Note. The copy of O2 illustrated is actually a sample and only one white band has been applied. Issued cards have two white bands.

T - TEST CARDS

Test cards have been produced from 1982 to the present but no specific information on them is available so far. They are reported to be all of the same type.

Magnetic cards were originally manufactured by Autelca on behalf the Bahrain Telecommunications Company B.S.C..   Control numbers are in black. New cards by GPT, UK, were introduced in 1988.

1 Autelca Magnetic Cards.

Single Series

AD1

№	Ill.	Units	Date	Description		Value
AD1	*AD1*	25	1986	Dark blue, black / white	(160,000)	5.00 ▢
AD2	*(AD1)*	50	1986	Green, black / white	(160,000)	7.50 ▢
AD3	*(AD1)*	100	1986	Blue, black / white	(300,000)	12.00 ▢
AD4	*(AD1)*	200	1986	Red, black / white	(80,000)	20.00 ▢

Note. The instructions on the reverse are in both English and Arabic.

GPT Magnetic Cards

First Issue. Modern Bahrain.

№	Ill.	Units	Date	Description		Value
D1	*D1*	25	1989	THE SAIL, MANAMA, Multicoloured	(15,000)	4.00 ▢
D2	*D2*	50	1989	ENTRANCE TO HAMAD TOWN, Multicoloured	(15,000)	6.00 ▢
D3	*D3*	100	1989	CITY CENTRE, MANAMA, Multicoloured	(21,250)	10.00 ▢
D4	*D4*	200	1989	AL-TA'AWAN MONUMENT, Multicoloured	(10,000)	20.00 ▢

Second Issue. Bahrain by Night

D5	*D5*	25	1989	SUNSET, Multicoloured	(15,000)	4.00 ▢
D6	*D6*	50	1989	ISA TOWN GATE, Multicoloured	(15,000)	6.00 ▢
D7	*D7*	100	1989	ARAD FORT, Multicoloured	(21,250)	10.00 ▢
D8	*D8*	200	1989	DIPLOMATIC AREA, MANAMA, Multicoloured	(20,000)	20.00 ▢

Note. A full production run of 20,000 copies of a 100 unit card with the design of D7 was prepared in error and not issued. It is not clear what did happen to them but copies may appear on the market.

Third Issue. Traditional Crafts.

D9	*D9*	25	1989	A'ALI POTTERY, Multicoloured	(15,000)	4.00 ▢
D10	*D10*	50	1989	WEAVER, BANI JAMRA, Multicoloured	(15,000)	6.00 ▢
D11	*D11*	100	1989	COFFEE POTS REPAIR SHOP, Multicoloured	(21,250)	10.00 ▢
D12	*D12*	200	1989	BASKET MAKER, Multicoloured	(10,000)	20.00 ▢

Fourth Issue. Traditional Bahrain

D13	*D13*	25	1989	A'ALI BURIAL MOUNDS, Multicoloured	(15,000)	4.00 ▢
D14	*D14*	50	1989	TRADITIONAL DOOR, Multicoloured	(15,000)	6.00 ▢
D15	*D15*	100	1989	SIYADI HOUSE, MUHARRAQ, Multicoloured	(21,250)	10.00 ▢
D16	*D16*	200	1989	AL-KHAMIS MOSQUE, Multicoloured	(10,000)	20.00 ▢

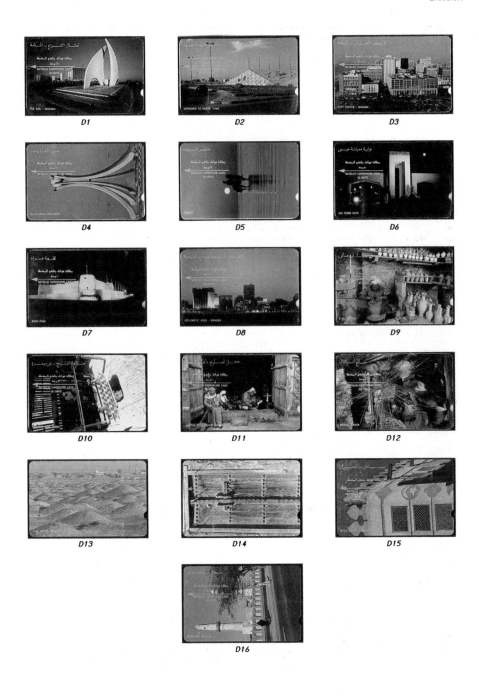

D1

D2

D3

D4

D5

D6

D7

D8

D9

D10

D11

D12

D13

D14

D15

D16

BARBADOS

Magnetic cards by GPT (UK) are about to be introduced.

First Issue. Magnetic cards by GPT.

D1

№	Ill.	Units	Date	Description		Value	
D1	*D1*	BD$4	1989	Multicolour	(1000)	20.00 ☐	
D2	*(D1)*	BD$10	1989	Multicolour	(9000)	10.00 ☐	
D3	*(D1)*	BD$20	1989	Multicolour	(11,000)	15.00 ☐	

Note.   D1 is included in the Cable and Wireless collectors pack of British West Indies cards (see under Promotional Cards at the end of this book).

BELGIUM

Optical cards are manufactured by Landis and Gyr, Switzerland. Control numbers follow th usual pattern for Landis and Gyr cards (see Austria), the first digit indicating year of manufacture and the second two the month.   The first definitive issues were in solid orange on silver but operational improvements necessitated the addition of a white band over the optical strip the width of which has varied in later issues as for those of Austria.   Special or commemorative cards began to appear late in 1988 and the first advertising card was issued in August, 1989. The unit corresponds to 10BF (about 18 UK pence) and the 20 and 105 unit cards cost 200 and 1000BF respectively.   There is thus a bonus of five units for buying the 105 unit card.

D - DEFINITIVE CARDS

First Series. 'A' in circle. Seventeen lines within arrow. No white band over optical strip.

№	Ill.	Units	Date	Description		Value			
D1	*(D1)*	25	2/77	Orange / silver	(3500)	500.00 ☐	250.00 ☐		
D2	*(D1)*	100	2/77	·· ·· ·· ··	(3978)	600.00 ☐	350.00 ☐		

Note.   It has not been possible to obtain samples of D1 and D2 to illustrate. They are very similar to D3 and D4 except in that their printed scales go to 25 and 100.   D2 was apparently encoded with an extra 5 units making it a 105 unit card but its printed scale only went up 100.

Second Series. Values changed to 20 and an indicated 105 units.

№	Ill.	Units	Date	Description		Value		
D3	*(D1)*	20	3/79	Orange / silver	(41,000?)	100.00 ☐	45.00 ☐	
D4	*D1*	105	3/79	·· ·· ·· ··	(58,000?)	200.00 ☐	55.00 ☐	

Third Series. Number of vertical silver stripes in arrow reduced to six.

№	Ill.	Units	Date	Description		Value		
D5	*(D2)*	20	5/84	Orange / silver	(1,000,000)	25.00 ☐	10.00 ☐	
D6	*D2*	105	5/84	·· ·· ·· ··	(138,000)	40.00 ☐	20.00 ☐	

Fourth Issue. 1.5mm white band over optical strip. 'B' in circle. '105' and 'u'(for 'unités') added.

№	Ill.	Units	Date	Description		Value		
D7	*D3*	105	9/84	Metallic orange, white / silver	(60,000?)	50.00 ☐	25.00 ☐	

Fifth Series. 1.5mm white band. 'u' omitted after denomination.

№	Ill.	Units	Date	Description	Value		
D8	*D4*	20	10/84	Metallic orange, white / silver	45.00 ☐	7.00 ☐	
D9	*(D4)*	105	10/84	·· ·· ·· ·· ·· ·· ·· ··	80.00 ☐	10.00 ☐	

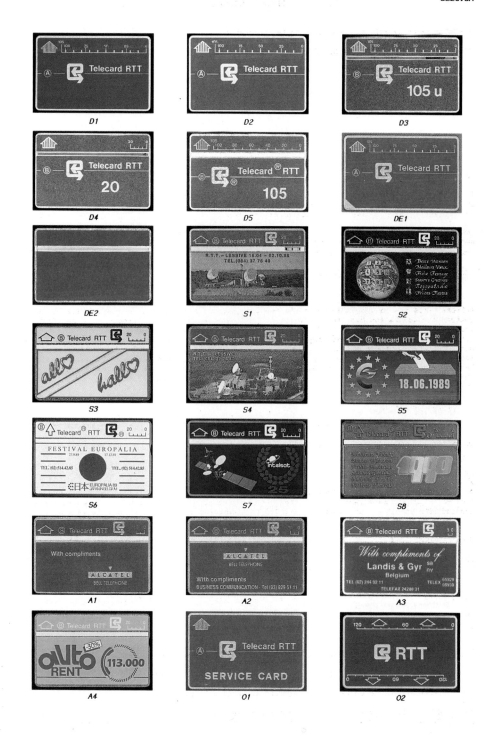

Note 1. It is now known that the two cards with white bands over the optical strip but with 'A' in the circle, listed as D5 and D6 in the first edition of this book, do not exist.

Note 2. Similarly the 20 unit card with a 'u' after the denomination, listed as D7 in the first edition, was never issued although a few samples are said to exist. It seems that when the '105 u' card was issued it was realised that, while 'u' stands for 'unités' in French, it does not stand for the equivalent word in Flemish so the '20 u' card was not produced and it was decided to have only simple numbers in the future.

Note 3. All the metallic orange cards exhibit shade variations from red-orange to a more yellow-orange.

Sixth Series. 2mm white band in 3.2mm gap (as for fifth series).

D10	*(D4)*	20	7/85	Metallic orange, white / silver	25.00 ▢	10.00 ▢
D11	*(D4)*	105	7/85	.. ..	40.00 ▢	15.00 ▢

Seventh Series. 2mm white band in 4.5mm gap (as for eighth series).

D12	*(D4)*	20	7/85	Metallic orange, white / silver	8.00 ▢	2.50 ▢
D12(a)				Control No. misplaced to left	15.00 ▢	6.00 ▢
D13	*(D4)*	105	7/85	Metallic orange, white / silver	30.00 ▢	7.50 ▢

Note. As in France, the orange design was redrawn for the change from a 1.5mm white band to a 2mm white band, the gap far the optical track and white band being increased from 3.2mm to 4.5mm. Some of the first cards to bear the 2mm bands were made with the older type blanks and these are relatively rare. All such 20 unit cards seem to have controls beginning 5B4 and the 105 unit cards 5B2 but these controls are more often found on 1.5mm band cards.

Eighth Series. 4mm white band.

D14	*(D4)*	20	1/87	Metallic orange, white / silver	6.00 ▢	2.00 ▢
D14(a)				Control No. inverted	10.00 ▢	6.00 ▢
D15	*(D4)*	105	1/87	Metallic orange, white / silver	20.00 ▢	3.50 ▢
D15(a)				Control No. error - 117K.. instead of 711K..	70.00 ▢	10.00 ▢

Ninth Series. 3mm white band.

D16	*(D4)*	20	10/87	Metallic orange, white / silver	4.50 ▢	1.00 ▢
D16(a)				Control No. inverted	4.50 ▢	1.00 ▢
D17	*(D4)*	105	10/87	Metallic orange, white / silver	25.00 ▢	2.50 ▢
D17(a)				control No. inverted	40.00 ▢	2.00 ▢

Tenth Series. 3mm white band. Design changed. Notched.

D18	*(D5)*	20	1/90	Metallic orange, white / silver	5.00 ▢	1.50 ▢
D18(a)				Without notch	5.00 ▢	1.50 ▢
D19	*D5*	105	1/90	Metallic orange, white / silver	20.00 ▢	2.50 ▢

DE - DEFINITIVE EXPERIMENTAL CARDS

The three experimental cards below, were made in very small quantities to deal with specific problems that arose at those times. All are very rare. They have been given a 'D' for definitive prefix since they were, unlike Test and Service cards, to be used in telephones in the ordinary way although they were not issued to the public and cannot therefore be listed in the main definitive series.

DE1	-	20	2/77	Orange / silver (20?)	--- ▢	--- ▢
DE2	*DE6*	105	1984?	Orange / silver (20?)	--- ▢	--- ▢
DE3	*DE3*	20?	1985?	Orange, white / silver (50?)	--- ▢	--- ▢

Note. No card is available to provide an illustration of DE1. The card is absolutely plain, non-metallic orange, with no band or other markings of any sort except for the margin. These three cards are refered to as 'anti-fraud cards' in Belgium.

S - SPECIAL/COMMEMORATIVE CARDS

Nº	Ill.	Units	Date	Description	Value	
S1	*S1*	20	4/88	LESSIVE I Multicolour (shades) (270,000)	20.00 ☐	3.00 ☐
S1				Control inverted	20.00 ☐	3.50 ☐
S2	*S2*	20	11/88	VOEUX '89 Multicolour (shades) (250,000)	7.00 ☐	2.50 ☐
S2				Control inverted	8.00 ☐	3.00 ☐

Note. In S1 there are shade variations in both the orange area at the top and in the picture below where the foreground varies from green to light brown. In S2 the main variations are best seen in the 'poles' of the world where some are bluish and others pinkish.

Nº	Ill.	Units	Date	Description	Value	
S3	*S3*	20	2/89	VALENTINE Red, black / pale blue (310,000)	12.00 ☐	1.50 ☐
S3(a)				/ deeper blue	15.00 ☐	2.50 ☐
S3(b)				/ pale bluish grey	20.00 ☐	4.00 ☐
S4	*S4*	20	4/89	LESSIVE II Multicolour (shades) (268,000)	12.00 ☐	1.50 ☐

Note. In S4 shade differences in the picture are slight but the orange top area does vary.

Nº	Ill.	Units	Date	Description	Value	
S5	*S5*	20	6/89	EURO-ELECTIONS Multicolour (shades)(157,000)	10.00 ☐	1.50 ☐
S5(a)				Control inverted	10.00 ☐	2.50 ☐
S5(b)				Purple lower background	15.00 ☐	3.00 ☐
S6	*S6*	20	10/89	FESTIVAL EUROPALIA Red, black/white (400,000)	8.00 ☐	1.50 ☐
S6(a)				Control inverted	8.00 ☐	3.50 ☐
S7	*S7*	20	10/89	INTELSAT Shades of blue, gold, white(372,000)	10.00 ☐	1.50 ☐
S7(a)				Control not inverted	14.00 ☐	2.50 ☐
S7(b)				Yellow-gold wreath	12.00 ☐	1.50 ☐
S8	*S8*	20	11/89	VOEUX '90, Multicolour (350,000)	10.00 ☐	1.50 ☐
S8(a)				Control not inverted	12.00 ☐	1.50 ☐
S8(b)				Deeper clear blue background	20.00 ☐	2.50 ☐

A - ADVERTISING CARDS

Nº	Ill.	Units	Date	Description	Value	
A1	*A1*	10	9/88	ALCATEL, Orange / silver (2000)	125.00 ☐	100.00 ☐
A2	*A2*	10	9/88	ALCATEL, Orange / silver (1000)	175.00 ☐	120.00 ☐
A3	*A3*	5	11/88	LANDIS & GYR, Blue, orange, white/silver (2000)	200.00 ☐	150.00 ☐
A4	*A4*	20	8/89	AUTO-RENT, Blue, white / yellow (300,000)	8.00 ☐	1.50 ☐
A4(a)				Inverted control	10.00 ☐	1.50 ☐

O - OFFICIAL/SERVICE CARDS

It is now known that there are at least four different Service cards from Belgium. That given as O1 in the first edition now becomes O2.

Nº	Ill.	Units	Date	Description	Value	
O1	*O1*	(120)	1977?	Orange / silver	200.00 ☐	150.00 ☐
O2	*O2*	240	1984?	Orange / silver	100.00 ☐	45.00 ☐
O2(a)				Control No. inverted	120.00 ☐	50.00 ☐
O3	*O3*	240	1985	Orange, white / silver (2mm band)	30.00 ☐	30.00 ☐
O4	*(O3)*	240	1989	Orange, white / silver (4mm band)	40.00 ☐	30.00 ☐

T - TEST CARDS

Nº	Ill.	Units	Date	Description	Value	
T1	*T1*	—	1977?	Orange / matt silver	80.00 ☐	50.00 ☐
T2	*(T1)*	—	1984?	Orange / polished silver	40.00 ☐	30.00 ☐
T3	*(T1)*	—	1988?	Orange / polished silver, as *T2* on reverse	30.00 ☐	30.00 ☐

Note. These cards have no units and no control numbers. They can reportedly be used within the telephone some thirty times to check the voltages and are then discarded. The figures in the silver area differ from card to card. The only way of telling whether a card is used or not is from general condition and, especially, the presence or absence of rubbing marks about 16 mm from each short edge.

G - CLOSED USER GROUP CARDS

Nº	Ill.	Units	Date	Description	Value	
CUG1	*CUG1*	120	4/83	BELL TELEPHONE, Blue/silver (5900 - see below)	200.00 ☐	150.00 ☐
CUG2	*CUG2*	20	2/88	TAGAWA HOTEL, Orange, white / silver (1000)	150.00 ☐	100.00 ☐

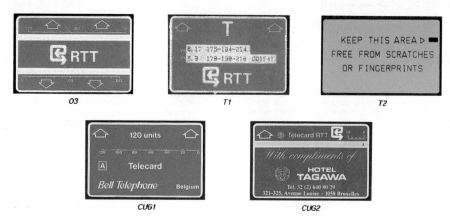

O3   T1   T2

CUG1   CUG2

Note 1.   CUG1, the Bell Telephone card, has been used by Bell Telephone SA, Brussels, for demonstrating international calls.   Printings were 900 in 1983 and 5000 in 1985.

Note 2.   CUG2 is no longer available from the Tagawa Hotel.   Collectors are asked not to write to the Hotel seeking cards.

General Note.   Many of the earlier Belgian (and other Landis and Gyr) cards show yellow, light brown or even dark brown bands over the optical strip.   This is an aging effect on the early thermographic coatings used at that time and varies to some extent with the way in which the cards have been stored.   They are sometimes listed or even offered for sale as varieties.   This is not, in my view, correct.   They were all white originally.   The more recent coatings have been improved and should prove more stable with time.   Similarly cards stored under certain conditions (or chemically tampered with) can show blackening of the silver areas.   The reasons for this are not fully understood but, again, they were all originally silver and these do not constitute varieties in my view.

Belgian telephone cards may be obtained from: Regie van Telefonie en Telegrafie, / CO1, / E. Jacqmainlaan 166, / 1210 BRUSSELS, / BELGIUM

BERMUDA

Optically encoded cards are manufactured by Landis and Gyr, Switzerland, for the Bermuda Telephone Company, Ltd, in association with Cable and Wireless.   The unit cost is 25 cents.   Magnetic cards by Autelca, Switzerland, have also been issued through Cable and Wireless and have since been destroyed.

M1

D1

1   MAGNETIC CARDS (Autelca)

Nº	Ill.	Units	Date	Description	Value
M1	*(M1)*	$10	1986	Blue, dark blue / white (15,000)	40.00 □
M2	*(M1)*	$20	1986	Green, blue / white (13,000)	40.00 □
M3	*M1*	$50	1986	Red, blue / white (10,000)	100.00 □

Note.   M3 has been illustrated because it was the only card of the set available but this card was, in fact, never issued.

2 OPTICAL CARDS (Landis and Gyr)

First Series. 4mm white strip.

Nº	Ill.	Units	Date	Description					Value	
D1	(D1)	40	2/87	Blue, white / silver (11,000)					10.00 ▢	5.00 ▢
D2	D1	100	2/87	..	..	..	..	.. (6000)	20.00 ▢	15.00 ▢
D3	(D1)	200	2/87	..	..	..	..	.. (5000)	40.00 ▢	25.00 ▢

Second Issue. 3mm white strip. Not notched.

Nº	Ill.	Units	Date	Description	Value	
D4	(D1)	40	12/87	Blue, white / silver (10,000)	8.00 ▢	3.00 ▢

Third Issue. 3mm white strip. Notched.

Nº	Ill.	Units	Date	Description	Value	
D5	(D1)	100	7/88	Blue, white / silver (5000)	18.00 ▢	6.00 ▢

BRAZIL

Magnetic telephone cards supplied by GPT, UK, are about to be introduced on a trial basis.

D - DEFINITIVE CARDS

Field Trial Cards.

D1

Nº	Ill.	Units	Date	Description	Value
D1	(D1)	5	1990	Dark blue, light blue, white (45,000)	4.00 ▢
D2	(D1)	10	1990	Dark blue, light blue, white (30,000)	6.00 ▢
D3	(D1)	100	1990	Dark blue, light blue, white (20,000)	10.00 ▢
D4	D1	500	1990	Dark blue, light blue, white (10,000)	25.00 ▢

P - PROMOTIONAL CARD

P1

P1	P1	1000	1987	Multicolour (1500)	60.00 ▢

Magnetic cards supplied by GPT (UK) are about to be introduced for the Island of Tortola in the British Virgin Islands. Following the disastrous effects of Hurricane Hugo in 1989, a special card is also about to be issued and 10% of the proceeds will go to the disaster fund.

D - DEFINITIVE CARDS

First Issue. Magnetic cards by GPT.

D1   S1

№	Ill.	Units	Date	Description	Value
D1	*D1*	US$2	1989	Multicolour (1000)	20.00 ☐
D2	*(D1)*	US$5	1989	Multicolour (20,000)	4.00 ☐
D3	*(D1)*	US$10	1989	Multicolour (10,000)	8.00 ☐
D4	*(D1)*	US$20	1989	Multicolour (5000)	18.00 ☐

Note. D1 is included in the Cable and Wireless collectors pack of British West Indies cards (see under Promotional Cards at the end of this book).

S - SPECIAL CARD

S1	*S1*	US$10	1989	HURRICANE HUGO, Multicolour (4500)	10.00 ☐

Note. This card is a charity card in that $1 will be given to the Hurricane Hugo Relief Fund for each card sold.

BRUNEI

Magnetic cards are supplied by Autelca Ltd to the Brunei Darussalam telephone authority, JTB. Control numbers are in black.

D1   S1 (reverse)   S2 (reverse)

D - DEFINITIVE CARDS

№	Ill.	Units	Date	Description	Value
D1	*(D1)*	B$10	1988	Dark green, gold / white (180,000)	10.00 ☐
D2	*(D1)*	B$20	1988	·· ·· ·· ·· ·· ·· (150,000)	12.00 ☐
D3	*(D1)*	B$50	1988	·· ·· ·· ·· ·· ·· (120,000)	20.00 ☐
D4	*D1*	B$100	1988	·· ·· ·· ·· ·· ·· (100,000)	30.00 ☐

S - SPECIAL CARDS

S1	*(D1)*	B$10	1989	Dark green, gold / white (100) Reverse as *S1*	200.00 ☐
S2	*(D1)*	B$10	1989	·· ·· ·· ·· ·· ·· (100) Reverse as *S2*	200.00 ☐

Note. These rare cards were issued to promote the introduction of the TelcaStar CARD payphone in Brunei.

BULGARIA

Bulgaria introduced a magnetic telephone card system in late 1988 or early 1989. The cards seem to have been produced by a local manufacturer and few details are available at present. Wording is in French and Bulgarian and a code on the reverse of the only specimens I have seen suggests that they were made in 1988. The control number is black.

D1

Nº	Ill.	Units	Date	Description	Value
D1	*D1*	1AB	1989?	Brown, pale green / white	5.00 ☐
D2	*(D1)*	2AB	1989?	Brown, orange / white	10.00 ☐
D3	*(D1)*	5AB	1989?	Brown, pale blue / white	15.00 ☐
D4	*(D1)*	10AB	1989?	Brown, yellow / white	25.00 ☐

Note. Quantities issued are not known but the highest control numbers noted for the four values are 021555, 004321, 022901 and 023171 respectively.

BURUNDI

Optical cards are supplied to the Burundi telephone company, ONATEL, by Landis and Gyr, Switzerland.

D1

Nº	Ill.	Units	Date	Description	Value	
D1	*(D1)*	20	2/90	Blue, white / silver	6.00 ☐	3.00 ☐
D2	*(D1)*	50	2/90	Green, white / silver	10.00 ☐	5.00 ☐
D3	*D1*	100	2/90	Red, white / silver	20.00 ☐	12.00 ☐

CAMEROON

Magnetic cards are supplied by Autelca to the Cameroon Ministry of Posts and Telecommunications. Values are in Cameroon Francs. Control numbers are in black. There appear to have been no new issues since the last edition of this book.

D1

Nº	Ill.	Units	Date	Description	Value
D1	*(D1)*	F1500	1987	Red, yellow, green, black / white (50,000)	10.00 ☐
D2	*(D1)*	F3000	1987	.. .. (30,000)	15.00 ☐
D3	*D1*	F5000	1987	.. .. (15,000)	25.00 ☐

Note. It is reported that only the 3000F value is currently in service.

CANADA

A field trial of the GPT magnetic card system was conducted at the Goose Bay military base in Labrador from September, 1988, to March, 1989. Two cards based on the standard GPT service card were used. The 500 unit card cost $25 and the 1000 unit card $50.

D1

№	Ill.	Units	Date	Description	Value
D1	*D1*	500	9/88	Red, blue, white (1000)	60.00 ▢
D2	*(D1)*	1000	9/88	·· ·· ·· ·· (1000)	80.00 ▢

CAYMAN ISLANDS

Magnetic cards are supplied by Autelca to Cable and Wireless who run the telephone service for the islands. Values are given in both units and in Cayman Island Dollars at 10 cents per unit. Control numbers are in black.

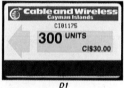

D1

№	Ill.	Units	Date	Description	Value
D1	*(D1)*	75	1986	Green, blue / white (50,000)	6.00 ▢
D2	*D1*	300	1986	Yellow, blue / white (30,000)	10.00 ▢
D3	*(D1)*	500	1986	Red, blue / white (15,000)	20.00 ▢

CENTRAL AFRICAN REPUBLIC

Optical cards are supplied by Landis and Gyr, Switzerland.

D - DEFINITIVE CARDS

First Issue. 4mm white band.

D1

№	Ill.	Units	Date	Description	Value	
D1	*(D1)*	60	6/87	Green, white / silver (5000)	10.00 ▢	5.00 ▢
D2	*(D1)*	120	6/87	Red, white / silver (3600)	20.00 ▢	12.00 ▢

Second Issue. 3mm white band. Notched.

| D3 | *(D1)* | 60 | 1989 | Green, white / silver (5000) | 8.00 ▢ | 5.00 ▢ |
| D4 | *D1* | 120 | 1989 | Red, white / silver (3000) | 15.00 ▢ | 10.00 ▢ |

BEIJING (PEKIN)

Magnetic cards by Tamura, Japan, are in use. Both definitives and advertising cards have been issued. Field trials of magnetic cards and telephones by Alcatel (Bell Telephone), Belgium, are about to begin.

DT - DEFINITIVE CARDS (Tamura)

№	Ill.	Units	Date	Description		Value	
DT1	DT1	¥10	21/9/89	PALACE MUSEUM, Multicolour (?000)		4.00 ☐	2.50 ☐
DT2	DT2	¥10	21/9/89	PANDA, Multicolour (?000)		4.00 ☐	2.50 ☐
DT3	DT3	¥20	21/9/89	GREAT WALL, Multicolour (?000)		8.00 ☐	5.00 ☐
DT4	DT4	¥20	21/9/89	HE BAO, Multicolour (?000)		8.00 ☐	5.00 ☐
DT5	DT5	¥50	21/9/89	SUMMER PALACE, Multicolour (?000)		15.00 ☐	8.00 ☐
DT6	DT6	¥100	21/9/89	HEAVEN TEMPLE, Multicolour (?000)		25.00 ☐	15.00 ☐

Second Issue.

№	Ill.	Units	Date	Description		Value	
DT7	DT7	¥10	25/9/89	WIRELESS TELEPHONE, Multicolour (?000)		8.00 ☐	4.00 ☐
DT8	(DT7)	¥20	25/9/89	·· ·· ·· ·· ·· ·· ·· (?000)		10.00 ☐	5.00 ☐
DT9	(DT8)	¥50	25/9/89	·· ·· ·· ·· ·· ·· ·· (?000)		15.00 ☐	6.00 ☐
DT10	DT8	¥100	25/9/89	·· ·· ·· ·· ·· ·· ·· (?000)		20.00 ☐	8.00 ☐

AT - ADVERTISING CARDS

№	Ill.	Units	Date	Description		Value	
AT1	*AT1*	¥10	25/9/89	NTT, Multicolour (?000)		4.00 ☐	2.50 ☐
AT2	*AT2*	¥20	25/9/89	ANA, Multicolour (?000)		4.00 ☐	2.50 ☐
AT3	*AT3*	¥50	25/9/89	ANA, Multicolour (?000)		8.00 ☐	5.00 ☐
AT4	*AT4*	¥50	25/9/89	KDD, Multicolour (?000)		8.00 ☐	5.00 ☐

CA & DA - COMPLIMENTARY AND DEFINITIVE CARDS (Alcatel - Bell)

№	Ill.	Units	Date	Description	Value	
CA1	*CA1*	¥1	1990	MAP OF CHINA, Yellow, brown, red / white	4.00 ☐	2.50 ☐
DA1	*(DA1)*	¥10	1990	Multicolour.	4.00 ☐	2.50 ☐
DA1	*(DA1)*	¥30	1990	Multicolour.	7.00 ☐	4.50 ☐
DA1	*DA1*	¥50	1990	Multicolour.	10.00 ☐	6.00 ☐

Note. It seems that the same complimentary card, CA1, will be used in Beijing, Guangzhou and Shanghai. All cards have their value and magnetic strip on the reverse

GUANGZHOU

Cards by a Japanese company, Tamura, are being tested. Only the two cards illustrated below have come to light and reports differ as to whether others exist. Both would seem to be advertising cards and have been provisionally listed as such. Tests of a second magnetic system by Alcatel, Belgium, are about to begin. No cards have yet been seen but they will be similar to and in the same values as those for Beijing and Shanghai.

AT - ADVERTISING CARDS (Tamura)

AT1   AT2

№	Ill.	Units	Date	Description		Value	
AT1	*AT1*	¥20	1989	TAMURA, Multicolour (?000)		10.00 ☐	5.00 ☐
AT2	*AT2*	¥50	1989	NEC, Multicolour (?000)		12.00 ☐	6.00 ☐

CA & DA - COMPLIMENTARY AND DEFINITIVE CARDS (Alcatel - Bell)

№	Ill.	Units	Date	Description	Value	
CA1	–	¥1	1990	MAP OF CHINA, Yellow, brown, red / white	4.00 ☐	2.50 ☐
DA1	–	¥10	1990	Multicolour.	4.00 ☐	2.50 ☐
DA1	–	¥30	1990	Multicolour.	7.00 ☐	4.50 ☐
DA1	–	¥50	1990	Multicolour.	10.00 ☐	6.00 ☐

Note. No illustrations are yet available. It is understood that CA1 is exactly the same as that for Beijing above and the designs for the definitives will similar to those of Beijing.

SHANGHAI

Magnetic cards by Autelca have been supplied to the Post and Telecommunication Administration of Shanghai for use on international calls. Magnetic cards supplied by GPT, UK, have since been introduced. Field trials of cards and telephones by Tamura of Japan are in progress and further trials of cards by Alcatel, Belgium, are about to begin.

1 Autelca cards.

№	Ill.	Units	Date	Description	Value
D1	*(D1)*	¥25	1987	Black / white (20,000)	10.00 ☐
D2	*(D1)*	¥60	1987	·· ·· ·· (15,000)	50.00 ☐
D3	*D1*	¥100	1987	·· ·· ·· (10,000)	25.00 ☐

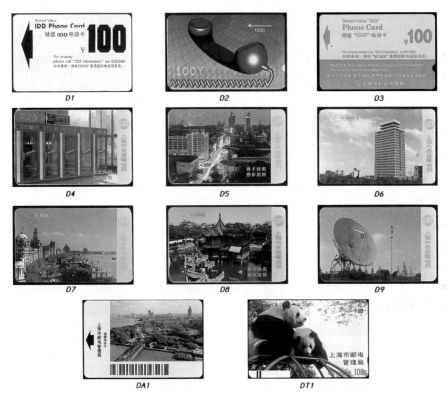

D1   D2   D3

D4   D5   D6

D7   D8   D9

DA1   DT1

2 GPT Cards.

The first issue of GPT trial cards consisted of very small numbers of 'provisional' cards made by overprinting the standard engineering test card with the values in yuan. The cards consist of the standard GPT service card design (including the service card value of 1000 units) with the new value over-printed in the left bottom corners. They are, of course, encoded with the Shanghai values rather than those of the service cards. There appears to be no distinction between definitives and special cards in later GPT Shanghai cards.

First Issue.

№	Ill.	Units	Date	Description	Value
D4	*(D2)*	¥25	1988	Red and blue (200)	400.00 ☐
D5	*(D2)*	¥60	1988	,, ,, ,, (200)	400.00 ☐
D6	*D2*	¥100	1988	,, ,, ,, (100)	750.00 ☐

Second Issue.

D7	*(D3)*	¥25	1988	Blue and yellow (5000)	45.00 ☐
D8	*(D3)*	¥60	1988	,, ,, ,, ,, (4500)	45.00 ☐
D9	*D3*	¥100	1988	,, ,, ,, ,, (500)	400.00 ☐

Third Issue.

D10	*D4*	¥25	1989	Multicolour (13,750)	5.00 ☐
D11	*D5*	¥25	1989	Multicolour (13,750)	5.00 ☐
D12	*D6*	¥60	1989	Multicolour (27,500)	7.00 ☐
D13	*D7*	¥60	1989	Multicolour (22,313)	7.00 ☐
D14	*D8*	¥25	1989	Multicolour (13,750)	10.00 ☐
D15	*D9*	¥25	1989	Multicolour (13,750)	10.00 ☐

CHINA (SHANGHAI-SHENZHEN)

CA & DA - COMPLIMENTARY AND DEFINITIVE CARDS (Alcatel - Bell)

№	Ill.	Units	Date	Description	Value	
CA1	-	¥1	1990	MAP OF CHINA, (Same as *CA1* for Beijing)	4.00 ▯	2.00 ▯
DA1	*(DA1)*	¥10	1990	Multicolour.	5.00 ▯	2.50 ▯
DA2	*DA1*	¥30	1990	Multicolour.	8.00 ▯	4.00 ▯
DA3	*(DA1)*	¥50	1990	Multicolour.	15.00 ▯	6.00 ▯

DT - DEFINITIVE CARD (Tamura)

DT1	*(DT1)*	¥10	1989	Multicolour.	5.00 ▯	2.50 ▯

Note. Only this card has come to light and it seems to be fairly common. It seems likely, however, that others exist

SHENZHEN

Magnetic cards were initially supplied by Autelca to the Shenda Telephone Co. Ltd. for use in Shenzhen Province, bordering on Hong Kong in the south of China. Later cards have been produced by GPT, UK.

D1 *D2* *D3*
D4 *D5* *D6*
D7 *D8* *D9*
D10 *D11*

1. Autelca Cards.

D1	*(D1)*	¥12	1985	Green / white	(15,000)	15.00 ▯
D2	*(D1)*	¥25	1985	·· ·· ··	(20,000)	15.00 ▯
D3	*D1*	¥50	1985	·· ·· ··	(20,000)	25.00 ▯

2. GPT Cards.

№	Ill.	Units	Date	Description			Value
D4	*D2*	¥25	1989	No. 1 XIAO MEI SHA BEACH,	Multicolour	(5200)	8.00 ☐
D5	*D3*	¥25	1989	No. 2 FAIRY LAKE,	Multicolour	(5200)	8.00 ☐
D6	*D4*	¥50	1989	No. 3 HONEY LAKE PARK,	Multicolour	(5200)	10.00 ☐
D7	*D5*	¥50	1989	No. 4 EVENING IN SHENZHEN,	Multicolour	(5200)	10.00 ☐
D8	*D6*	¥50	1989	No. 5 XILI LAKE COMPLEX,	Multicolour	(5200)	10.00 ☐
D9	*D7*	¥50	1989	No. 6 MODERN SHENZHEN,	Multicolour	(5200)	10.00 ☐
D10	*D8*	¥50	1989	No. 7 SEA WORLD,	Multicolour	(5200)	10.00 ☐
D11	*D9*	¥100	1989	No. 8 LIZHI LAKE,	Multicolour	(5200)	15.00 ☐
D12	*D10*	¥100	1989	No. 9 SHIYAN LAKE,	Multicolour	(5200)	15.00 ☐
D13	*D11*	¥100	1989	No. 10 CHUNG YING STREET,	Multicolour	(5200)	15.00 ☐

Second Issue. As above but date at bottom right changed to 1990.

№	Ill.	Units	Date	Description			Value
D14	*(D2)*	¥25	1990	No. 1 XIAO MEI SHA BEACH,	Multicolour	(?000)	8.00 ☐
D15	*(D3)*	¥25	1990	No. 2 FAIRY LAKE,	Multicolour	(?000)	8.00 ☐
D16	*(D4)*	¥50	1990	No. 3 HONEY LAKE PARK,	Multicolour	(?000)	10.00 ☐
D17	*(D5)*	¥50	1990	No. 4 EVENING IN SHENZHEN,	Multicolour	(?000)	10.00 ☐
D18	*(D6)*	¥50	1990	No. 5 XILI LAKE COMPLEX,	Multicolour	(?000)	10.00 ☐
D19	*(D7)*	¥50	1990	No. 6 MODERN SHENZHEN,	Multicolour	(?000)	10.00 ☐
D20	*(D8)*	¥50	1990	No. 7 SEA WORLD,	Multicolour	(?000)	10.00 ☐
D21	*(D9)*	¥100	1990	No. 8 LIZHI LAKE,	Multicolour	(?000)	15.00 ☐
D22	*(D10)*	¥100	1990	No. 9 SHIYAN LAKE,	Multicolour	(?000)	15.00 ☐
D23	*(D11)*	¥100	1990	No. 10 CHUNG YING STREET,	Multicolour	(?000)	15.00 ☐

The cards of Shenzhen and other Chinese areas may be obtained by writing to: Mr Xian Shao Hua, / Shenda Telephone Co. Ltd. / The Local Telephone Building, /HuaFu Road, / ShangBu District, / SHENZHEN/ People's Republic of China.

COSTA RICA

Trials of a pay-phone system using cards supplied by GPT, UK, were due to begin in 1989. What actually happened is not clear at present. Only definitive cards exist and cost 50, 100 and 800 Colones respectively, i.e. the unit is 1 Colone.

D - DEFINITIVE CARDS

D1

№	Ill.	Units	Date	Description		Value
D1	*(D1)*	50	1989?	Multicolour / white	(15,000)	15.00 ☐
D2	*D1*	100	1989?	Multicolour / pink	(7500)	25.00 ☐
D3	*(D1)*	800	1989?	Multicolour / pale blue (2500)		40.00 ☐

CURAÇAO

Curaçao, which used to be known as the Netherlands Antilles, consists of a group of islands off the coast of Venezuela in the Caribbean Sea. Optical cards are manufactured by Landis and Gyr for Telecommunication Netherlands Antilles. Definitive cards are produced for each of the main islands of the group and for the Company as a whole. General test cards as described and illustrated under Algeria but with the number '22' in the arrow are used but are not separately listed.

DG1

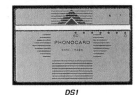

DS1

DS2

DM1

1 GENERAL

Nº	Ill.	Units	Date	Description	Value	
DG1	–	240	1987	Green / silver (?000)	40.00 ☐	15.00 ☐
DG2	DG1	240	10/87	Dark & light grey, red / silver (3000)	25.00 ☐	10.00 ☐

Note. DG1 was a standard Landis and Gyr 'PHONOCARD' card with '22' in the four arrows and coloured green instead of the more usual blue. No illustration is available.

2 SATEL SABA

DS1	DS1	60	10/87	Dark & light grey, red / silver (500)	50.00 ☐	35.00 ☐
DS2	DS2	240	10/87	·· ·· ·· ·· ·· ·· ·· ·· (500)	60.00 ☐	40.00 ☐

3 TELBO – BONAIRE   As above but marked "TALBO – BONAIRE"

DB1	(DS1)	60	10/87	Dark & light grey, red / silver (1000)	40.00 ☐	25.00 ☐
DB2	(DS2)	240	10/87	·· ·· ·· ·· ·· ·· ·· ·· (1000)	50.00 ☐	30.00 ☐

4 EUTEL – St EUSTATIUS   As above but marked "EUTEL – St EUSTATIUS"

DE1	(DS1)	60	10/87	Dark & light grey, red / silver (500)	50.00 ☐	35.00 ☐
DE2	(DS2)	240	10/87	·· ·· ·· ·· ·· ·· ·· ·· (500)	60.00 ☐	40.00 ☐

5 TELEM – St MAARTEN   As above but marked "TELEM – St MAARTEN"

First Issue.

DM1	(DS1)	60	10/87	Dark & light grey, red / silver (2000)	35.00 ☐	20.00 ☐
DM2	(DS2)	240	10/87	·· ·· ·· ·· ·· ·· ·· ·· (2000)	40.00 ☐	25.00 ☐

Second Issue. New design.

DM3	(DM1)	60	1989	Grey / silver (70,000)	10.00 ☐	3.00 ☐
DM4	DM1	120	1989	Pale grey / silver (70,000)	20.00 ☐	7.00 ☐

CYPRUS

Magnetic cards have been manufactured by GPT, UK., for use in the southern half of the island. They are denominated in Cypriot pounds rather than units. Recently a £2 value has been introduced along with a complimentary.

C1

D1

D2

D3

D4

C - COMPLIMENTARY CARD

Nº	Ill.	Units	Date	Description	Value
C1	*C1*	£2	1989	Multicolour (10,000)	6.00 ▢

D - DEFINITIVE CARDS

Nº	Ill.	Units	Date	Description	Value
D1	*(D1)*	£2	1989	Dull green / white (?0,000)	4.00 ▢
D2	*(D1)*	£5	11/87	·· ·· ·· ·· ·· (20,000)	8.00 ▢
D3	*D1*	£10	11/87	·· ·· ·· ·· ·· (5000)	25.00 ▢

Second Issue. As above but with a small notch.

Nº	Ill.	Units	Date	Description	Value
D4	*(D1)*	£2	1989	Dull green / white (?0,000)	4.00 ▢
D5	*(D1)*	£5	1989	·· ·· ·· ·· ·· (388,350)	5.00 ▢
D6	*(D1)*	£10	1989	·· ·· ·· ·· ·· (94,292)	12.00 ▢

Note. The numbers issued of the large and small notched varieties are not certain. The total printing of £2 cards is known to have been 100,000 at the time of writing. At present the two varieties are about equally common and have been priced accordingly.

Nº	Ill.	Units	Date	Description	Value
D7	*D2*	£2	1/90	APHRODITE'S ROCK AT PAPHOS, Multicoloured,	3.00 ▢
D8	*D3*	£5	1/90	HARBOUR AND CASTLE AT PAPHOS, Multicoloured,	7.00 ▢
D9	*D4*	£10	1/90	KOLOSSI CASTLE, Multicoloured,	10.00 ▢

DENMARK

1 COPENHAGEN TELEPHONE COMPANY (KTAS)

Optical cards including a single definitive, a complimentary and a service card, manufactured by Landis and Gyr, Switzerland, were introduced in Copenhagen in 1983. These cards are given the prefix 'OC', 'OD' and 'OO' respectively below. Subsequently magnetic cards supplied by GPT, UK, were adopted and recently trials of a magnetic system by System Card of Denmark have begun at Elsinore.

O - OPTICAL CARDS

OC - COMPLIMENTARY CARD

Nº	Ill.	Units	Date	Description	Value	
OC1	*OC1*	(5)	6/83	Deep orange / silver (30,000)	2.00 ▢	1.50 ▢

Note. OC1 can be distinguished from OD1 only by the asterisk (*) after 'korttelefon'. There were printings of 15,000 in 1982 and 1983.

OC1   OD1   OO1

OD - DEFINITIVE CARD

OD1 **OO1** (120) 6/83   Deep orange / silver (60,000 + 139,000 in 1982/3) 6.00 ▯   2.00 ▯

Note. OD1 is without stated denomination but was actually of 120 (0.25 DKr) units. The two printings, one in late 1982 and the other in 1983, are probably not distinguishable from their control numbers since they were made before dates were incorporated in the controls.

OO - OFFICIAL/SERVICE CARD

OO1 **OO1** (120) 6/83   Deep orange / silver (2870)   ---- ▯   40.00 ▯

GPT MAGNETIC CARDS

Only definitive cards of two values, denominated in Danish Kroner, have so far been issued. The lower value, however, is issued in no less than nine different designs which fit together to form a pattern known collectivly as the Copenhagen puzzle. There are now two versions of each of these designs. Some or all of the 20 DKr cards of the 1988 printing exist with both rough and smooth surfaces.

D1-9

№	Ill.	Units	Date	Description							Value
D1	**D1-9**	20 kr	11/86	Red, blue, yellow, black / white (2500)							6.00 ▯
D2	··	··	··	··	··	··	··	··	··	(2500)	6.00 ▯
D2(a)	··	··	··	··	··	··	··	··	··	Rough Surface. (6000)	10.00 ▯
D3	··	··	··	··	··	··	··	··	··	(2500)	6.00 ▯
D4	··	··	··	··	··	··	··	··	··	(2500)	6.00 ▯
D4(a)	··	··	··	··	··	··	··	··	··	Rough Surface. (6000)	10.00 ▯
D5	··	··	··	··	··	··	··	··	··	(2500)	6.00 ▯
D6	··	··	··	··	··	··	··	··	··	(2500)	6.00 ▯
D6(a)	··	··	··	··	··	··	··	··	··	Rough Surface. (6000)	10.00 ▯

Nº	Ill.	Units	Date	Description		Value
D7					(2500)	6.00 □
D7(a)					Rough Durface. (6000)	10.00 □
D8					(2500)	6.00 □
D9					(2500)	6.00 □
D9(a)					Rough Durface. (6000)	10.00 □
D10	*D10*	90 kr	11/86	Red, blue, yellow (shades), black / white ()		20.00 □
D10(a)					Rough Surface. (?000)	30.00 □

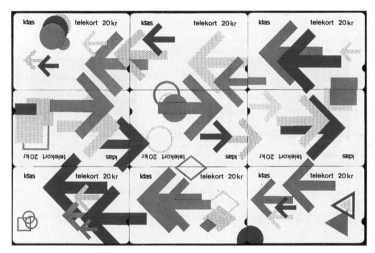

D11-19

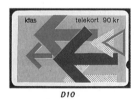

D10

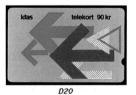

D20

D11	*D11-19*	20 kr	11/86	Red, blue, yellow, black / white (2500)		3.50 □
D12					(2500)	3.50 □
D13					(2500)	3.50 □
D14					(2500)	3.50 □
D15					(2500)	3.50 □
D16					(2500)	3.50 □
D17					(2500)	3.50 □
D18					(2500)	3.50 □
D19					(2500)	3.50 □
D20	*D20*	90 kr	11/86	Red, blue, yellow, black / white (?000)		20.00 □

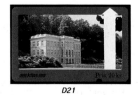

D21

D22

D23

Elsinore Trial Cards by System Cards, Denmark

№	Ill.	Units	Date	Description		Value
D21	*D21*	20DKr	4/89	Multicolour	(5000)	5.00 ▢
D22	*D22*	50DKr	4/89	Blue-grey, yellow	(3000)	12.00 ▢
D23	*D23*	100DKr	4/89	Multicolour	(2000)	25.00 ▢

Note. D22 and D23 give additional values of 2 and 5 DKr respectively. D21 shows a manor house in Elsinore called Marienlyst, D22 shows Holgar the Dane who will awaken from his sleep in the cellars of Kronborg Castle in Denmark's hour of greatest need and D23 shows Kronborg Castle, Elsinore.

2. FYNS TELEFON

Two cards by GPT, UK, were introduced in March(?), 1989.

	D1		D2

D1	*D1*	20DKr	3/89	Multicolour (8000)	10.00 ▢
D2	*D2*	50DKr	3/89	Black / red-brown and white (2000)	25.00 ▢

Note. These cards were designed by local artists Finn Hillerup and Sonia Brandes respectively.

3 JUTLAND TELEPHONE COMPANY (JYDSK TELEFON)

Magnetic cards manufactured by GPT, UK, are in use. Field trials of cards produced by Data-z of Denmark have recently begun in the town of Holstebro in Jutland.

C1

D1

D2

D3

S1

S2

S3

C - COMPLIMENTARY CARD

Nº	Ill.	Units	Date	Description	Value
C1	*C1*	5 KR	1988	Blue, red / white (10,000)	5.00 ☐

D - DEFINITIVE CARDS

Nº	Ill.	Units	Date	Description	Value
D1	*(D1)*	20 KR	1988	Blue, red / white (35,000)	3.00 ☐
D2	*D1*	50 KR	1988	·· ·· ·· ·· (15,000)	8.00 ☐

Holstebro Trial Cards by Data-z, Denmark

D3	*D2*	20 KR	9/89	Multicolour (12,000)	6.00 ☐
D4	*D3*	50 KR	9/89	Multicolour (8000)	12.00 ☐

S - SPECIAL CARDS

S1	*S1*	20 KR	7/89	WORLD MASTERS GAMES, Multicolour (12,500)	6.00 ☐
S2	*S2*	50 KR	7/89	·· ·· ·· ·· ·· ·· ·· ·· (12,500)	10.00 ☐
S3	*S3*	100 KR	7/89	·· ·· ·· ·· ·· ·· ·· ·· (5000)	25.00 ☐

Note. The World Masters Games took place in Herning, Aalborg and Aarhus from 22 July to 6 August, 1989. The first such games took place in Toronto, Canada, in 1985 and the next will be in Minnesota, USA, in 1993. S1 shows beached fishing boats, S2 a Danish farm and S3 the Concert Hall in Aarhus.

DIEGO GARCIA

Diego Garcia is an island in the Indian Ocean which is of note largely for its military base. Magnetic cards are supplied by Autelca for use in the telephone system which is operated by Cable and Wireless. Only definitive cards have been issued. Control numbers are in black and are now, I understand, prefixed by the letter 'D'..

D - DEFINITIVE CARDS

D1

Nº	Ill.	Units	Date	Description	Value
D1	*(D1)*	17	1985	Blue, deep grey / white (80,000)	10.00 ☐
D2	*(D1)*	50	1985	Blue, green / white (60,000)	12.00 ☐
D3	*D1*	100	1985	Blue, pale blue / white (30,000)	15.00 ☐
D4	*(D1)*	200	1985	Blue, red / white (15,000)	22.00 ☐

Note. D2 to D4 have "CONDITIONS OF USE / 1. This card is not refundable / 2. Do not bend / 3. Payphone will not accept damaged cards / 4. For time per unit please see display in booth / 5. Valid for use in Diego Garcia only" on the reverse and may thus be distinguished from those of the Falkland Islands (q.v.) while D1 has the general form which has "5. Valid in country of purchase only", without mentioning the name of the island, and is otherwise the same.

DJIBOUTI

Electronic or 'smart' cards by Schlumberger Industries, France, were introduced in 1989.

D1

№	Ill.	Units	Date	Description		Value
D1	(D1)	10	1989	Yellow / white	(15,000)	6.00 ◻
D2	(D1)	25	1989	Greenish yellow / white	(25,000)	10.00 ◻
D3	(D1)	50	1989	Olive / white	(20,000)	12.00 ◻
D4	(D1)	100	1989	Pale green / white	(45,500)	12.00 ◻
D5	(D1)	200	1989	Bluish green / white	(15,500)	20.00 ◻
D6	D1	300	1989	Green-black / white	(32,000)	20.00 ◻

Note. The card illustrated is a punched sample kindly supplied by Schlumberger.

DOMINICA

Magnetic cards supplied by GPT (UK) are about to be introduced.

First Issue. Magnetic cards by GPT.

D1

№	Ill.	Units	Date	Description		Value
D1	(D1)	EC$5.40	1989	Multicolour	(1000)	20.00 ◻
D2	(D1)	EC$10	1989	Multicolour	(7000)	8.00 ◻
D3	D1	EC$20	1989	Multicolour	(4000)	15.00 ◻
D4	(D1)	EC$40	1989	Multicolour	(1000)	25.00 ◻

Note. D1 is included in the Cable and Wireless collectors pack of British West Indies cards (see under Promotional Cards at the end of this book).

EGYPT

Magnetic telephone cards, possibly manufactured by Mantegazza of Milan, Italy, and the corresponding payphones, manufactured by Urmet S.P.A. of Turin, Italy, are in use. The cards are of thin paper-board and the top left corner must be snapped off along a perforated line before they are first used. Used and unused cards may thus easily be distinguished. Only definitive cards of 20 and 40 Egyptian Lira have so far been issued.

D1

№	Ill.	Units	Date	Description	Value	
D1	*D1*	EL 20	1/88	Green, black / white	8.00 U	4.00 U
D2	*(D1)*	EL 40	1989	Green, black / white	25.00 ☐	10.00 ☐

FALKLAND ISLANDS

The Falklands Islands telephone service is operated by Cable and Wireless and magnetic cards are supplied by Autelca. The 50 unit card is identical to the Ascension Island card and all three have the general "country of purchase" wording on the reverse. The Falklands Island 50 unit card may be distinguished by its control number which is prefixed with an 'F' while the Ascension card has no prefix or is prefixed 'A'. All control numbers are in black and vary, as do those of all Autelca cards, in size and type. A collector in the Falkland Islands reports six different control types on the 50 unit value and two on each of the others. There are also said to be distinct shade differences between earlier and later printings.

D1

№	Ill.	Units	Date	Description		Value
D1	*(D1)*	50	1985	Blue, green / white	(170,000)	4.00 ☐
D2	*D1*	100	1985	Blue, pale blue / white	(60,000)	10.00 ☐
D3	*(D1)*	200	1985	Blue, red / white	(20,000)	20.00 ☐

FINLAND

There are 58 independent telephone companies in Finland, each owned by the subscribers in their areas of operation. Fortunately, perhaps, only three of them have issued telephone cards. These are the PTT of Finland, Hämeen Puhelin Oy and Tampereen Puhelinosuuskunta. Optical cards have been manufactured by Landis and Gyr, Switzerland. The unit is 0.2 FMk. The general test card described and illustrated under Algeria was also used in Finland but is not separately listed. Magnetic cards by Autelca, also of Switzerland, were field-tested in Finland. Mpre recently magnetic cards have been supplied by GPT, UK.

PTT OF FINLAND

DM1   *DO1*   *DO2*

MAGNETIC CARD (Autelca) This card was field tested in 1985.

№	Ill.	Units	Date	Description	Value
DM1	*DM1*	50FMk	1985	Black / yellow (20,000)	25.00 ☐

Note. This card is made of thin, stiff paper-board rather than the usual plastic.

OPTICAL CARDS. (Landis and Gyr)

№	Ill.	Units	Date	Description			Value	
DO1	*(DO1)*	50	3/82	Dark blue / silver	"SAMSTALSKORT"	(3000)	30.00 ☐	20.00 ☐
DO2	*DO2*	50	1984	Blue / silver	"SAMSTALSKORT"	(26,000)	20.00 ☐	10.00 ☐
DO3	*DO1*	120	3/82	Dark blue / silver	"SAMSTALSKORT"	(1000)	50.00 ☐	40.00 ☐

Note. The extra 'S' in 'SAMSTALSKORT' was an error in the first production run and was corrected in the second.

FINLAND

MAGNETIC CARDS (GPT)

D1

D2

D3

D4

№	Ill.	Units	Date	Description	Value
D1	*D1*	10FMk	1989	Multicoloured (10,000)	4.00 ☐
D2	*D2*	30FMk	1989	Multicoloured (90,000)	8.00 ☐
D3	*D3*	50FMk	1989	Multicoloured (50,000)	12.00 ☐
D4	*D4*	100FMk	1989	Multicoloured (50,000)	18.00 ☐

Note. The cards of P&T TELE of Finland can be bought from their: Philatelic Centre, / PL 654, / SF-00101 HELSINKI, / FINLAND

HÄMEEN PUHELIN OY

D1

Three Issues. 2mm white band, 4mm white band, 3mm white band with notch.

D1	*D1*	90	9/84	Dark blue, white / silver, 2mm band	25.00 ☐	10.00 ☐
D2	*(D1)*	90	12/87	Dark blue, white / silver, 4mm band	20.00 ☐	6.00 ☐
D3	*(D1)*	90	1/89	Dark blue, white / silver, 3mm band, notched	10.00 ☐	3.00 ☐

Note. An earlier card, also by Landis and Gyr, was used in internal experiments but no further details are known.

TAMPEREEN PUHELINOSUUSKKUNTA

Only one card, a 'standard' card by Landis and Gyr, was field tested. Only 60 out of the 1000 supplied were sold. The telephones are no longer available so no further used cards should appear.

D1

D1	*D1*	120	9/84	Blue, white / silver (1000)	50.00 ☐	150.00 ☐

Optical cards, manufactured by Landis and Gyr, Switzerland, were used in France from 1980 to 1986 but it was then decided that, for public use, the electronic system which employs the 'smart cards' described in following sections would be adopted. The optical cards were recalled against a money refund for unused units and are now rare. Unusually the denomination was in franks as well as in 'units'. The use of optical cards was however retained for closed user groups — ski-stations in the Haute-Savoie region until late 1983 and in military bases and prisons until the end of 1987. Magnetic cards of with detachable corners similar to recent Italian cards were used in the Savoie region from early 1981 to 1984. Optical cards have been given an 'O' prefix and magnetic cards an 'M' prefix to distinguish them from the current electronic types which have no general prefix. There were a number of ommissions and misplacements in the first edition of this book and it has been necessary, unfortunately, to change the numbering system extensively.

1 OPTICAL CARDS

OC - COMPLIMENTARY CARD

№	Ill.	Units	Date	Description	Value	
OC1	*OC1*	3	4/80	Dark blue / silver (3000)	200.00 ◻	160.00 ◻

OD - DEFINITIVE CARDS

First Series - Promotional issue.

OD1	*OD1*	20(10F)	4/80	Dark blue / silver (8000)	150.00 ◻	90.00 ◻
OD2	*OD2*	105(50F)	4/80	·· ·· ·· ·· ·· (11,000)	170.00 ◻	100.00 ◻

Note. For promotional purposes OD2 gave 5% more units at no extra cost.

Second Series.

OD3	*(OD3)*	20(10F)	6/80	Dark blue / silver (25.000)	120.00 ◻	70.00 ◻
OD4	*(OD4)*	100(50F)	6/80	·· ·· ·· ·· ·· (12,000)	150.00 ◻	90.00 ◻

Third Series - As for OD3 and OD4 but in lighter blue

OD5	*OD3*	20(10F)	3/82	Blue / silver (54,000)	120.00 ◻	70.00 ◻
OD6	*OD4*	100(50F)	3/82	·· ·· ·· (19,000)	150.00 ◻	90.00 ◻

Fourth Series

OD7	*(OD5)*	· 40	12/83	Blue / silver (636,200)	50.00 ◻	30.00 ◻
OD8	*OD5*	120	12/83	·· ·· ·· (275,000)	50.00 ◻	30.00 ◻

Note. These cards and those below replaced the magnetic cards used in the Savoie region.

Fifth Series. 1.5mm white band.

OD9	*(OD6)*	40	2/85	Red, white / silver (692,000)	50.00 ◻	45.00 ◻
OD10	*OD6*	120	2/85	·· ·· ·· ·· ·· (68,000)	40.00 ◻	30.00 ◻

Sixth Issue. 2mm white band. 3mm space for optical strip.

OD11	*(OD6)*	40	12/85	Red, white / silver (190,000)	35.00 ◻	25.00 ◻

Seventh Issue. 2mm white band. Redrawn with 4mm space for optical strip.

OD12	*(OD6)*	40	1987?	Red, white / silver (50,000)	35.00 ◻	25.00 ◻

Note. 120 unit cards with a 2mm white band are now known not to have been issued. The fifth, sixth and seventh issues were used in the Savoie region ski resorts (Courchevel, Val Thorens, Les Menuires and Méribel-Mottaret) up to the autumn of 1986 when they were replaced by electronic telephones and cards. Their use continued in closed user application in some military camps and prisons until the end of 1987.

OS - SPECIAL/COMMEMORATIVE CARD

21st European Telecommunications Congress, Bordeaux, 6-11 September, 1982.

OS1	*OS1*	100	6/9/82	Blue / silver (800)	350.00 ◻	200.00 ◻

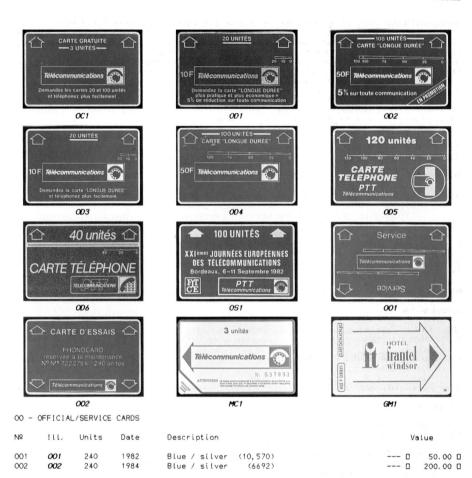

OC1   OD1   OD2

OD3   OD4   OD5

OD6   OS1   OO1

OO2   MC1   GM1

OO - OFFICIAL/SERVICE CARDS

Nº	Ill.	Units	Date	Description		Value
001	*OO1*	240	1982	Blue / silver (10,570)	--- ☐	50.00 ☐
002	*OO2*	240	1984	Blue / silver (6692)	--- ☐	200.00 ☐

Note. 001 was the original card used from the outset. 002 was that used in the Savoie at the end of 1983 and may have been in general use by then. Both are rare but the later one is more so. There must presumably have been a test card as well but no information on it has come to light.

M - MAGNETIC CARDS

These cards were used in the "Trois Vallees" ski resorts. Twelve telephones manufactured by C.G.A. (Compagnie Générale d'Automation) and Telic were installed in January, 1981 - four in Courchevel, two in Meribel-Mottaret, and three each in Les Menuires and Val Thorens. It is not known who made the actual cards. These telephones were replaced by 250 Landis and Gyr telephones throughout the Savoie resort region at the end of 1983.

MC - COMPLIMENTARY CARD

MC1	*(MC1)*	3	1/81	Blue / white (blue control)	70.00 ☐	40.00 ☐
MC2	*(MC1)*	3	1/81	Blue / white (control without letter N)	100.00 ☐	60.00 ☐

MD - DEFINITIVE CARDS

MD1	*(MC1)*	20	1/81	Blue (shades) / white (blue control)	40.00 ☐	25.00 ☐
MD2	*(MC1)*	20	1982?	Darker blue / white (smaller black control)	65.00 ☐	40.00 ☐
MD3	*(MC1)*	100	1/81	Blue / white (blue control)	45.00 ☐	30.00 ☐
MD4	*(MC1)*	100	1/81	Light blue / white (blue control)	45.00 ☐	30.00 ☐
MD5	*(MC1)*	100	1982?	Darker blue / white (smaller black control)	65.00 ☐	40.00 ☐

CLOSED USER GROUP CARD: HOTEL CARD

This card was field tested at the Hotel Frantel Windsor in Paris in 1978 making it one of the earliest telephone cards. Although made by Landis and Gyr (Switzerland) it was actually a magnetic card. Like some recent Bull CP8/Autelca smart cards used in Switzerland, these cards had no fixed value but could be charged with however many units the customer wanted to buy.

№	Ill.	Units	Date	Description	Value
GM1	*GM1*	–	1978	Light blue / white	3000.00 □

Note. Only one specimen of this card is known to have come onto the market although others exist.

3 ELECTRONIC CARDS

Electronic cards replaced the optical cards described above in 1986 and are currently in use. There is an extraordinarily wide variation in the definitive series of French electronic telephone cards. They differ in shade of colour, in surface texture, in detail of design, in type of control number and in the pattern of the gold contacts through which the silicon chip embedded in the card is accessed. This variation derives from the fact that French telephone cards have been simultaniously manufactured by four different companies, Schlumberger Industries, Solaic, Bull CP8 and Gemplus. Definitive cards are listed below by manufacturer for the sake of simplicity. Control or, probably, batch numbers are indented on the reverse in most cases. Also found in France (and Germany and, perhaps, Spain) is the 'Carte Télécom' or Pastel card. These are effectively transfer charge cards activated with a PIN (Personal Identification Number) which store the number of units used up to a preset number at which they are automatically charged to an account through the telephone. Although these are used in the same telephones they are not prepayment cards they have not been listed in this book. Only one 'collector's value' is given for each electronic card listed below because, without access to a suitable French public telephone, there is no means of knowing whether a card has been used or not. Effectively they are prices for used cards. Unused cards, still sealed in the plastic sachets in which they are supplied, command a premium over the prices given in this book in most cases.

D - DEFINITIVE CARDS

There are now two types of 'definitive' card in France - those blue and white striped cards listed as definitives in the last edition, known to French collectors as 'pyjamas', are no longer being issued. The "POUR TÉLÉPHONER CHOISISSEZ VOTRE HEURE" cards, now known to French collectors as 'cordons' from the telephone cord in the design and listed (mistakenly) as A9 to A14 in the last edition, are the current definitive cards. Both are now listed as definitives but distinguished as DP for pyjamas and DC for cordons. The four different manufacturers are distinguished by 'SI' for Schlumberger, 'SO' for Solaic, 'BU' for Bull CP8 and 'GP' for Gemplus both for the definitives and for the Special and Private cards that follow. Contacts vary in form as described below and, particularly in cordons, may be against a pale background or a dark background. These two types are indicated by a 'p' or a 'd' after the Roman numeral of the contact type in the Contact column if both types can be found on otherwise similar cards. Thus IVd means a type IV (i.e. Schlumberger) contact on a dark background. In addition there are, in this case, type IV contacts on a hatched dark background known as TI (for Texas Instruments) and silver contacts indicated by IV Ag.

Two new columns of information have been introduced to indicate the type of surface and the type of control number on the reverse. Surfaces include

        (a) Smooth Glazed - flat and shiney like a mirror (SG),
        (b) coarsely textured or Rough Glazed like orange peel (RG),
        (c) finely textured or Fine Glazed (FG),
        (d) Smooth Lustrous - midway between glazed and smooth matt (SL),
        (e) Finely textured Lustrous (FL),
        (f) Rough Lustrous (RL),
        (g) Smooth Matt (SM)
        (h) finely textured or Fine Matt (FM)
        (i) Rough Matt (RM).

There are variations within these basic surface types, especially in the degree of glossiness of 'smooth matt' surfaces, which may be collected as sub-varieties. Silk screen printed Pyjamas sometimes show a rough glazed design on a smooth matt surface and this is shown as RG/SM. The surface of the reverse, where significant, is shown by a prefixed 'r', e.g. rSM means that the reverse is smooth matt.

Control numbers are normally present on all but some of the Bull CP8 cards. They would seem to be batch numbers rather than individual card numbers and bear no obvious relationship to date of manufacture or indeed to anything else. There are several types of control number which specialist collectors see as generating collectably different cards. The types listed below are the main ones found on both pyjamas and cordons (and on the special and advertising cards). They may be found upright, inverted or at an angle, incompletely struck, doubly struck, etc, providing further scope for specalisation. French listings also often distinguish controls with different numbers of digits but these have not been distinguished in this book. Only main types are listed here.

i.	1.6mm	impressed (SI)
ii.	1.6mm	impressed with 13.5mm blue-green disk (SI)
iii.	2 - 2.25mm	apparantly hand-scratched (SI)
iv.	2.2mm	hot-pressed (BU)
v.	2.5mm	impressed (SI)
vi.	2.5mm	dotted engraving (apparantly done with drill but actually a laser) (SI)
vii.	2.5mm	rough engraving but not dotted (SI)
viii.	2.5mm	printed numerals of medium thickness (GP)
ix.	2.5mm	thin printed numerals (GP)
x.	2.8mm	thick printed numerals (GP)
xi.	2.8mm	impressed (SI)
xii.	3.0mm	hot-pressed (BU)

The listings below are intended to include the main types. More specialised listings have been prepared and published in France. The ordering of the definitives has been changed in this edition in that both Pyjamas and Cordons are now grouped by contact type. It has not proved possible to obtain reliable dates of issue and it is felt that this arrangement will make identification of cards easier for the collector. Gaps in the numbering have been left to accomodate future additions.

PYJAMAS

All pyjamas are on a white background and only the other colour is listed below. All are prefixed DP (for Definitive Pyjama) followed by the manufacturer, SI, SO, BU or GP as above.

SCHLUMBERGER PYJAMAS. Contact patterns are of the four main types shown below. The holes containing the silicon chips go right through the cards and are sealed behind with a black or (with Type IV contacts) brown or, rarely, red resin spot. Schlumberger cards are of two types - laminated and moulded. Laminations or the absence of them can be seen by examining the edge of a card under a magnifier but these types are not distinguished in this catalogue.

Type I   Type II   Type III   Type IV

DPSI1   DPSI2   DPSI3

№	Ill.	Units	Description	Surface	Control	Contact	Value
DPSI1	(DPSI2)	40	Pale blue (silk screened)	SM/SG	None	I	10.00 ☐
DPSI2	(DPSI1)	40	Pale blue ·· ·· ·· ··	SM/SG	None	I	20.00 ☐
DPSI3	DPSI1	120	Deep blue ·· ·· ·· ··	SM/SG	None	I	40.50 ☐
DPSI3(a)			Contact inverted	SM/SG	None	(I)	75.00 ☐
DPSI4	(DPSI2)	120	Deep blue ·· ·· ·· ··	SM/SG	None	I	40.00 ☐

DPSI4

DPSI5

DPSI6

DPSI7

DPSI8

DPSI9

№	Ill.	Units	Description	Surface	Control	Contact	Value
DPSI5	(DPSI2)	40	Pale blue (offset) Height 47.8mm	SL	i.	II	4.00 ☐
DPSI6	(DPSI2)	40	Pale blue (offset) Height 48.3mm	SG	i.	II	4.00 ☐
DPSI7	DPSI2	40	Pale blue (offset) Ht.48.8mm	SL	i.	II	5.00 ☐
DPSI8	(DPSI2)	40	Pale blue (screened)	SM/SG	i.	II	6.00 ☐
DPSI9	(DPSI2)	40	Pale blue (screened)	SM/SG	None	II	6.00 ☐
DPSI10	(DPSI1)	40	Pale blue (screened)	SL	i.	II	6.00 ☐
DPSI11	DPSI3	120	Dark blue (offset) Ht.47.8	FL	i.	II	6.00 ☐
DPSI12	DPSI4	120	Dark blue (typo) Ht.48.8	FM	i.	II	6.00 ☐
DPSI13	(DPSI4)	120	Dark blue (screened)	SM/SG?	i.	II	4.00 ☐
DPSI14	(DPSI1)	120	Dark blue (screened)	SM/SG?	i.	II	4.00 ☐
DPSI15	(DPSI4)	120	Dark blue (screened)	SM/SG?	None	II	4.00 ☐
DPSI16	(DPSI5)[1]	40	Pale blue (offset) Ht.48.0mm	SG	i.	III	2.00 ☐
DPSI17	(DPSI5)[1]	40	Pale blue (offset) Ht.48.0mm	SL	i.	III	2.00 ☐
DPSI18	(DPSI5)[1]	40	Pale blue (offset) Ht.48.8mm	SGrSG	i.	III	2.00 ☐
DPSI19	(DPSI5)[1]	40	Pale blue (offset) Ht.48.8mm	SGrSG	i.	III	2.00 ☐
DPSI20	(DPSI5)[2]	40	Pale blue (offset) I<1mm Ht.48.8mm	SL	i.	III	2.00 ☐
DPSI21	DPSI5[2]	40	Pale blue (offset) I<0.4mm Ht.48.8	SL	i.	III	2.00 ☐
DPSI22	DPSI5[2]	40	Pale blue (offset) I<0.4mm Ht.48.0	SGrSG	i.	III	2.00 ☐
DPSI23	DPSI5[2]	40	Pale blue (offset) I<0.4mm Ht.48.5mm	SG	i.	III	2.00 ☐
DPSI24	(DPSI5)[3]	40	Pale blue (offset) I<1mm Ht.48.0mm	SL	i.	III	2.00 ☐

Note. The offset-printed 40 unit cards with Type III contacts are found with three basic design variations - in those with a superscript [1] the point of the arrow (<) meets a stripe below centre, in those with [2] (illustrated as DPSI5) at centre and in that with [3] above centre. Heights (Ht.) are those of the design (not the card) from top to bottom and 'I<1mm' etc. indicates distances from the point of the arrow at top left to the edge of the colour.

DPSI25	(DPSI6)	40	Light blue (recess) Ht.48.0mm	FM	i.	III	4.00 ☐
DPSI26	DPSI6	40	Light blue (recess) Ht.48.4mm	FM	i.	III	4.00 ☐
DPSI27	(DPSI6)	40	Light blue (recess) Ht.49.0mm	FM	i.	III	5.00 ☐
DPSI28	(DPSI6)	40	Light blue (recess) Ht.49.4mm	FM	i.	III	5.00 ☐
DPSI29	(DPSI5)	40	Pale blue (screened)	FG/SG	i.	III	2.50 ☐
DPSI30	(DPSI5)	40	Pale blue (typo) Ht.48.5mm	FM	i.	III	2.50 ☐
DPSI31	(DPSI7)	50	Purple (shades)(recess) Ht.48.9mm	FM	i.	III	1.50 ☐
DPSI32	(DPSI7)	50	Same but amber resin under contact	FM	i.	III	1.50 ☐
DPSI33	(DPSI7)	50	Same but brown resin	FM	i.	III	1.50 ☐
DPSI34	(DPSI7)	50	Same but red resin	FM	i.	III	500.00 ☐
DPSI35	(DPSI7)	50	Purple (shades)(recess) Ht.49.3mm	FM	i.	III	1.50 ☐
DPSI36	(DPSI7)	50	Purple (shades) Ht.49.7mm	FM	i.	III	1.50 ☐
DPSI37	(DPSI7)	50	Violet (shades)(offset) Ht.47.8mm	SM	i.	III	1.50 ☐
DPSI38	(DPSI7)	50	Same but brown resin under contact	SM	i.	III	1.50 ☐
DPSI39	(DPSI7)	50	Violet < meets gap between lines	SM	i.	III	20.00 ☐
DPSI40	DPSI7	50	Deep violet-blue (offset)	SM	i.	III	3.00 ☐
DPSI41	(DPSI7)	50	Violet (screened)	RG/SM?	i.	III	10.00 ☐
DPSI42	(DPSI7)	50	Violet (screened)	RG/SM?	None	III	10.00 ☐

№	Ill.	Units	Description	Surface	Control	Contact	Value
DPS143	*DPS18*	120	Dark blue (offset) Ht.49.0mm	SM	i.	III	5.00 ▢
DPS144	*(DPS18)*	120	Dark blue (offset) Ht.48.5mm	SM	i.	III	5.00 ▢
DPS145	*DPS19*	120	Dark blue (offset) Ht.48.5mm	SM	i.	III	5.00 ▢
DPS146	*(DPS18)*	120	Dark blue (offset) Ht.48.5mm	SG	i.	III	5.00 ▢
DPS147	*(DPS19)*	120	Dark blue (offset) Ht.48.5mm	SM	i.	III	5.00 ▢
DPS148	*(DPS18)²*	120	Dark blue (offset) Ht.48.5mm	SM	i.	III	5.00 ▢
DPS149	*(DPS18)²*	120	Dark blue (offset) Ht.48.5mm	SM	i.	III	5.00 ▢
DPS150	*(DPS18)²*	120	Dark blue (offset) Ht.48.5mm	SG	i.	III	5.00 ▢
DPS151	*(DPS18)*	120	Dark blue (offset) Ht.48.0mm	SG	i.	III	4.00 ▢
DPS152	*·(DPS18)*	120	Dark blue (offset) Ht.48.0mm	SM	i.	III	4.00 ▢
DPS153	*(DPS18)*	120	Same but white contact area flat	FL	i.	III	10.00 ▢
DPS154	*(DPS18)*	120	Dark blue (offset) Ht.47.7mm	SG	i.	III	4.00 ▢
DPS155	*(DPS18)*	120	Dark blue (offset) Ht.47.7mm	SM	i.	III	4.00 ▢
DPS156	*(DPS18)²*	120	Dark blue (offset) Ht.47.7mm I<1mm	SM	i.	III	4.00 ▢
DPS157	*(DPS18)³*	120	Dark blue (offset) Ht.47.7mm	SM	i.	III	4.00 ▢
DPS158	*(DPS18)³*	120	Same but amber resin below contact	SM	i.	III	4.00 ▢
DPS159	*(DPS18)²*	120	Dark blue (offset)				
			Ht.47.7mm I<0.8mm	SL	i.	III	3.00 ▢
DPS160	*(DPS18)*	120	Dark blue (screened)	SG-SM	i.	III	3.00 ▢
DPS161	*(DPS18)*	120	Dark blue (recess) Ht.49.3mm	SL	i.	III	3.00 ▢
DPS162	*(DPS18)*	120	Dark blue (recess) Ht.49.0mm	SL	i.	III	4.00 ▢
DPS163	*(DPS18)*	120	Dark blue (recess) Ht.48.5mm	SL	i.	III	4.00 ▢
DPS164	*(DPS18)*	120	Same but amber resin below contact	SL	i.	III	4.00 ▢
DPS165	*(DPS18)*	120	(Offset) 11mm black ● below contact	SG	i.	III	4.00 ▢
DPS166	*(DPS19)*	120	(Offset) 11mm black ● below contact	FM	i.	III	4.00 ▢

Note 1. Those with a superscript ² have the arrow meeting the centre of a coloured stripe and on those with ³ the point of the arrow is above the centre of a stripe. On those without superscript it is below the centre of a stripe.

Note 2. DPS153 has a flat white area round the contact inset to take a Type IV contact.

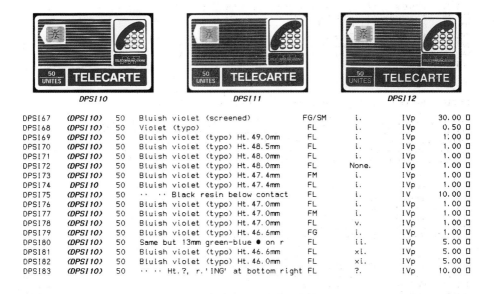

DPS110 DPS111 DPS112

DPS167	*(DPS110)*	50	Bluish violet (screened)	FG/SM	i.	IVp	30.00 ▢
DPS168	*(DPS110)*	50	Violet (typo)	FL	i.	IVp	0.50 ▢
DPS169	*(DPS110)*	50	Bluish violet (typo) Ht.49.0mm	FL	i.	IVp	1.00 ▢
DPS170	*(DPS110)*	50	Bluish violet (typo) Ht.48.5mm	FL	i.	IVp	1.00 ▢
DPS171	*(DPS110)*	50	Bluish violet (typo) Ht.48.0mm	FL	i.	IVp	1.00 ▢
DPS172	*(DPS110)*	50	Bluish violet (typo) Ht.48.0mm	FL	None.	IVp	1.00 ▢
DPS173	*(DPS110)*	50	Bluish violet (typo) Ht.47.4mm	FM	i.	IVp	1.00 ▢
DPS174	*DPS110*	50	Bluish violet (typo) Ht.47.4mm	FL	i.	IVp	1.00 ▢
DPS175	*(DPS110)*	50	·· ·· Black resin below contact	FL	i.	IV	10.00 ▢
DPS176	*(DPS110)*	50	Bluish violet (typo) Ht.47.0mm	FL	i.	IVp	1.00 ▢
DPS177	*(DPS110)*	50	Bluish violet (typo) Ht.47.0mm	FM	i.	IVp	1.00 ▢
DPS178	*(DPS110)*	50	Bluish violet (typo) Ht.47.0mm	FL	v.	IVp	1.00 ▢
DPS179	*(DPS110)*	50	Bluish violet (typo) Ht.46.6mm	FG	i.	IVp	1.00 ▢
DPS180	*(DPS110)*	50	Same but 13mm green-blue ● on r	FL	ii.	IVp	5.00 ▢
DPS181	*(DPS110)*	50	Bluish violet (typo) Ht.46.6mm	FL	xi.	IVp	5.00 ▢
DPS182	*(DPS110)*	50	Bluish violet (typo) Ht.46.0mm	FL	xi.	IVp	5.00 ▢
DPS183	*(DPS110)*	50	·· ·· Ht.?, r.'ING' at bottom right	FL	?.	IVp	10.00 ▢

General Note. French specialists also distinguish between various minor differences in the surface texture on the reverse, in the numbers of digits in the control numbers on the reverse and in the location and orientation of the control numbers. They also recognise more gradations of front surface type than listed above. Specialist catalogues covering French definitive cards have been published in France.

№	Ill.	Units	Description	Surface	Control	Contact	Value
DPSI84	*DPSI11*	50	Reddish violet (typo) Ht. 48.5mm	FL	i.	IVp	1.00 ☐
DPSI85	*(DPSI11)*	50	Reddish violet (typo) Ht. 48.0mm	FL	i.	IVp	1.00 ☐
DPSI86	*(DPSI11)*	50	Reddish violet (typo) Ht. 47.5mm	FL	i.	IVp	1.00 ☐
DPSI87	*(DPSI11)*	50	Reddish violet (typo) Ht. 46.5mm	FL	i.	IVp	1.00 ☐
DPSI88	*DPSI12*	50	Reddish violet (typo) Ht. 50.0mm	FL	i.	IVp	1.00 ☐
DPSI89	*(DPSI12)*	50	Reddish violet (typo) Ht. 49.0mm	FL	i.	IVp	1.00 ☐
DPSI90	*(DPSI12)*	50	Reddish violet (typo) Ht. 48.5mm	FL	i.	IVp	1.'00 ☐
DPSI91	*(DPSI12)*	50	Reddish violet (typo) Ht. 48.0mm	FL	i.	IVp	1.00 ☐

Note. The arrow in Type DPSI11 has a less acute angle and type DPSI12 has a narrow space between the ends of the stripes and the box to the right.

DPSI13

DPSI14

DPSI15

DPSI16

DPSI17

№	Ill.	Units	Description	Surface	Control	Contact	Value
DPSI92	*(DPSI13)*	50	Bluish violet (screened)	FG/FM	None	IVp	1.00 ☐
DPSI93	*(DPSI13)*	50	Bluish violet (screened)	FG/FM	i.	IVp	1.00 ☐
DPSI94	*(DPSI13)*	50	Bluish violet (screened)	FG/FM	iii.	IVp	1.00 ☐
DPSI95	*DPSI13*	50	Bluish violet (shades) (screened)	FG/FM	vi.	IVp	1.00 ☐
DPSI96	*(DPSI13)*	50	Bluish violet (typo)	FL	i.	IVp	1.00 ☐
DPSI97	*(DPSI13)*	50	Bluish violet (typo)	FL	iii.	IVp	1.00 ☐
DPSI98	*(DPSI13)*	50	Bluish violet (typo)	FL	vi.	IVp	1.00 ☐
DPSI99	*(DPSI14)*	120	Dark blue (typo) Ht. 48.5mm	FL	i.	IVp	5.00 ☐
DPSI100	*DPSI14*	120	Dark blue (typo) Ht. 47.8mm	FL	i.	IVp	1.00 ☐
DPSI101	*(DPSI14)*	120	Darkish blue (typo) Ht. 47.4mm	FL	i.	IVp	3.00 ☐
DPSI102	*(DPSI14)*	120	Dark blue (typo) Ht. 47.0mm	FL	i.	IVp	3.00 ☐
DPSI103	*(DPSI14)*	120	Dark blue (typo) Ht. 47.0mm	FG	i.	IVp	3.00 ☐
DPSI104	*(DPSI14)*	120	Darkish blue (typo) Ht. 47.0mm	FL	i.	IVp	3.00 ☐
DPSI105	*(DPSI14)*	120	Darkish blue (typo) Ht. 46.8mm	FL	xi.	IVp	30.00 ☐
DPSI106	*(DPSI14)*	120	Darkish blue (typo) Ht. 46.8mm	FL	i. & xi.	IVp	30.00 ☐
DPSI107	(DPSI14)	120	Darkish blue (typo) Ht. 46.2mm	FL	i.	IVp	5.00 ☐
DPSI108	*(DPSI14)*	120	Dark blue (typo)	FL	i. & v.	IVp	10.00 ☐
DPSI109	*(DPSI14)*	120	Dark blue (typo)	FL	v.	IVp	8.00 ☐
DPSI110	*(DPSI14)*	120	Bluish violet (error)	FL	i.	IVp	10.00 ☐

Note. Several of the above cards may be found with the contact posts standing well proud of the contact surface and this is regarded as a collectable variety by some.

№	Ill.	Units	Description	Surface	Control	Contact	Value
DPSI111	*DPSI15*	120	Dark blue (typo)	FL	i.	IVp	30.00 ☐
DPSI112	*DPSI16*	120	Dark blue (typo)	FL	i.	IVp	1.00 ☐
DPSI113	*(DPSI16)*	120	Dark blue (typo)	FL	iii.	IVp	1.00 ☐
DPSI114	*DPSI17*	120	Darkish blue (screened)	FL	i.	IVp	1.00 ☐
DPSI115	*(DPSI17)*	120	Darkish blue (screened)	FL	vi.	IVp	1.00 ☐
DPSI116	*(DPSI17)*	120	Darkish blue (screened)	FL	vii.	IVp	1.00 ☐
DPSI117	*(DPSI17)*	120	Darkish blue (typo)	FL	vii.	IVp	20.00 ☐

SOLAIC PYJAMAS. Contact patterns are of Types V and VI below. Solaic Type VI contacts measure 10mm high by 11.5mm wide and have a smooth, slightly convex surface (rf Gemplus contacts below). There are two types: in the first and earlier type the dark area of resin below the contact, which can be seen through the slots in the contact pattern, measures 7.5mm high by 8.5mm wide while in the other it measures 8.8mm high by 10.2mm wide; these are listed below as contact types VIa and VIb respectively. Some French specialists also distinguish between large and small slots in the contact pattern. All Solaic 'pyjamas' are printed by offset lithography. The hole for the chip does not extend to the back of the card which is therefore plain. Controls, where present, are of type i. and are normally inverted at bottom right on the reverse. They may be so lightly struck as to be almost invisible. Solaic cards are indicated by 'SO' throughout.

Type V

Type VI

DPS01

DPS02

DPS03

DPS04

DPS05

DPS06

№	Ill.	Units	Description	Surface	Control	Contact	Value
DPS01	*DPS01*	40	Pale blue	SM	None	V	10.00 ☐
DPS02	*DPS02*	50	Violet	SM	None	V	8.00 ☐
DPS03	*(DPS02)*	50	Violet	SM	i.	V	8.00 ☐
DPS04	*(DPS02)*	50	Violet, 3/87, 1,000,000th. Note 1.	SM	?.	V	150.00 ☐
DPS05	*(DPS02)*	50	Violet, 3/87, 1,000,000th. Note 1.	SM	?.	V	150.00 ☐

Note 1. 500 each of DPS04 and DPS05 were issued to mark the production of 1,000,000 cards by Solaic. DPS04 has "MARS 1987...DEJA 1 000 000 / DE CARTES A MEMOIRE PRODUITES PAR: / SLIGOS-SOLAIC / 92067 PARIS-LA-DEFENCE (16.1.49.00.90.00)" printed by ink-jet on four lines at the bottom of the reverse while DPS05 has only the lower two lines with "33" in place of "16" in the telephone number. These cards are extremely rare.

DPS06	*(DPS03)*	50	Dk violet blue (contact area 15mm)	SM	i.	V	30.00 ☐
DPS07	*DPS03*	50	Dk violet blue (contact area 16mm)	SM	i.	V	15.00 ☐
DPS08	*(DPS04)*	120	Darkish blue	SM	None	V	10.00 ☐
DPS09	*(DPS04)*	120	Dark blue	SM	None	V	10.00 ☐
DPS010	*DPS04*	120	Dark blue	SM	i.	V	10.00 ☐
DPS011	*DPS05*	50	Dark violet blue	SM	i.	VIa	15.00 ☐
DPS012	*DPS05*	50	Dark violet blue	SL	i.	VIa	15.00 ☐
DPS013	*DPS05*	50	Dark violet blue	SM	i.	VIb	15.00 ☐
DPS014	*DPS06*	120	Blue	SM	i.	VIa	3.00 ☐
DPS015	*DPS06*	120	Blue	SM	i.	VIb	3.00 ☐
DPS016	*DPS06*	120	Blue	SM	None	VIb?	3.00 ☐
DPS017	*DPS06*	120	Dark blue	SM	i.	VIb	3.00 ☐
DPS018	*DPS06*	120	Dark blue (Ht. contact area 16mm)	SM	i.	VI?	15.00 ☐

BULL CP8 PYJAMAS. All Bull CP8 cards issued in France have the same Type VII contact pattern and all Bull CP8 pyjamas were printed by offset lithography. The hole for the chip does not penitrate to the back. The cards always have wording on the reverse but control numbers are oftem absent. There are seven lines of text on the back of each card (except for the first card which has ten) and this is in the same colour as the printing on the front unless otherwise indicated. Some cards have a small star printed in the bottom right corner on the reverse - indicated by a * in the control column. One finds some variation in the distance between the white arrow and the contact and also in the level of the contact with respect to the stripes; these would seem not to be varieties but rather to depend on the centering of the design on the card since the contact must be at a constant location with respect to the edges of the card in order to operate the telephone. Bull CP8 issues are indicated by 'BU' throughout.

Type VII

| DPBU1 | | | | | DPBU2 (reverse) |

Nº	Ill.	Units	Description	Surface	Control	Contact	Value
DPBU1	(DPBU1)	40	Pale blue (r. black, 10 lines)	SG	None	VIId	20.00 ☐
DPBU2	(DPBU1)	40	Pale blue (r. black, 7 lines)	SG	None	VIId	10.00 ☐
DPBU3	(DPBU1)	40	Pale blue	SG	iv.	VIId	2.00 ☐
DPBU4	(DPBU1)	40	Pale blue	RM	None	VIId	2.00 ☐
DPBU5	*DPBU1*	50	Purple (rev. star)	SG	None*	VIId	1.00 ☐
DPBU6	(DPBU1)	50	Dark violet blue	SG	iv.	VIId	1.00 ☐
DPBU7	(DPBU1)	50	Dark violet blue	FG	None	VIId	1.00 ☐
DPBU8	(DPBU1)	50	Dark violet blue (r. star)	SG	None*	VIIp	1.00 ☐
DPBU9	(DPBU1)	50	Violet-blue	FG	None	VIId	1.00 ☐
DPBU10	(DPBU1)	50	Violet-blue	SL	None	VIId	1.00 ☐
DPBU11	(DPBU1)	50	Violet-blue	FG	iv.	VIId	1.00 ☐
DPBU12	(DPBU1)	50	Violet-blue (r. star)	FG	None*	VIId	1.00 ☐
DPBU13	(DPBU1)	50	Violet-blue (r. star)	FG	None*	VIIp	1.00 ☐
DPBU14	(DPBU1)	50	Violet-blue	SG	iv.	VIId	1.00 ☐
DPBU15	(DPBU1)	50	Violet-blue	FL	None	VIId	1.00 ☐
DPBU16	(DPBU1)	50	Violet-blue	SG	xii.	VIId	1.00 ☐
DPBU17	(DPBU1)	50	Purple	SG	xii.	VIId	1.00 ☐
DPBU18	(DPBU1)	50	Violet-blue	SG	None	VIIp	1.00 ☐
DPBU19	(DPBU1)	50	Violet-blue	SL	None	VIIp	1.00 ☐
DPBU20	(DPBU1)	50	Violet-blue (r. black star)	SG	None*	VIIp	1.00 ☐
DPBU21	(DPBU1)	50	Violet-blue (r. black star)	SL	None*	VIIp	1.00 ☐
DPBU22	(DPBU1)	50	Violet-blue (r. black star)	FG	None*	VIIp	1.00 ☐
DPBU23	(DPBU1)	50	Violet-blue	SG	xii.	VIIp	1.00 ☐
DPBU24	(DPBU1)	50	Violet-blue	SL	xii.	VIIp	1.00 ☐
DPBU30	(DPBU1)	120	Darkish blue (r. black text)	SG	xii.	VIId	10.00 ☐
DPBU31	(DPBU1)	120	Darkish blue (r. black text)	SG	None	VIId	10.00 ☐
DPBU32	(DPBU1)	120	Blue	SG	xii.	VIId	1.50 ☐
DPBU33	(DPBU1)	120	Dark blue	SG	None	VIId	2.00 ☐
DPBU34	(DPBU1)	120	Dark blue	SG	xii.	VIId	2.00 ☐
DPBU35	(DPBU1)	120	Pale blue (colour of 40 unit card)	SG	None	VIId	100.00 ☐

Nº	Ill.	Units	Description	Surface	Control	Contact	Value
DPBU36	*(DPBU1)*	120	Darkish blue	FM	xii.	VIId	3.00 ☐
DPBU37	*(DPBU1)*	120	Darkish blue	FM	None	VIId	3.00 ☐
DPBU38	*(DPBU1)*	120	Darkish blue	FG	xii.	VIId	3.00 ☐
DPBU39	*(DPBU1)*	120	Darkish blue	SL	None	VIId	3.00 ☐
DPBU40	*(DPBU1)*	120	Darkish blue	SL	xii.	VIId	3.00 ☐
DPBU41	*(DPBU1)*	120	Darkish grey-blue	SG	None	VIId	3.00 ☐

GEMPLUS PYJAMAS. Gemplus began making telephone cards for France Telecom in June/July, 1988, in place of Bull CP8. All Gemplus pyjamas were printed by offset lithography. The contact pattern used is virtually identical to Type VI used by Solaic but can be distinguished in that the Solaic contacts measure 11.5 mm wide by 10.2 mm high while the Gemplus contacts are a little larger measuring 11.8 wide by 10.5 mm high. Another distinguishing feature is a pronounced hump round the centre of the Gemplus contacts whereas Solaic contacts are even. All Gemplus control numbers appear to be printed in colour while Solaic controls are impressed. Gemplus cards are indicated by the letters 'GP' throughout.

DPGP1

DPGP2

Nº	Ill.	Units	Description	Surface	Control	Contact	Value
DPGP1	*DPGP1*	50	Violet (green control 0111 and spot)	SL	viii.	VI	5.00 ☐
DPGP2	*(DPGP1)*	50	Violet (green control 2300 and spot)	SL	viii.	VI	15.00 ☐
DPGP3	*(DPGP1)*	50	Violet (violet control and spot)	FL	viii.	VI	5.00 ☐
DPGP4	*(DPGP1)*	50	Violet (violet control)	FL	viii.	VI	1.00 ☐
DPGP5	*(DPGP2)*	50	Violet (violet control)	FL	viii.	VI	1.00 ☐
DPGP6	*DPGP2*	50	Violet (black control)	FL	viii.	VI	1.00 ☐
DPGP10	*(DPGP2)*	120	Blue (blue control)	FL	viii.	VI	1.50 ☐
DPGP11	*(DPGP2)*	120	Blue (black control)	FL	viii.	VI	1.50 ☐

CORDONS

The colours of the cordon design are essentially the same for all cards (except for the Schlumberger cards with a white background) so the colour space in the listing below has been used only to indicate departures from the norm. Cordons show many points of variation making them rather difficult to list in an economic yet comprehensive way. These variables (apart from errors) include:

1. Manufacturer
2. Contact
3. Background to contact
4. Front design features such as white areas round contact, lettering, etc
5. Major shade variations - usually background or telephone mouthpiece
6. Surface textures on both front and reverse.
7. (Reverse) Date of validity of information
8. (Reverse) Control type and location
9. (Reverse) Colour of resin over the chip on Schlumberger cards
10. (Reverse) Wording variations at the right
11. (Reverse) Other design changes, e.g. coloured spots and stars on Bull cards

Cards are listed by manufacturer and it has again proved impossible to determine reliable dates of issue. They are therefore listed in approximate issue order where systematic changes in design have allowed this to be determined. Most cards give the date from which the tariffs given apply as 1-1-88 at the bottom on the reverse and this can be assumed unless otherwise stated. On the reverse there are two main forms of the address of the publisher, Régie T, below the control box at bottom right, one having three lines and one four. These correlate with with seven and six line layouts respectively above the control boxes and are indicated by '3 lines' and '4 lines' in the listings below. All cordons can be assumed to be offset-printed unless otherwise stated.

SCHLUMBERGER CORDONS

There are two independent design variations found on the fronts of Schlumberger cordons. Most cards have an accent over the 'E' in UNITÉS in the tablet on the front (but not, for some obscure reason, on the reverse). On some 120 unit cards however the accent is missing and in these cases the words stop just over 1mm from the logo as compared with almost 3mm where the accent is present. The accent or its absence is indicated by É or E for 120 unit cards below; it is always present on 50 unit cards. There are also two settings of the wording at bottom left. In type 1 the tail of the 'P' in POUR ends over the centre of the 'O' in CHOISISSEZ while in type 2 it ends rather to the right of the centre of the 'O'. These variations seem to occur randomly in time and possibly come from different production lines. The space between the arrow at top left and the white area round the contact also varies but it is probable that this arises because there are slight variations in the registration of the design relative to the edges of the card while the position of the contact in the card must be constant. All Schlumberger cordons with type IV gold (or silver) contacts, whether they have pale or dark backgrounds to the contacts, have their chips set in transparant brown resin which is ground flat such that the chip and eight contact posts are visible from the reverse. Schlumberger have recently introduced a silver coloured type IV contact and this is designated IV Ag. IV Agd thus means a silver type IV contact on a dark background. Type IV contacts with dark backgrounds due to a dark, hatched backing layer set in clear resin are often refered to as Texas Instruments (TI) contacts.

Offset-printed Blue Cordons

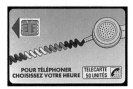

DCSI1

DCSI2 (reverse)

№	Ill.	Units	Description	Surface	Control	Contact	Value
DCSI1	*(DCSI1)*	50	Dated 1-6-1987	SM	i.'	IIId	250.00 ⊡

Note 1. The control is located in the centre of the left sector of the reverse rather than in its box and is inverted. This card was given out at the annual SICOB exhibition.

№	Ill.	Units	Description	Surface	Control	Contact	Value
DCSI2	*DCSI1*	50	Type 1, 3 lines, 45° (see Note 1.)	SL	i.	IIId	0.50 ⊡
DCSI3	*(DCSI1)*	50	Type 1, 3 lines, 15° (see Note 1.)	SL	i.	IIId	0.50 ⊡
DCSI4	*(DCSI1)*	120	Type 1, É, 3 lines, 45°	SL	i.	IIId	0.50 ⊡
DCSI5	*(DCSI1)*	120	Type 1, É, 3 lines, 15°	SL	i.	IIId	0.50 ⊡
DCSI6	*(DCSI1)*	50	As DCSI3 but reverse highly glazed	SG	i.	IIId	1.00 ⊡
DCSI7	*(DCSI1)*	50	As DCSI2 but w. France Telecom tel. no. printed vertically on reverse	SL	i.	IIId	50.00 ⊡
DCSI8	*(DCSI1)*	50	Type 2, 3 lines	SG	i.	IIId	1.00 ⊡
DCSI9	*(DCSI1)*	50	Same but yellow area round contact	SG	i.	IIId	1.50 ⊡
DCSI10	*(DCSI1)*	50	Error. 120 unités on reverse	SG	i.	IIId	40.00 ⊡
DCSI11	*(DCSI1)*	120	Type 2, no accent on E, 3 lines	SG	i.	IIId	1.00 ⊡
DCSI12	*(DCSI1)*	120	Same but yellow area round contact	SG	i.	IIId	1.50 ⊡
DCSI13	*(DCSI1)*	50	Type 2, brown resin, 4 lines, 45°	SG	i.	IIIp	0.50 ⊡
DCSI14	*(DCSI1)*	50	Type 2, brown resin, 4 lines, 45°	FG	i.	IIIp	0.50 ⊡
DCSI15	*(DCSI1)*	50	Type 2, brown resin, 4 lines, 15°	SG	i.	IIIp	1.00 ⊡
DCSI16	*(DCSI1)*	50	Same but rounded corners to contact area (i.e. card intended for Type IV contact)	SG	i.	IIIp	8.00 ⊡
DCSI17	*(DCSI1)*	50	Type 2, black resin, 4 lines, 15°,	SG	i.	IIId	1.50 ⊡
DCSI18	*(DCSI1)*	50	Same but rounded corners to contact area (i.e. card intended for Type IV contact)	SG	i.	IIId	8.00 ⊡
DCSI19	*(DCSI1)*	50	Error. As DCSI17 w. 120 unités on reverse	SG	i.	IIId	40.00 ⊡
DCSI20	*(DCSI1)*	120	Type 2, brown resin, E, 4 lines, 45°	SG	i.	IIIp	0.50 ⊡
DCSI21	*(DCSI1)*	120	Type 2, brown resin, E, 4 lines, 45°	SG	2.5mm laser	IIIp	0.50 ⊡
DCSI22	*(DCSI1)*	120	Type 2, brown resin, E, 4 lines, 15°	SG	i.	IIIp	1.00 ⊡
DCSI23	*(DCSI1)*	120	Same but rounded corners to contact area (i.e. card intended for Type IV contact)	SG	i.	IIIp	8.00 ⊡

Note 1. Under high magnification the pale blue background is seen to be made up of a square matrix of small dots. Normally this matrix is set at 45° to the horizontal (or vertical) but in some the whole matrix is rotated such as to be at about 15° to the horizontal.

| | | DCS13 | | DCS14 | | DCS15 |

Nº	Ill.	Units	Description	Surface	Control	Contact	Value
DCS130	(DCS13)	50	Type 1, 4 lines	SM	i.	IVp	5.00 ☐
DCS131	(DCS13)	120	Type 1, É, 4 lines	SM	i.	IVp	8.00 ☐
DCS132	(DCS13)	120	Type 1, E, 4 lines	SM	i.	IVp	8.00 ☐
DCS133	(DCS13)	120	Type 2, E, 4 lines, 45°	SG	i.	IVp	8.00 ☐
DCS134	(DCS14)	120	Type 2, É, 4 lines	SM	i.	IVp	10.00 ☐
DCS135	(DCS14)	120	Type 2, É, 4 lines, 45°	SL 2.5mm laser		IVp	10.00 ☐
DCS140	(DCS13)	50	Type 1, 3 lines, 45°	SL	i.	IVd	1.00 ☐
DCS141	(DCS13)	50	Type 1, 3 lines, 15°	SL	i.	IVd	1.00 ☐
DCS141(a)			Type 1, 3 lines, 15° (double control)	SL	i. ×2	IVd	5.00 ☐
DCS142	(DCS13)	50	Type 1, 3 lines	SL	v.	IVd	1.00 ☐
DCS143	(DCS13)	50	Type 1, 3 lines, red spot in control box	SL	i.	IVd	8.00 ☐
DCS144	(DCS13)	50	Type 1, 3 lines	SL	vii.	IVd	1.00 ☐
DCS145	(DCS13)	120	Type 1, É, 3 lines, 45°	SL	i.	IVd	1.00 ☐
DCS146	(DCS13)	120	Type 1, É, 3 lines, 15°	SL	i.	IVd	1.00 ☐
DCS147	(DCS13)	50	Type 2, 3 lines	SG	i.	IVd	1.00 ☐
DCS148	(DCS13)	50	Same but green ring round reverse contact	SG	i.	IVd	20.00 ☐
DCS149	(DCS13)	120	Type 2, E, 3 lines	SG	i.	IVd	1.00 ☐
DCS150	(DCS13)	50	Type 1, 4 lines, 45°	SL	i.	IVd	1.00 ☐
DCS151	(DCS13)	50	Type 1, 4 lines, 15°	SL	i.	IVd	1.00 ☐
DCS152	(DCS13)	50	Type 1, 4 lines, 15°, Control 2.8mm laser	SL	(xi.)	IVd	3.00 ☐
DCS153	(DCS13)	120	Type 1, É, 4 lines, 45°	SL	i.	IVd	1.00 ☐
DCS154	(DCS13)	120	Type 1, É, 4 lines, 15°	SL	i.	IVd	1.00 ☐
DCS155	(DCS13)	120	Type 1, É, 4 lines	SM	vii.	IVd	1.00 ☐
DCS156	(DCS13)	50	Type 2, 4 lines	SG	None	IVd	1.00 ☐
DCS157	(DCS13)	50	Type 2, 4 lines	SG	i.	IVd	1.00 ☐
DCS158	(DCS13)	120	Type 2, É, 4 lines	SG	i.	IVd	1.00 ☐
DCS159	(DCS14)	50	Type 1, 4 lines, 45°	SM	i.	IVd	1.00 ☐
DCS160	(DCS14)	50	Type 1, 4 lines, 15°	SL	i.	IVd	0.50 ☐
DCS161	(DCS14)	50	Type 1, 4 lines, 45°	SG	i.	IVd	1.00 ☐
DCS162	(DCS14)	50	Type 1, 4 lines, 15°	SG	i.	IVd	0.50 ☐
DCS163	(DCS14)	50	Type 2, 4 lines	SG	i.	IVd	4.00 ☐
DCS164	(DCS14)	120	Type 2, E, 4 lines	SG	i.	IVd	10.00 ☐
DCS170	(DCS13)	120	Type 1, E, 3 lines, 15°	SL	i.	IVAg(TI)	8.00 ☐
DCS171	(DCS13)	50	Type 1, 4 lines, 15°	SL	i.	IVAg(TI)	5.00 ☐
DCS172	(DCS13)	120	Type 1, E, 4 lines, 15°	SL	i.	IVAg(TI)	8.00 ☐
DCS173	(DCS13)	120	Type 1, É, 4 lines, 15°	SL	i.	IVAg(TI)	8.00 ☐
DCS174	(DCS14)	50	Type 1, É, 4 lines, 15°	SL	i.	IVAg(TI)	5.00 ☐
DCS175	(DCS14)	120	Type 1, É, 4 lines, 15°	SL	i.	IVAg(TI)	8.00 ☐

Silk Screened Blue Cordons. Blue background formed of regular spots of colour. There are two sizes of contact space in the design — 11.2mm X 13.5mm (in effect no white surround) and 13.2mm X 15mm (white border of about 1mm round the contact) — refered to below as Ht 11.2mm and HT 13.2mm respectively. All are of 50 units and all have a CVH text of Type 2.

DCS190	(DCS15)	50	3 lines, Ht 11.2mm	FG/SM	None	IVp	6.00 ☐
DCS191	(DCS15)	50	3 lines, Ht 11.2mm	FG/SM	i.¹	IVp	3.00 ☐
DCS192	(DCS15)	50	3 lines, Ht 11.2mm, deeper blue	FG/SM	i.¹	IVp	3.00 ☐
DCS193	(DCS15)	50	3 lines, Ht 11.2mm	FG/SM	v.	IVp	3.00 ☐
DCS194	(DCS15)	50	3 lines, Ht 11.2mm	FG/SM	vi.	IVp	3.00 ☐

№	Ill.	Units	Description	Surface	Control	Contact	Value
DCBU1	(DCBU1)	40	5/87? Two white twists on cord	??	None	VII	200.00 ⊡
DCBU2	(DCBU2)	50	r. star	FG	None*	VIId	0.50 ⊡
DCBU3	(DCBU2)	50	r. star	FL	None*	VIId	0.50 ⊡
DCBU4	(DCBU2)·	50	no star	SM	None	VIId	0.50 ⊡
DCBU5	(DCBU2)	50	r. star	FL	None*	VIIp	0.50 ⊡
DCBU6	(DCBU2)	50	r. star	SL	None*	VIIp	0.50 ⊡
DCBU7	(DCBU2)	50	r. star, purple logo	FL	None*	VIIp	0.50 ⊡
DCBU8	(DCBU2)	50	r. star, blue-purple logo	SL	None*	VIIp	1.00 ⊡
DCBU9	(DCBU2)	50	r. no star	FG	None	VIIp	0.50 ⊡
DCBU10	(DCBU2)	50	r. blue spot in control box	FL	None	VIIp	5.00 ⊡
DCBU11	(DCBU2)	50	r. blue spot in control box, purple logo	FL	None	VIIp	5.00 ⊡
DCBU12	(DCBU2)	120	r. star, 4 line address	FL	None*	VIId	10.00 ⊡

GEMPLUS CORDONS

All are printed by offset lithography. There are two types according to the design of the front –
with and without a white patch around the contact. The white area in Gemplus cards is 15mm wide
compared with 16mm in the very similar Solaic cards. Those without a white area round the contact
show three types of reverse, the 3 line or the 4 line address of Régie T found in other makes and a
second type of 4 line address with Publicité and Télécarte having capital letters – listed as '4 line
T' below. All have black printed controls: 2.8mm (type x.) initially and, more recently, medium or thin
2.5mm figures (types viii. and ix.). Later ones add a lower or upper case letter after the four-figure
number. Some specialists collect different letters as varieties. All controls without letters I have
seen have been of the first type while those with letters can be of any type. All have CVH wording
of type 1 and there is no variation in the value/logo tablets. All are dated 1-1-88. There is some
variation of shade of the light blue background to the design of the front and of the deep blue
right-hand blocks of colour on the reverse. There is also considerable variation in the shade of grey
of the telephone mouthpiece (m/p) with some being pale grey and others being quite distinctly brownish
grey. The blue backgrounds are in arrays of dots at 25° or 45° to the edges as indicated.

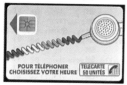

DCGP1

DCGP2

№	Ill.	Units	Description	Surface	Control	Contact	Value
DCGP1	DCGP1	50	3 lines, mouthpiece pale grey, 45°	FL	x.	VI	6.00 ⊡
DCGP2	(DCGP1)	120	3 lines, ...	FL	x.	VI	15.00 ⊡
DCGP3	(DCGP2)	50	3 lines, pale blue, m/p pale grey, 45°	FL	x.	VI	0.50 ⊡
DCGP4	(DCGP2)	120	3 lines, pale blue, ...	FL	x.	VI	0.50 ⊡
DCGP5	(DCGP2)	50	3 lines, darker blue, m/p brownish, 45°	FL	x.	VI	0.50 ⊡
DCGP6	DCGP2	120	3 lines, darker blue, ...	FL	x.	VI	0.50 ⊡
DCGP7	(DCGP2)	50	4 lines, m/p grey, 45°	FL	x.	VI	0.50 ⊡
DCGP8	(DCGP2)	50	4 lines, m/p grey, r. orange instead of red	FL	x.	VI	0.50 ⊡
DCGP9	(DCGP2)	120	4 lines, m/p grey, 45°	FL	x.	VI	0.50 ⊡
DCGP10	(DCGP2)	50	4 lines, blue, mouthpiece brownish grey 45°	FL	viii.	VI	0.50 ⊡
DCGP11†	(DCGP2)	120	4 lines, ...	FL	viii.	VI	0.50 ⊡
DCGP12	(DCGP2)	50	4 lines, pale blue, m/p pale grey, 25°	FL	viii.	VI	0.50 ⊡
DCGP13	(DCGP2)	120	4 lines, pale blue, ...	FL	viii.	VI	0.50 ⊡
DCGP14	(DCGP2)	50	4 lines T, blue, mouthpiece pale grey, 25°	FL	viii.	VI	1.00 ⊡
DCGP15	(DCGP2)	120	4 lines T, ...	FL	viii.	VI	1.00 ⊡
DCGP16	(DCGP2)	50	4 lines T, pale blue, m/p pale grey, 25°	FL	viii.	VI	1.00 ⊡
DCGP17	(DCGP2)	120	4 lines T, pale blue, ...	FL	viii.	VI	1.00 ⊡
DCGP18	(DCGP2)	50	4 lines T, pale blue, m/p pale grey, 25°	FL	ix.	VI	1.00 ⊡
DCGP19	(DCGP2)	120	4 lines T, pale blue, ...	FL	ix.	VI	1.00 ⊡

For France (and also for Germany and for Mercury in the UK) it has been decided to introduce a new category — Private cards. These are cards which were never on general sale to the public . Most were produced in small or very small quantities, often 1000, and distributed by the customer for which they were made as advertising material, as gifts or to collectors. Cards refered to as Promotional cards in the first edition are also now included in this category since they are essentially private cards distributed by, usually, the manufacturers as advertising or promotional material. Similarly it has been decided that all those cards, whether commemorative or advertising, (except for definitives — pyjamas and cordons) which were on general sale to the public should be grouped together into a single category. There are now therefore two sections below — Special/Advertising (S), distributed regionally (Paris, Marseille, Lyon, Nice, Cannes, Bordeaux and Lille) by France Telecom, and Private (P).

S - SPECIAL/ADVERTISING (PUBLIC) CARDS

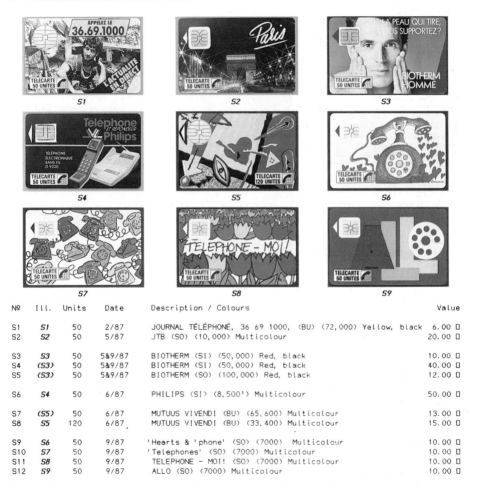

№	Ill.	Units	Date	Description / Colours	Value
S1	S1	50	2/87	JOURNAL TÉLÉPHONÉ, 36 69 1000, (BU) (72,000) Yellow, black	6.00 ☐
S2	S2	50	5/87	JTB (SO) (10,000) Multicolour	20.00 ☐
S3	S3	50	5&9/87	BIOTHERM (SI) (50,000) Red, black	10.00 ☐
S4	(S3)	50	5&9/87	BIOTHERM (SI) (50,000) Red, black	40.00 ☐
S5	(S3)	50	5&9/87	BIOTHERM (SO) (100,000) Red, black	12.00 ☐
S6	S4	50	6/87	PHILIPS (SI) (8,500') Multicolour	50.00 ☐
S7	(S5)	50	6/87	MUTUUS VIVENDI (BU) (65,600) Multicolour	13.00 ☐
S8	S5	120	6/87	MUTUUS VIVENDI (BU) (33,400) Multicolour	15.00 ☐
S9	S6	50	9/87	'Hearts & 'phone' (SO) (7000) Multicolour	10.00 ☐
S10	S7	50	9/87	'Telephones' (SO) (7000) Multicolour	10.00 ☐
S11	S8	50	9/87	TELEPHONE — MOI! (SO) (7000) Multicolour	10.00 ☐
S12	S9	50	9/87	ALLO (SO) (7000) Multicolour	10.00 ☐

Note 1. S3 has square corners to the white contact area; S4 has rounded corners.

Note 2. A further 1500 copies of S6 but with a rectangular box at bottom right on the reverse were distributed privately and are listed as P19 below.

S10

S11

S12

S13

S14

S15

S16

S17

S18

S19

S20

S21

S22

S23

S24

Nº	Ill.	Units	Date	Description / Colours	Value
S13	*(S10)*	50	11/87	'Red' Cortot (SI) (270,000) Multicolour	2.00 ☐
S13(a)				Thick black line on reverse	4.00 ☐
S14	*S10*	120	11/87	'Red' Cortot (SI) (130,000) Multicolour	4.00 ☐
S15	*S11*	50	15/12/87	'télécom, ma planéte' (SO) (21,160) Multicolour	25.00 ☐
S16	*S12*	50	12/87	CLÉ DE LUNE (BU - dark background)(46,680) Multicolour	60.00 ☐
S17	*(S12)*	50	12/88?	CLÉ DE LUNE (BU - pale background) (?) Multicolour	50.00 ☐
S18	*S13*	120	12/87	AIGUILLE DU MIDI (SO) (15,000) Multicolour	35.00 ☐
S19	*(S14)*	50	5/88	TRANSFERT D'APPEL (SO) (100,000) Multicolour	10.00 ☐
S20	*(S14)*	50	5/88	TRANSFERT D'APPEL (SO) 50 overprinted on 120 (1000?)	35.00 ☐
S21	*S14*	120	··	TRANSFERT D'APPEL (SO) (50,000)	15.00 ☐
S22	*S15*	50	6/88	FÊTE SANS FRONTIERE / LYON (SI) (20,000) Multicolour	35.00 ☐
S23	*S16*	120	7/88	F.I.T.E.M. '88 (SI) (1500) Multicolour	40.00 ☐
S24	*S17*	50	7/88	CHATEAUVALLON (SI) (10,000) Black and white	40.00 ☐
S25	*S18*	50	7/88	TOULON CABLE (SO) (10,000) Multicolour	30.00 ☐
S26	*S19*	50	7/88	WAGNER (SI, contact type III) (400,000?) Multicolour	4.00 ☐
S27	*(S19)*	120	7/88	WAGNER (SI, contact type III) (200,000?) Multicolour	8.00 ☐
S28	*(S19)*	50	7/88	WAGNER (SI, contact type IV) (400,000?) Multicolour	6.00 ☐
S29	*(S19)*	120	7/88	WAGNER (SI, contact type IV) (200,000?) Multicolour	12.00 ☐

№	Ill.	Units	Date	Description / Colours	Value
S30	*S20*	50	7/88	ALLO LE CIEL? (SO) (58,000) Multicolour	12.00 □
S31	*(S20)*	120	7/88	ALLO LE CIEL? (SO) (16,000) Multicolour	16.00 □
S32	*S21*	50	8/88	POLIO PLUS (SI, contact type III) (35,000?) Multicolour	8.00 □
S32(a)		50	8/88	Error - 50 front on 120 reverse	70.00 □
S33	*(S21)*	50	8/88	POLIO PLUS (SI, contact type IV) (35,000?) Multicolour	8.00 □
S34	*(S21)*	120	8/88	POLIO PLUS (SI, contact type III) (15,000) Multicolour	12.00 □
S34(a)		120	8/88	Error: Tête bêche (i.e. reverse inverted)	30.00 □
S35	*S22*	50	9/88	SUR NOS APPAREILS / PF1 (SO) (10,000) Multicolour	25.00 □
S36	*S23*	50	9/88	Blue Sun (SO) (400,000) Shades of blue	3.00 □
S36(a)		50	9/88	Error: 50 on front, 120 on reverse	100.00 □
S37	*(S23)*	120	9/88	Blue Sun (SO) (200,000) Shades of blue	5.00 □
S38	*S24*	50	10/88	CACHAREL CHEMISERIE (SI) (66,000) Blue, white, black	8.00 □
S38(a)		50	10/88	Error: 50 on front, 120 on reverse	90.00 □
S38(b)		50	10/88	Error: Tête bêche (i.e. reverse inverted)	30.00 □
S39	*(S24)*	120	10/88	CACHAREL CHEMISERIE (SI) (34,000) Blue, white, black	12.00 □

S25

S26

S27

S28

S29

S30

S31

S32

S33

№	Ill.	Units	Date	Description / Colours	Value
S40	*S25*	50	11/88	4th Dimension - Women (SO) (400,000) Multicolour	2.00 □
S41	*(S25)*	120	11/88	4th Dimension - Women (SO) (200,000) Multicolour	4.00 □
S42	*S26*	50	11/88	4th Dimension - Men (SO) (400,000) Multicolour	2.00 □
S43	*(S26)*	120	11/88	4th Dimension - Men (SO) (200,000) Multicolour	4.00 □
S44	*S27*	50	11/88	CROIX-ROUGE (SO) (10,000) Multicolour, No № on front	25 □
S45	*(S28)*	50	11/88	1918-1988 (SI) (10,000) Multicolour, No № on front.	25 □
S46	*S29*	50	11/88	NANCY - PLACE STANISLAS (SI) (10,000) Multicolour	40.00 □
S47	*S30*	50	11/88	OYONNAX - GYMNASTIQUE (SO) (10,000) Multicolour	40.00 □
S48	*S31*	50	11/88	HALLE TONY-GARNIER (SO) (20,000) Multicolour	12.00 □
S48(a)		50	11/88	Error: Tête bêche (i.e. reverse inverted)	25.00 □
S49	*S32*	50	12/88	GYMNASTIQUE - DIJON (SI) (2000) Multicolour	40.00 □
S50	*S33*	50	12/88	MANOUKIAN (SO) (266,852) Multicolour	4.00 □
S51	*(S33)*	120	12/88	MANOUKIAN (SO) (130,354) Multicolour	8.00 □

S34	*S35*	*S36*

S37	*S38*	*S39*

№	Ill.	Units	Date	Description / Colours	Value
S52	*(S34)*	50	1/89	ISO THOMSON (SO) (?000) Multicolour	2.00 ☐
S53	*(S34)*	120	1/89	ISO THOMSON (SO) (?000) Multicolour	3.00 ☐
S54	*(S34)*	50	1/89	ISO THOMSON (SI - III) (?000) Multicolour, Surface SG	1.50 ☐
S55	*(S34)*	120	1/89	ISO THOMSON (SI - III) (?000) Multicolour, Surface SG	2.50 ☐
S56	*(S34)*	50	1/89	ISO THOMSON (SI - III) (?000) Multicolour, Surface SL	1.50 ☐
S57	*(S34)*	120	1/89	ISO THOMSON (SI - III) (?000) Multicolour, Surface SL	2.50 ☐
S58	*(S34)*	50	1/89	ISO THOMSON (SI - IVp) (?000) Multicolour	10.00 ☐
S59	*(S34)*	50	1/89	ISO THOMSON (SI - IVd^1) (?000) Surface FM, Control i.	1.50 ☐
S59(a)		50	1/89	Reverse screen printed (?000) Surface FM, Control i.	6.00 ☐
S60	*(S34)*	120	1/89	ISO THOMSON (SI - IVd^1) (?000) Surface FM, Control i.	2.50 ☐
S61	*(S34)*	50	1/89	ISO THOMSON (SI - IVd^1) (?000) Surface FM, Control vi.	1.50 ☐
S62	*(S34)*	120	1/89	ISO THOMSON (SI - IVd^1) (?000) Surface FM, Control vi.	2.50 ☐
S63	*S34*	50	1/89	ISO THOMSON (SI - IVd^2) (?000) Surface SG, Control i.	1.50 ☐
S64	*(S34)*	120	1/89	ISO THOMSON (SI - IVd^2) (?000) Surface SG, Control i.	2.50 ☐
S65	*(S34)*	50	1/89	ISO THOMSON (SI - IVd^2) (?000) Surface FM, Control i.	1.50 ☐
S66	*(S34)*	120	1/89	ISO THOMSON (SI - IVd^2) (?000) Surface FM, Control i.	2.50 ☐
S67	*(S34)*	50	1/89	ISO THOMSON (SI - IVd^2) (?000) Surface FM, Control vi.	1.50 ☐
S68	*(S34)*	120	1/89	ISO THOMSON (SI - IVd^2) (?000) Surface FM, Control vi.	2.50 ☐

Note. Some of the 120 unit values above have been assumed from the existence of 50 unit values. the Schlumberger contacts with superscript 1 are surrounded by a very narrow white line while those with superscript 2 are set in a larger, square cornered white area as in the illustration. In addition to the above basic types there are many marked shade variations and differences to be found in the positions of the text on the reverse. Specialised collections of these cards are possible. The numbers of the various types printed are not known but the total for all types is reported to be around 6,000,000. If the normal practice of France Telecom was followed 4,000,000 would be of 50 units and 2,000,000 of 120 units.

№	Ill.	Units	Date	Description / Colours	Value
S69	*S35*	50	1/89	BASTILLE TREICHVILLE (SI) (12,200) Multicolour	3.00 ☐
S70	*(S35)*	120	1/89	BASTILLE TREICHVILLE (SI) (8000?) Multicolour	7.00 ☐
S71	*S36*	50	1/89	LUCY (Paris-Moscow)(SI-III)(?000), White logo. Multicolour	2.50 ☐
S71(a)		50	1/89	Error: Tête bêche (i.e. reverse inverted)	20.00 ☐
S72	*(S36)*	120	1/89	LUCY (Paris-Moscow)(SI-III)(?000), White logo. Multicolour	4.00 ☐
S73	*(S36)*	50	1/89	LUCY (Paris-Moscow)(SI-IV)(?000), White logo. Multicolour	2.50 ☐
S74	*(S36)*	120	1/89	LUCY (Paris-Moscow)(SI-IV)(?000), White logo. Multicolour	4.00 ☐
S75	*S37*	50	2/89	BALTHAZAR II (SO) (8000?) Multicol., Two 't's in Monttessuy	3.00 ☐
S76	*(S37)*	120	2/89	BALTHAZAR II (SO) (5000?) Multicol., ·· ·· ·· ·· ·· ··	5.00 ☐
S77	*(S38)*	50	2/89	FOLON - BICENTINARY (No № on front)(SI)(97,000) Multicol.	25.00 ☐
S78	*S39*	50	4/89	NORD PAS DE CALAIS (GP) (100,000?) Multicolour	3.50 ☐
S78(a)		50	4/89	Error: Tête bêche (i.e. reverse inverted)	25.00 ☐
S79	*(S39)*	120	4/89	NORD PAS DE CALAIS (GP) (50,000?) Multicolour	7.00 ☐

Note. Copies of S69, S71, S73 and S75 with one 't' in 'Monttessuy' on the reverse are private issues; P93 etc. below.

S40   S41   S42

S43   S44   S45

S46   S47   S48 (reverse)

S49 (reverse)   S50   S51 (reverse)

№	Ill.	Units	Date	Description / Colours	Value
S80	**S40**	50	4/89	CHENONCEAUX – REGION CENTRE (SO) (???000) Shades of brown	3.00 □
S80(a)		50	4/89	Error: Tête bêche (i.e. reverse inverted)	10.00 □
S81	**(S40)**	120	4/89	CHENONCEAUX – REGION CENTRE (SO) (???000) Shades of brown	5.00 □
S82	**S41**	50	4/89	BRAHMS – METZ (GP) (7000) Multicolour	7.00 □
S83	**(P41)**	120	4/89	BRAHMS – METZ (GP) (3000) Multicolour	10.00 □
S84	**S42**	50	4/89	BERCY GYMNASTIQUE – Women (SI) (400,000?) Multicolour	2.00 □
S84(a)		50		Error – 120 units on reverse	35.00 □
S85	**(S42)**	120	4/89	BERCY GYMNASTIQUE – Women (SI) (200,000?) Multicolour	4.00 □
S85(a)		120		Error: Tête bêche (i.e. reverse inverted)	15.00 □
S86	**S43**	50	4/89	BERCY GYMNASTIQUE – Men (SO) (400,000?) Multicolour	2.00 □
S87	**(S43)**	120	4/89	BERCY GYMNASTIQUE – Men (SO) (200,000?) Multicolour	4.00 □
S88	**S44**	50	4/89	EPINAL CABLE (SO) (??,000) Multicolour	5.00 □
S88(a)		50		Error: Tête bêche (i.e. reverse inverted)	10.00 □
S89	**(S44)**	120	4/89	EPINAL CABLE (SO) (??,000) Multicolour	5.00 □
S89(a)		120		Error: Tête bêche (i.e. reverse inverted)	20.00 □
S90	**S45**	50	4/89	JTB – MONT ST. MICHEL (SO) (31,000) Multicolour	15.00 □

Note. 1000 of S90 were privately distributed in France and the other 30,000 in Japan. Many og the latter seem to have found their way home again.

№	Ill.	Units	Date	Description / Colours	Value
S91	**S46**	50	4/89	LOR-HIS-TEL (SI) (12,000) Multicolour	5.00 □
S91(a)		50	4/89	Error: Tête bêche (i.e. reverse inverted)	10.00 □
S92	**(S46)**	120	4/89	LOR-HIS-TEL (SI) (8000) Multicolour	12.00 □
S93	**S47**	50	5/89	CHAPELLE ROYALE (SI) (?000) Multicolour, Reverse as **S48r**	15.00 □
S94	**(S47)**	50	5/89	CHAPELLE ROYALE (SI) (?000) Multicolour, Reverse as **S49r**	5.00 □
S94(a)		50		Error: Tête bêche (i.e. reverse inverted)	10.00 □
S95	**(S47)**	120	5/89	CHAPELLE ROYALE (SI) (?000) Multicolour, ·· ·· ·· ··	8.00 □
S95(a)		120		Error: Tête bêche (i.e. reverse inverted)	15.00 □
S96	**S50**	50	5/89	CHAPELLE ROYALE (SI) (?000) Multicolour/Rose, Rev. as **S51r**	5.00 □
S97	**(S50)**	120	5/89	CHAPELLE ROYALE (SI) (?000) Multicolour/Rose, ·· ·· ··	8.00 □

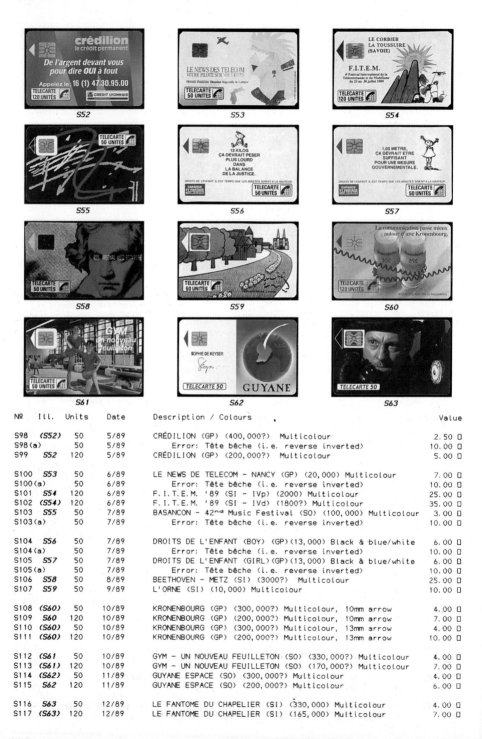

S52

S53

S54

S55

S56

S57

S58

S59

S60

S61

S62

S63

№	Ill.	Units	Date	Description / Colours	Value
S98	*(S52)*	50	5/89	CRÉDILION (GP) (400,000?) Multicolour	2.50 ▢
S98(a)		50	5/89	Error: Tête bêche (i.e. reverse inverted)	10.00 ▢
S99	*S52*	120	5/89	CRÉDILION (GP) (200,000?) Multicolour	5.00 ▢
S100	*S53*	50	6/89	LE NEWS DE TELECOM - NANCY (GP) (20,000) Multicolour	7.00 ▢
S100(a)		50	6/89	Error: Tête bêche (i.e. reverse inverted)	10.00 ▢
S101	*S54*	120	6/89	F.I.T.E.M. '89 (SI - IVp) (2000) Multicolour	25.00 ▢
S102	*(S54)*	120	6/89	F.I.T.E.M. '89 (SI - IVd) (1800?) Multicolour	35.00 ▢
S103	*S55*	50	7/89	BASANCON - 42nd Music Festival (SO) (100,000) Multicolour	3.00 ▢
S103(a)		50	7/89	Error: Tête bêche (i.e. reverse inverted)	10.00 ▢
S104	*S56*	50	7/89	DROITS DE L'ENFANT (BOY) (GP)(13,000) Black & blue/white	6.00 ▢
S104(a)		50	7/89	Error: Tête bêche (i.e. reverse inverted)	10.00 ▢
S105	*S57*	50	7/89	DROITS DE L'ENFANT (GIRL)(GP)(13,000) Black & blue/white	6.00 ▢
S105(a)		50	7/89	Error: Tête bêche (i.e. reverse inverted)	10.00 ▢
S106	*S58*	50	8/89	BEETHOVEN - METZ (SI) (3000?) Multicolour	25.00 ▢
S107	*S59*	50	9/89	L'ORNE (SI) (10,000) Multicolour	10.00 ▢
S108	*(S60)*	50	10/89	KRONENBOURG (GP) (300,000?) Multicolour, 10mm arrow	4.00 ▢
S109	*S60*	120	10/89	KRONENBOURG (GP) (200,000?) Multicolour, 10mm arrow	7.00 ▢
S110	*(S60)*	50	10/89	KRONENBOURG (GP) (300,000?) Multicolour, 13mm arrow	4.00 ▢
S111	*(S60)*	120	10/89	KRONENBOURG (GP) (200,000?) Multicolour, 13mm arrow	10.00 ▢
S112	*(S61)*	50	10/89	GYM - UN NOUVEAU FEUILLETON (SO) (330,000?) Multicolour	4.00 ▢
S113	*(S61)*	120	10/89	GYM - UN NOUVEAU FEUILLETON (SO) (170,000?) Multicolour	7.00 ▢
S114	*(S62)*	50	11/89	GUYANE ESPACE (SO) (300,000?) Multicolour	4.00 ▢
S115	*S62*	120	11/89	GUYANE ESPACE (SO) (200,000?) Multicolour	6.00 ▢
S116	*S63*	50	12/89	LE FANTOME DU CHAPELIER (SI) (330,000) Multicolour	4.00 ▢
S117	*(S63)*	120	12/89	LE FANTOME DU CHAPELIER (SI) (165,000) Multicolour	7.00 ▢

S64

S65

S66

S67

№	Ill.	Units	Date	Description / Colours	Value
S118	S64	50	12/89	1889 - 1989 TELEPHONE PUBLIC (SI) (330,000) Multicolour	4.00 ☐
S119	(S64)	120	12/89	1889 - 1989 TELEPHONE PUBLIC (SI) (165,000) Multicolour	7.00 ☐
S120	S65	50	12/89	ASPIRINE OBERLIN (GP) (?0,000) Multicolour	4.00 ☐
S121	(S65)	120	12/89	ASPIRINE OBERLIN (GP) (?0,000) Multicolour	7.00 ☐
S122	S66	50	1/90	INSTITUTIONNEL EUROPE (SO) (330,000) Multicolour	4.00 ☐
S123	(S66)	120	1/90	INSTITUTIONNEL EUROPE (SO) (165,000) Multicolour	7.00 ☐
S124	S67	50	1/90	ENTREZ DANS LA 4ème DIMEMSION (SI) (330,000) Multicolour	4.00 ☐
S125	(S67)	120	1/90	ENTREZ DANS LA 4ème DIMENSION (SI) (!65,000) Multicolour	7.00 ☐

P - PRIVATE CARDS

P1

P2

P3

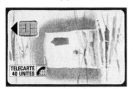

P4

P5

P6

P1	P1	40	12/86	"Flip Clip Amor" (BU) (186) Multicolour (numbered & signed)	1100 ☐
P1(a)		40	12/86	"Flip Clip Amor" (BU) (200) Multicolour (not signed)	1000 ☐
P2	P2	40	12/86	"Ecce Homo Dial" (BU) (186) Multicolour (numbered & signed)	1100 ☐
P2(a)		40	12/86	"Ecce Homo Dial" (BU) (200) Multicolour (not signed)	500 ☐
P3	P3	40	12/86	Akhras I (SI) (180) Multicolour (numbered & signed)	2500 ☐
P3(a)		40	12/86	Akhras I (SI) (200) Multicolour (not signed)	2000 ☐
P4	P4	40	12/86	Akhras II (SI) (180) Multicolour (numbered & signed)	2500 ☐
P4(a)		40	12/86	Akhras II (SI) (200) Multicolour (not signed)	2000 ☐
P5	P5	40	12/86	LE CLOAREC I (SO) (180) Multicolour (numbered & signed)	2500 ☐
P5(a)		40	12/86	LE CLOAREC I (SO) (200) Multicolour (not signed)	2000 ☐
P6	P6	40	12/86	LE CLOAREC II (SO) (180) Multicolour (numbered & signed)	2500 ☐
P6(a)		40	12/86	LE CLOAREC II (SO) (200) Multicolour (not signed)	2000 ☐

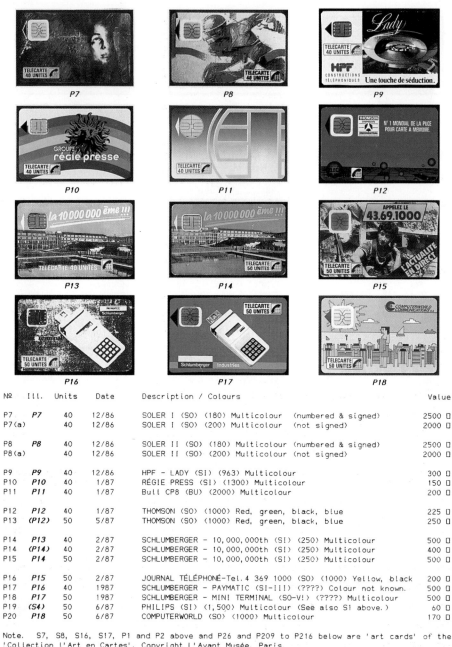

№	Ill.	Units	Date	Description / Colours	Value
P7	P7	40	12/86	SOLER I (SO) (180) Multicolour (numbered & signed)	2500 □
P7(a)		40	12/86	SOLER I (SO) (200) Multicolour (not signed)	2000 □
P8	P8	40	12/86	SOLER II (SO) (180) Multicolour (numbered & signed)	2500 □
P8(a)		40	12/86	SOLER II (SO) (200) Multicolour (not signed)	2000 □
P9	P9	40	12/86	HPF - LADY (SI) (963) Multicolour	300 □
P10	P10	40	1/87	RÉGIE PRESS (SI) (1300) Multicolour	150 □
P11	P11	40	1/87	Bull CP8 (BU) (2000) Multicolour	200 □
P12	P12	40	1/87	THOMSON (SO) (1000) Red, green, black, blue	225 □
P13	(P12)	50	5/87	THOMSON (SO) (1000) Red, green, black, blue	250 □
P14	P13	40	2/87	SCHLUMBERGER - 10,000,000th (SI) (250) Multicolour	500 □
P14	(P14)	40	2/87	SCHLUMBERGER - 10,000,000th (SI) (250) Multicolour	400 □
P15	P14	50	2/87	SCHLUMBERGER - 10,000,000th (SI) (250) Multicolour	500 □
P16	P15	50	2/87	JOURNAL TÉLÉPHONÉ-Tel. 4 369 1000 (SO) (1000) Yellow, black	200 □
P17	P16	40	1987	SCHLUMBERGER - PAYMATIC (SI-III) (????) Colour not known.	500 □
P18	P17	50	1987	SCHLUMBERGER - MINI TERMINAL (SO-V!) (????) Multicolour	500 □
P19	(S4)	50	6/87	PHILIPS (SI) (1,500) Multicolour (See also S1 above.)	60 □
P20	P18	50	6/87	COMPUTERWORLD (SO) (1000) Multicolour	170 □

Note. S7, S8, S16, S17, P1 and P2 above and P26 and P209 to P216 below are 'art cards' of the 'Collection l'Art en Cartes', Copyright L'Avant Musée, Paris.

GENERAL NOTE. All cards are the property of the telephone company or sponsor which commissions them. The manufacturers and the publisher (Régie T) cannot supply cards directly to collectors and should not be approached for cards.

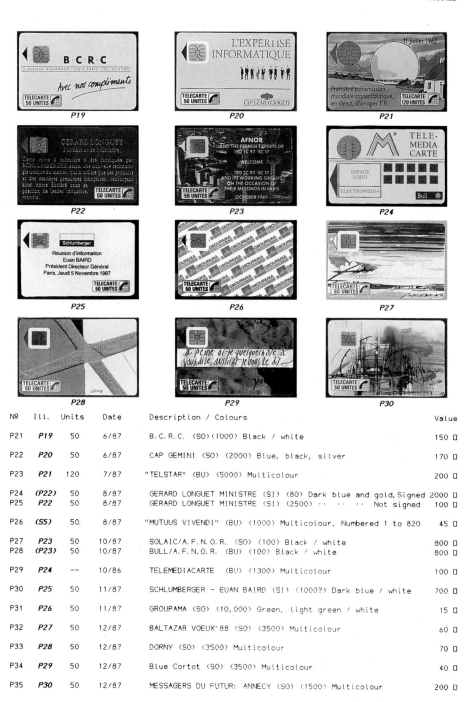

№	Ill.	Units	Date	Description / Colours	Value
P21	*P19*	50	6/87	B.C.R.C. (SO)(1000) Black / white	150 ▢
P22	*P20*	50	6/87	CAP GEMINI (SO) (2000) Blue, black, silver	170 ▢
P23	*P21*	120	7/87	"TELSTAR" (BU) (5000) Multicolour	200 ▢
P24	*(P22)*	50	8/87	GERARD LONGUET MINISTRE (SI) (80) Dark blue and gold, Signed	2000 ▢
P25	*P22*	50	8/87	GERARD LONGUET MINISTRE (SI) (2500) ·· ·· ·· Not signed	100 ▢
P26	*(S5)*	50.	8/87	"MUTUUS VIVENDI" (BU) (1000) Multicolour, Numbered 1 to 820	45 ▢
P27	*P23*	50	10/87	SOLAIC/A.F.N.O.R. (SO) (100) Black / white	800 ▢
P28	*(P23)*	50	10/87	BULL/A.F.N.O.R. (BU) (100) Black / white	800 ▢
P29	*P24*	--	10/86	TELEMEDIACARTE (BU) (1300) Multicolour	100 ▢
P30	*P25*	50	11/87	SCHLUMBERGER – EUAN BAIRD (SI) (1000?) Dark blue / white	700 ▢
P31	*P26*	50	11/87	GROUPAMA (SO) (10,000) Green, light green / white	15 ▢
P32	*P27*	50	12/87	BALTAZAR VOEUX'88 (SO) (3500) Multicolour	60 ▢
P33	*P28*	50	12/87	DORNY (SO) (3500) Multicolour	70 ▢
P34	*P29*	50	12/87	Blue Cortot (SO) (3500) Multicolour	40 ▢
P35	*P30*	50	12/87	MESSAGERS DU FUTUR: ANNECY (SO) (1500) Multicolour	200 ▢

Nº	Ill.	Units	Date	Description / Colours	Value
P36	*P31*	50	12/87	DGT Ministerial (BU) (2500) Multicolour¹	300 ⊡

Note. P36 was given as an official Christmas present. The card fits in to a larger sheet of the same material which continues the design and has a greeting on it. P36, complete with its surround, commands a large premium.

Nº	Ill.	Units	Date	Description / Colours	Value
P37	*P32*	50	12/87	CGB CITIBANK (SO) (250) Blue, black, silver, white (Les Ternes, Paris)	200 ⊡
P38	*(P32)*	··	··	·· ·· ·· ·· ·· ·· ·· ·· ·· ·· (Marseille)	200 ⊡
P39	*(P32)*	··	··	·· ·· ·· ·· ·· ·· ·· ·· ·· ·· (Lyon)	200 ⊡
P40	*(P32)*	··	··	·· ·· ·· ·· ·· ·· ·· ·· ·· ·· (Toulouse)	200 ⊡
P41	*P33*	50	12/87	Renan RNIS (SO) (2000) Multicolour	120 ⊡
P42	*P34*	50	12/87	MERLIN GERIN (SO) (1000) Multicolour	120 ⊡
P43	*P35*	50	12/87	MEILLEURS VOEUX (SI) (10,000) Shades of blue	50 ⊡
P44	*(P35/6)*	50	12/87	Schlumberger Industries (SI) (1000) Shades of blue	40 ⊡
P45	*P36*	50	12/87	Schlumberger Technologies (SI) (1000) Shades of blue	40 ⊡
P46	*P37*	50	1/88	Reflet de l'Innovation (SI) (1000) Multicolour	180 ⊡
P47	*P38*	50	1/88	SG2 PARTAGÉ (SI) (1000) Multicolour	70 ⊡
P48	*P39*	50	1/88	E.A.G. (SO) (2000) Multicolour	50 ⊡
P49	*P40*	50	1/88	TEQUILLA I (SO) (1000 – numbered) Multicolour	60 ⊡
P50	*P41*	50	1/88	RÉUNION TÉLÉPHONE (SO) (1000) Telecom/Telecom	60 ⊡
P51	*(P41)*	50	?/88	RÉUNION TÉLÉPHONE (SO) (1000) Telecom/France Telecom	40 ⊡
P52	*(P41)*	50	12/88	RÉUNION TÉLÉPHONE (SO) (1300) France Telecom/France Telecom	70 ⊡
P53	*P42*	50	1/88	LA TÉLÉPHONIE (SO) (1500) Multicolour	100 ⊡
P53(a)		50	1/88	LA TÉLÉPHONIE (SO) (???) Multicolour, Coffret/album	200 ⊡

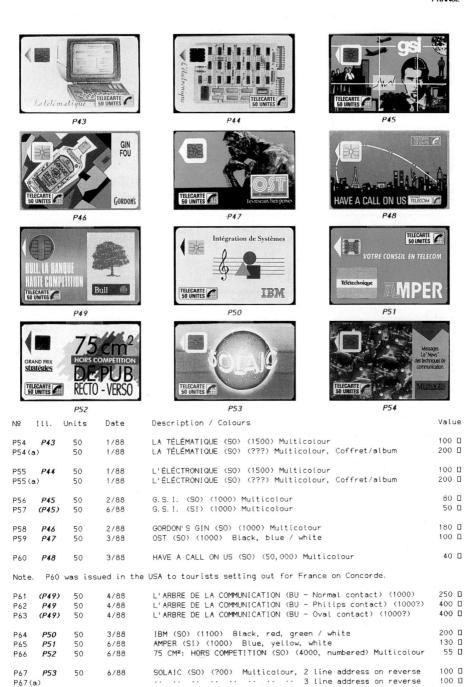

№	Ill.	Units	Date	Description / Colours	Value
P54	*P43*	50	1/88	LA TÉLÉMATIQUE (SO) (1500) Multicolour	100 ▢
P54(a)		50	1/88	LA TÉLÉMATIQUE (SO) (???) Multicolour, Coffret/album	200 ▢
P55	*P44*	50	1/88	L'ÉLÉCTRONIQUE (SO) (1500) Multicolour	100 ▢
P55(a)		50	1/88	L'ÉLÉCTRONIQUE (SO) (???) Multicolour, Coffret/album	200 ▢
P56	*P45*	50	2/88	G.S.I. (SO) (1000) Multicolour	80 ▢
P57	*(P45)*	50	6/88	G.S.I. (SI) (1000) Multicolour	50 ▢
P58	*P46*	50	2/88	GORDON'S GIN (SO) (1000) Multicolour	180 ▢
P59	*P47*	50	3/88	OST (SO) (1000) Black, blue / white	100 ▢
P60	*P48*	50	3/88	HAVE A CALL ON US (SO) (50,000) Multicolour	40 ▢

Note. P60 was issued in the USA to tourists setting out for France on Concorde.

P61	*(P49)*	50	4/88	L'ARBRE DE LA COMMUNICATION (BU – Normal contact) (1000)	250 ▢
P62	*P49*	50	4/88	L'ARBRE DE LA COMMUNICATION (BU – Philips contact) (1000?)	400 ▢
P63	*(P49)*	50	4/88	L'ARBRE DE LA COMMUNICATION (BU – Oval contact) (1000?)	400 ▢
P64	*P50*	50	3/88	IBM (SO) (1100) Black, red, green / white	200 ▢
P65	*P51*	50	6/88	AMPER (SI) (1000) Blue, yellow, white	130 ▢
P66	*P52*	50	6/88	75 CM²: HORS COMPETITION (SO) (4000, numbered) Multicolour	55 ▢
P67	*P53*	50	6/88	SOLAIC (SO) (?00) Multicolour, 2 line address on reverse	100 ▢
P67(a)				″ ″ ″ ″ ″ ″ ″ ″ 3 line address on reverse	100 ▢

Note. There were reportedly 900 of P67 and P67(a) together.

P68	*P54*	50	7/88	MESSAGES (SO) (1050) Multicolour	150 ▢

P55

P56

P57

P58

P59

P60

P61

P62

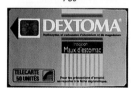

P63

P64

P65

P66

P67

P68

P69

№	Ill.	Units	Date	Description / Colours	Value
P69	*P55*	50	8/88	ORLEANS: ESPACE PROFESSIONNEL (SI) (1000) Multicolour	80 ◻
P70	*P56*	50	9/88	RENAULT ÉTOILE (SI) (1500) Blue, black, white	40 ◻
P71	*P57*	50	9/88	75 CM²: LA TÉLÉCARTE (SI) (5000) Multicolour	45 ◻
P72	*P58*	50	10/88	FR. TELECOM - MONTPELLIER (SO) (1000) Multicolour	80 ◻
P73	*P59*	50	10/88	DAAT (SO) (3000) Multicolour	60 ◻
P74	*P60*	50	10/88	SAGEM·SAT (SI) (2000) Blue, black / white	70 ◻
P75	*P61*	50	10/88	UNILOG (SI) (2000) Multicolour	30 ◻
P75(a)				Dark blue sky	40 ◻
P76	*P62*	50	10/88	MONTE CARLO '88 (SI) (1000) Multicolour	180 ◻
P77	*P63*	50	10/88	DEXTOMA (SI) (5020) Multicolour	35 ◻
P78	*(S27)*	50	11/88	CROIX-ROUGE (SO) (9000?) Multicolour, Numbered on front.	70 ◻
P79	*(S28)*	50	11/88	1918-1988 (SI) (?000) Multicolour, Numbered on front.	45 ◻
P80	*P64*	50	11/88	PONT A MOUSSON (SI) (2000) Multicolour	50 ◻
P81	*(P65)*	50	11/88	GRAND PRIX - ANGERS (SI-III) (1000) Multicolour	80 ◻
P82	*P65*	50	11/88	GRAND PRIX - ANGERS (SI-IV) (1000) Multicolour	60 ◻
P83	*P66*	50	11/88	TELECOMS. D'ENTREPRISE - ANGERS (SI) (1000) Multicolour	80 ◻
P84	*P67*	50	11/88	SEPT DE CAEN (GP) (1000) Blue, yellow, white	80 ◻
P85	*P68*	50	11/88	D.R. ROUEN 1989 (SI) (1300) Blue, yellow. white	80 ◻
P86	*(P69)*	50	11/88	PARC LOCATION (SO) (5000) Black, yellow, brown / white	25 ◻
P87	*P69*	50	11/88	PARC LOCATION (SI) (?000) Black, yellow, brown / white	35 ◻

Nº	Ill.	Units	Date	Description / Colours	Value
P88	P70	50	11/88	NUMERIS (SI) (2000) Black, blue / white	60 ☐
P89	P71	50	11/88	PAU (SO) (2000) Multicolour	65 ☐
P90	P72	50	11/88	STARANE 200 - PROCHIMAGRO (SI) (2500) Multicolour	40 ☐
P91	P73	50	12/88	BALTAZAR II (SI) (8000) Multicolour, "Montessuy"	40 ☐
P92	P74	50	12/88	LUCY (Paris, etc - Moscow)(SI)(8000), Black logo. Multicolour	40 ☐
P93	(S35)	50	12/88	TREICHVILLE BASTILLE (SI) (???) Multicolour, "Montessuy"	25 ☐
P94	P75	50	12/88	SATAS I (SO) (2000) Multicolour	90 ☐
P95	P76	50	12/88	ALPHAPAGE (SI) (1400) Multicolour	150 ☐
P96	P77	50	12/88	PONT DU GARD - CARCASSONNE (SI) (5000) Multicolour	30 ☐
P97	P78	50	12/88	MINISTERE PTE I (SI) (5000) Multicolour	80 ☐
P98	P79	50	12/88	MINISTERE PTE II (SO) (1000) Multicolour	60 ☐
P99	P80	50	12/88	AGENCE LYON AINAY (SO) (1000) Multicolour	120 ☐
P100	P81	50	12/88	RADIOCOM 2000 (SI) (1000) C. Pasquier, Multicolour	100 ☐
P101	P82	50	12/88	RADIOCOM 2000 (SI) (1000) Noël Pasquier, Multicolour	80 ☐
P102	P83	50	12/88	NEC (GP) (1600) Multicolour	60 ☐
P103	P84	50	12/88	OGER (SI) (1000) Multicolour	80 ☐

Note. P96, together with P124, are often listed as public cards but it seems that the conditions imposed on their purchase were such as to make them essentially private cards.

P85

P86

P87

P88

P89

P90

P91

P92

P93

P94

P95

P96

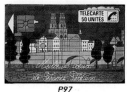

P97

P98

P99

Nº	Ill.	Units	Date	Description / Colours	Value
P104	*P85*	50	12/88	CGRCR (GP) (1000) Multicolour	70 ▢
P105	*P86*	50	12/88	THOMANN HANRY (SI) (1000) Multicolour	50 ▢
P106	*P87*	50	12/88	COGECOM (SI) (1000) Multicolour	100 ▢
P107	*P88*	50	12/88	BENCKISER-St MARC (GP) (2000) Gold, black, white	35 ▢
P108	*P89*	50	12/88	PA (SI) (5000) Red, black / gold	25 ▢
P109	*P90*	50	12/88	SG2 PROGRÉS (SO) (1000) Multicolour	70 ▢
P110	*P91*	50	12/88	CONSULT FR. TELECOM (SO) (3558) Blue, black, white	70 ▢
P111	*P92*	120	12/88	CHEMIN FAISANT I - TEXIER (SI) (1000) Multicolour	100 ▢
P112	*P93*	50	?/88?	E.P.R. (SO) (300) Black, gold, white	150 ▢
P113	*P94*	50	1/89	FT CERGY PONTOISE (SO) (1000) Multicolour	80 ▢
P114	*P95*	50	1/89	CONTESSE (SI) (1000) Blue, yellow, black, white	50 ▢
P115	*P96*	50	1/89	BIPE (SO) (1000) Multicolour	50 ▢
P116	*(S38)*	50	1/89	BI-CENTENAIRE, FOLON (SO) (3000) Multicolour, Numbered	15 ▢
P117	*P97*	50	1/89	MEILLIEURS VOEUX - ORLEANS (SO) (1000) Multicolour	70 ▢
P118	*P98*	50	1/89	BEHRING (SO) (1000) Multicolour	35 ▢
P119	*P99*	50	1989	TELEMEDIACARTE - AFRICABAT DAKAR (BU?)(?000) Red, grey, etc.	100 ▢

P100

P101

P102

P103

P104

P105

P106

P107

P108

P109

P110

P111

P112

P113

P114

№	Ill.	Units	Date	Description / Colours	Value
P120	*P100*	50	2/89	CHATEAU HOTEL DU TREMBLAY (SI) (1000) Black / cream	20 ▢
P121	*P101*	50	2/89	SYSTEMS CENTER (SI) (1000) Multicolour	60 ▢
P122	*P102*	50	3/89	FRANCE SOIR (SI) (1000) Multicolour	40 ▢
P123	*P103*	50	3/89	BORDEAUX – INTELLIGENT NETWORKS (SI) (1000?) Multicolour	70 ▢
P124	*P104*	50	3/89	BOURGES – MINITEL (GP) (2000) Multiicolour	35 ▢
P125	*P105*	50	3/89	PHILIPS – POCKET-MEMO (SI) (1000) Multicolour	40 ▢
P126	*P106*	50	3/89	ATR (GP) (1000) Multicolour	80 ▢
P127	*P107*	50	3/89	SODEXHO FRANCE (SO) (?000) Blue / white	80 ▢
P128	*P108*	50	3/89	GERCIF (SO) (?000) Red, black / white	60 ▢
P129	*P109*	50	3/89	COCHERY (SO) (?000) Blue, orange / white	50 ▢
P130	*P110*	50	4/89	QUALITE INDUSTRIELLE (SO) (1000) Multicolour	50 ▢
P131	*P111*	50	4/89	ABILIS (SI) (5000) Blue and white	30 ▢
P132	*P112*	50	4/89	PLESSIS BOUCHARD (GP) (2000) Multicolour	380 ▢
P133	*P113*	50	4/89	TEQUILA 89 – GAUMNITZ (SO) (1000?) Multicolour	80 ▢
P134	*P114*	50	4/89	SIEMEPHONE (SO) (1000) Multicolour	50 ▢

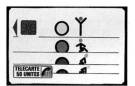

P115

P116

P117

P118

P119

P120

P121

P122

P123

P124

P125

P126

P127

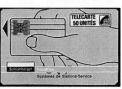

P128

P129

№	Ill.	Units	Date	Description / Colours	Value
P135	*P115*	50	4/89	FLOXYFRAL (SO) (20,000) Multicolour	30 ☐
P136	*P116*	50	4/89	ABEILLE VIE (SO) (2000?) Multicolour	35 ☐
P137	*P117*	50	4/89	BOURSE SCHAKO (SI) (1000?) Multicolour	30 ☐
P138	*P118*	50	4/89	L'ODA (SI) (1000) Multicolour (r. 6 figure 'fax no.')	40 ☐
P139	*(P118)*	50	4/89	L'ODA (SI) (1000) Multicolour (r. 8 figure 'fax no.')	40 ☐
P140	--	50	4/89	MOTOCYCLISTE DES HAUTS DE SEINE (??) (1000?) Multicolour	15 ☐
P141	--	50	4/89	UNION DES PHILATELISTES DES PTT (??) (1000?) Multicolour	40 ☐
P142	*P119*	50	4/89	LE FIGARO (SI) (1000) Black, white	35 ☐
P143	*P120*	50	4/89	VIA (GP) (1000) Multicolour	100 ☐
P144	*(P121)*	50	4/89	KRONENBOURG (SI - IVp) (400?) Multicolour	40 ☐
P145	*P121*	50	4/89	KRONENBOURG (SI - IVd) (600) Multicolour	30 ☐
P146	*P122*	50	4/89	BOSE (SI) (2000) Multicolour	25 ☐
P147	*P123*	50	4/89	WILLIAM SAURIN (SI) (2000) Multicolour	40 ☐
P148	*P124*	50	1989	NESTLÉ (SI) (1000) Multicolour	100 ☐
P149	*P125*	50	5/89	O.C.D.V. (SI) (1000) Multicolour	25 ☐
P150	*P126*	50	1989	Schlumberger: Production I (SI) (1000) Multicolour	60 ☐
P151	*P127*	50	1989	Schlumberger: Production II (SI) (1000) Multicolour	60 ☐
P152	*P128*	50	1989	Schlumberger: STATIONS-SERVICE (SI) (1000) Black, blue, white	60 ☐
P153	*P129*	50	5/89	SEITA (SI) (3500) Multicolour	60 ☐

Note.   In P135 the name of the product only appears in full when the card is unused in its sachet, the figures in the top line showing through to form the O and the Y.

P130

P131

P132

P133

P134

P135

P136

P137

P138

P139

P140

P141

P142

№	Ill.	Units	Date	Description / Colours	Value
P154	*P130*	50	5/89	L'APPEL MEDICAL (SI) (1000) Multicolour	60 □
P155	*P131*	50	5/89	D.O.T.R.N. (SI) (1000) Multicolour	60 □
P156	*P132*	50	5/89	ADEQUAT (SO) (1000) Multicolour	70 □
P157	*P133*	50	5/89	C.C.A.M. – Loustal 1 (SI) (250) Multicolour	120 □
P158	*P134*	50	5/89	C.C.A.M. – Loustal 2 (SI) (250) Multicolour	120 □
P159	*P135*	50	5/89	C.C.A.M. – Loustal 3 (SI) (250) Multicolour	120 □
P160	*P136*	50	5/89	C.C.A.M. – Loustal 4 (SI) (250) Multicolour	120 □
P161	*P137*	50	5/89	POULAIN (SI) (1000?) Multicolour	80 □
P162	*P138*	50	5/89	BALKALINE (SI) (1000) Blue, yellow, red, black	50 □
P163	*P139*	50	5/89	STARANE 200 II (SI) (2000) (Maize) Multicolour	40 □
P164	*P140*	50	5/89	GELAGRI BRETAGNE I (SI) (1000) Black, red, white	60 □
P165	*P141*	50	6/89	A.F.C.T.A. (SI) (1000) Grey / white	30 □
P166	*P142*	50	6/89	JAMET (GP) (1000) Multicolour	150 □

P143

P144

P145

P146

P147

P148

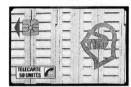
P149

P150

P151

P152

P153

P154

P155

P156

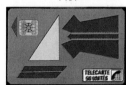
P157

N⁰	Ill.	Units	Date	Description / Colours	Value
P167	P143	50	6/89	JOHNNY HALLIDAY (SO) (1000) Multicolour	130 ▢
P168	P144	50	6/89	FRAIMONTAL (GP) (1000) Multicolour	60 ▢
P169	P145	50	6/89	C.A.T.S. (NERON) (SO?) (1000) Multicolour	50 ▢
P170	P146	50	6/89	PERRIER - ROLLAND GARROS (SO) (1000) Multicolour	100 ▢
P171	P147	50	6/89	ALCATEL ANSWARE (SO) (2000) Multicolour	65 ▢
P172	P148	50	6/89	CAVIA - GROUPE SOVAC (SO) (2000) Multicolour	30 ▢
P173	P149	50	6/89	T.I.M. (GP) (1000) Multicolour	60 ▢
P174	--	50	6/89	MONGOLFIERES (GP) (1000) Multicolour	20 ▢
P175	P150	50	6/89	SOFREQ (SO) (1000) Multicolour	120 ▢
P176	P151	50	6/89	BRIT AIR (GP) (1000) Multicolour	120 ▢
P177	P152	50	6/89	SKIP (SI) (1000) Multicolour	50 ▢
P178	P153	50	6/89	GRRREY (SO) (1000) Multicolour	40 ▢
P179	--	50	6/89	S.Q.B.B. ST. QUENTIN (SI) (1000) Multicolour	30 ▢
P180	P154	50	6/89	GERMINATION BLEUE (GP) (1000) Multicolour	40 ▢
P181	P155	120	6/89	U.I.T. NICE (SI) (?000) Multicolour	45 ▢
P182	P156	50	6/89	AEROSPATIALE (SI) (1000) Multicolour	50 ▢
P183	P157	50	6/89	ETS QUILFEN (SI) (1000) Red, yellow, blue	50 ▢

P158

P159

P160

P161

P162

P163

P164

P165

P166

P167

P168

P169

P170

P171

P172

Nº	Ill.	Units	Date	Description / Colours	Value
P184	*P158*	50	7/89	SEVRIER - LAC D'ANNECY (SO) (5000) Multicolour	15 ☐
P185	*P159*	50	7/89	BOZ (SI) (1000) Red, black, white	55 ☐
P186	*P160*	50	7/89	KODAK (SO) (800?) Multicolour	35 ☐
P187	*P161*	50	7/89	SOMMET DE L'ARCHE (SI) (10.000) Multicolour	25 ☐
P188	*P162*	50	7/89	SEPA (GP) (1000) Multicolour	25 ☐
P189	*P163*	50	7/89	EUROPE 93 (SI) (1000) Multicolour, 'Classic'	60 ☐
P190	*(P163)*	120	7/89	EUROPE 93 (SI) (200) Silver margin to card	150 ☐
P191	*(P163)*	120	7/89	EUROPE 93 (SI) (200) Gold margin to card	400 ☐
P192	*P164*	50	7/89	C.E.P.M.C.P. (SO) (380) Screen printed and signed by artist	120 ☐
P192(a)		50	9/89	Same but normal printing (SO) (1000) Red, blue, white	30 ☐
P193	*P165*	50	7/89	LUTECE DIFFUSION (FOOTBALL) (GP) (1000) Multicolour	25 ☐
P194	*P166*	50	7/89	O.C.D.V. (TENNIS) (GP) (1000) Multicolour	25 ☐
P195	*P167*	50	7/89	BALTEAU ENERTEC (SI) (1000) Multicolour	50 ☐
P196	*P168*	50	7/89	LA COMMUNICATION - VISAGE D'ENFANT (GP) (1000) Multicolour	50 ☐
P197	*P169*	50	7/89	SAUPIQUET - LES FILETINES (SI) (300?) Multicolour	60 ☐
P198	*P170*	50	7/89	FESTIVAL GERARD PHILIPE (SI) (1000) Brown, yellow, white	80 ☐
P199	*P171*	50	7/89	TELEMEDIACARTE - PUCE D'OR 89 (GP) (1000) Blue, gold, white	35 ☐
P200	*P172*	50	8/89	ARSENAL METZ MOZART (SI) (2000) red, green	15 ☐

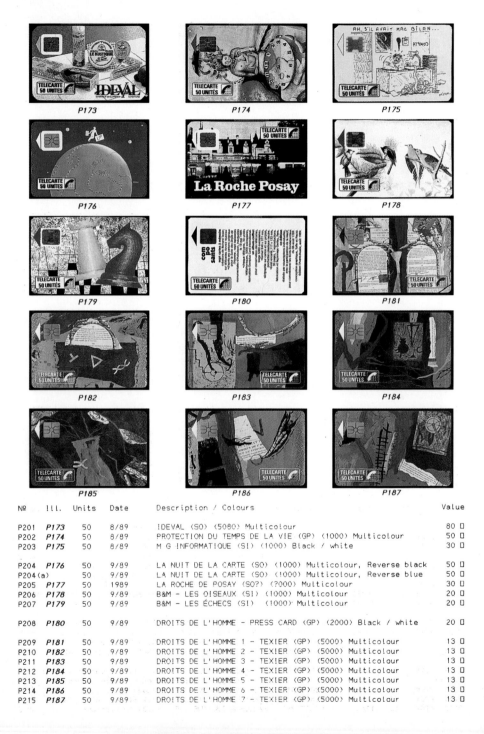

P173 P174 P175

P176 P177 P178

P179 P180 P181

P182 P183 P184

P185 P186 P187

№	Ill.	Units	Date	Description / Colours	Value
P201	P173	50	8/89	IDEVAL (SO) (5080) Multicolour	80 ▢
P202	P174	50	8/89	PROTECTION DU TEMPS DE LA VIE (GP) (1000) Multicolour	50 ▢
P203	P175	50	8/89	M G INFORMATIQUE (SI) (1000) Black / white	30 ▢
P204	P176	50	9/89	LA NUIT DE LA CARTE (SO) (1000) Multicolour, Reverse black	50 ▢
P204(a)		50	9/89	LA NUIT DE LA CARTE (SO) (1000) Multicolour, Reverse blue	50 ▢
P205	P177	50	1989	LA ROCHE DE POSAY (SO?) (?000) Multicolour	30 ▢
P206	P178	50	9/89	B&M - LES OISEAUX (SI) (1000) Multicolour	20 ▢
P207	P179	50	9/89	B&M - LES ÉCHECS (SI) (1000) Multicolour	20 ▢
P208	P180	50	9/89	DROITS DE L'HOMME - PRESS CARD (GP) (2000) Black / white	20 ▢
P209	P181	50	9/89	DROITS DE L'HOMME 1 - TEXIER (GP) (5000) Multicolour	13 ▢
P210	P182	50	9/89	DROITS DE L'HOMME 2 - TEXIER (GP) (5000) Multicolour	13 ▢
P211	P183	50	9/89	DROITS DE L'HOMME 3 - TEXIER (GP) (5000) Multicolour	13 ▢
P212	P184	50	9/89	DROITS DE L'HOMME 4 - TEXIER (GP) (5000) Multicolour	13 ▢
P213	P185	50	9/89	DROITS DE L'HOMME 5 - TEXIER (GP) (5000) Multicolour	13 ▢
P214	P186	50	9/89	DROITS DE L'HOMME 6 - TEXIER (GP) (5000) Multicolour	13 ▢
P215	P187	50	9/89	DROITS DE L'HOMME 7 - TEXIER (GP) (5000) Multicolour	13 ▢

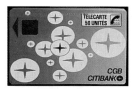

P188

P189

P190

P191

P192

P193

P194

P195

P196

P197

P198

P199

P200

P201

P202

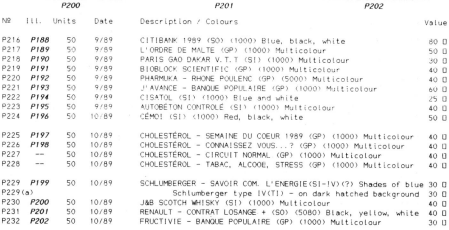

Nº	Ill.	Units	Date	Description / Colours	Value
P216	*P188*	50	9/89	CITIBANK 1989 (SO) (1000) Blue, black, white	80 ☐
P217	*P189*	50	9/89	L'ORDRE DE MALTE (GP) (1000) Multicolour	50 ☐
P218	*P190*	50	9/89	PARIS GAO DAKAR V.T.T (SI) (1000) Multicolour	30 ☐
P219	*P191*	50	9/89	BIOBLOCK SCIENTIFIC (GP) (1000) Multicolour	40 ☐
P220	*P192*	50	9/89	PHARMUKA – RHONE POULENC (GP) (5000) Multicolour	40 ☐
P221	*P193*	50	9/89	J'AVANCE – BANQUE POPULAIRE (GP) (1000) Multicolour	60 ☐
P222	*P194*	50	9/89	CISATOL (SI) (1000) Blue and white	25 ☐
P223	*P195*	50	9/89	AUTOBÉTON CONTROLÉ (SI) (1000) Multicolour	40 ☐
P224	*P196*	50	10/89	CÉMOI (SI) (1000) Red, black, white	50 ☐
P225	*P197*	50	10/89	CHOLESTÉROL – SEMAINE DU COEUR 1989 (GP) (1000) Multicolour	40 ☐
P226	*P198*	50	10/89	CHOLESTÉROL – CONNAISSEZ VOUS...? (GP) (1000) Multicolour	40 ☐
P227	--	50	10/89	CHOLESTÉROL – CIRCUIT NORMAL (GP) (1000) Multicolour	40 ☐
P228	--	50	10/89	CHOLESTÉROL – TABAC, ALCOOL, STRESS (GP) (1000) Multicolour	40 ☐
P229	*P199*	50	10/89	SCHLUMBERGER – SAVOIR COM. L'ENERGIE (SI-IV)(?) Shades of blue	30 ☐
P229(a)				Schlumberger type IV(TI) – on dark hatched background	30 ☐
P230	*P200*	50	10/89	J&B SCOTCH WHISKY (SI) (1000) Multicolour	40 ☐
P231	*P201*	50	10/89	RENAULT – CONTRAT LOSANGE + (SO) (5080) Black, yellow, white	40 ☐
P232	*P202*	50	10/89	FRUCTIVIE – BANQUE POPULAIRE (GP) (1000) Multicolour	30 ☐

P203

P204

P205

P206

P207

P208

P209

P210

P211

P212

P213

P214

P215

№	Ill.	Units	Date	Description / Colours	Value
P233	P203	50	10/89	STRAVINSKI - ARSENAL METZ (SI) (5000) Multicolour	15 ▢
P234	P204	50	10/89	S&M - SAMBRE ET MEUSE (GP) (1000) Multicolour	100 ▢
P235	P205	50	10/89	DAVID LANSKY - JOHNNY HALLYDAY () (?000) Multicolour	35 ▢
P236	P206	50	10/89	GOLF (SO) (1043) Multicolour	20 ▢
P237	P207	50	10/89	SIGMA CONSIEL (GP) (1000) Multicolour	30 ▢
P238	P208	50	10/89	DARE DO IT (GP) (1000) Multicolour	40 ▢
P239	P209	50	10/89	EVE ET LUI 1, p. SAYAC (GP) (500) Multicolour	150 ▢
P240	P210	50	10/89	EVE ET LUI 2, p. SAYAC (GP) (500) Multicolour	150 ▢
P241	P211	50	10/89	EVE ET LUI 3, p. SAYAC (GP) (500) Multicolour	150 ▢
P242	P212	50	10/89	EVE ET LUI 4, p. SAYAC (GP) (500) Multicolour	150 ▢
P243	--	50	10/89	S.A.S. (GP) (1000) Multicolour	40 ▢
P244	--	50	10/89	RUBENS (SO) (1043) Multicolour	40 ▢
P245	--	50	10/89	LE TEMPS RETROUVE (SO) (2043) Multicolour	20 ▢
P246	P213	50	11/89	GPL - L'AIR LIQUIDE (SI) (1000) Multicolour	100 ▢
P247	P214	50	11/89	MATT - CLOWN №. 1. (GP) (1000) Multicolour	40 ▢
P248	P215	50	11/89	MATT - CLOWN №. 2. (GP) (1000) Multicolour	40 ▢

| | P216 | | P217 | | P218 |

| | P219 | | P220 | | P221 |

| | P222 | | P223 | | P224 |

| | P225 | | P226 | | P227 |

| | P228 | | P229 | | P230 |

№	Ill.	Units	Date	Description / Colours	Value
P249	P216	50	11/89	NOVESPACE (SO) (1043) Multicolour	50 □
P250	P217	50	11/89	COMÉDIE D'AMOUR (GP) (1000) Multicolour	50 □
P251	P218	50	11/89	LOUISIANE (GP) (1000) Multicolour	20 □
P252	P219	50	11/89	Mc CAIN (GP) (1000) Multicolour	30 □
P253	P220	50	11/89	STUDIO MARCADET (GP) (1000) Black, yellow, red	40 □
P254	P221	50	11/89	LA JOCONDE (MONA LISA) (GP) (1000) Multicolour	60 □
P255	P222	50	11/89	REGIÉ T – 'L'ESPACE P U B' (SO) (5080) Multicolour	10 □
P256	(P222)	50	11/89	REGIÉ T – 'DEUX MOIS' (SO) (5080) Multicolour	10 □
P257	(P222)	50	11/89	REGIÉ T – 'PLANS MÉDIAS' (SO) (5080) Multicolour	10 □
P258	(P222)	50	11/89	REGIÉ T – 'CONTACTS UTILES' (SO) (5080) Multicolour	10 □
P259	(P222)	50	11/89	REGIÉ T – 'MÉDIA RÉGIONAL' (SO) (5080) Multicolour	10 □
P260	P223	50	11/89	TELEMARK (SI) (1000) Blue, yellow, white	35 □
P261	P224	50	11/89?	SCHLUMBERGER: LA COMMUNICATION FACILE (SI) (1000) Multicol.	40 □
P262	(P225)	50	11/89	SINORG (Named as on a visiting card) (SO) (c. 900) Multicol.	50 □
P263	P225	50	11/89	SINORG (Not named) (SO) (c. 100) Multicolour	80 □
P264	P226	50	11/89	KASS (GP) (1000) Shades of blue, yellow	50 □
P265	P227	50	11/89	DIAC ENTREPRISES (GP) (2000) Multicolour	20 □
P266	P228	50	11/89	BOSE – (CORTOT) (GP) (2000) Multicolour	30 □
P267	P229	50	11/89	GELAGRI BRETAGNE II (GP) (1000) Multicolour	60 □
P268	P230	50	11/89	MUSÉE DES ARTS ET TRADITIONS (GP) (1000) Multicolour	20 □

P231

P232

P233

P234

P235

P236

P237

P238

P239

P240

P241

P242

№	Ill.	Units	Date	Description / Colours	Value
P269	--	50	11/89	CIMENTS FRANCAIS (SO) (1043) Multicolour	50 ▢
P270	--	50	11/89	ARMAN (SO) (1043) Multicolour	30 ▢
P271	--	50	11/89	FLASH INTERIM (GP) (1000) Multicolour	20 ▢
P272	--	50	11/89	SPONTEX (SI) (1000) Multicolour	40 ▢
P273	*P231*	50	12/89	COMMUNAUTÉ EUROPÉEANNE – FR PRES. (SI Ag) (?000) Blue, red	50 ▢
P274	*P232*	50	12/89	S DIG (GP) (1000) Multicolour	60 ▢
P275	*P233*	50	12/89	SG2 – PARTENAIRES DU PROGRES (GP) (1000) Multicolour	50 ▢
P276	*P234*	50	12/89	RUFF (SI) (1000) Multicolour	40 ▢
P277	*P235*	50	12/89	BASTET – TRAVAUX PUBLICS (GP) (1000) Multicolour	60 ▢
P278	*P236*	50	12/89	DINERS CLUB INTERNATIONAL (GP) (5080) Multicolour	25 ▢
P279	*P237*	50	12/89	EOLE (SI) (1000) Blue, red, white	60 ▢
P280	*(P92)*	120	12/89?	CHEMIN FAISANT II – TEXIER (SI-TI)(1000) Multicol. New logo.	80 ▢
P281	--	50	1989	BERGICIEL (??) (?000) Multicolour?	30 ▢
P282	*P238*	50	12/89	CU – COMERCIAL UNION (GP) (1000) Blue, black, white	70 ▢
P283	*P239*	50	12/89	FR3 (GP) (5000) Blue, black, white	60 ▢
P284	--	50	12/89?	LUTTE CONTRE LE SIDA (GP) (1000) Multicolour	35 ▢
P285	*P240*	50	12/89?	A. F. T. (BATELIER) (GP) (1000) Multicolour	20 ▢
P286	--	50	12/89?	LE ST CLAIR (SI) (1000) Multicolour	50 ▢
P287	*P241*	50	12/89	CINERGY, p. ALERINI (GP) (1000) Multicolour	25 ▢
P288	*P242*	50	12/89	BOSE – POLE POSITION (BAKALIAN) (GP) (1100) Multicolour	30 ▢

P243

P244

P245

P246

Nº	Ill.	Units	Date	Description / Colours	Value
P289	*P243*	50	12/89	SCHLUMBERGER NOUVEAUX DEFIS 1990 (SI) (?000) Blue and white	50 ⊡
P290	*P244*	50	12/89	D.G.C. (JIMMY LOCCA) (SI) (1000) Multicolour	30 ⊡
P291	--	50	12/89	SCHLUMBERGER - OFF SHORE (SI) (?000) Multicolour?	35 ⊡
P292	--	50	12/89	RÉGIE T (GP) (300) Grey and white?	60 ⊡
P293	--	50	12/89	TECHNOBOLE METZ (??) (?000) Multicolour?	15 ⊡
P294	--	50	12/89	LUMINAIRES GUYOT (??) (1000) Multicolour?	15 ⊡
P295	--	50	12/89	GYM 'S.I.R.C.O.M.' (SO) (2000) Multicolour	20 ⊡
P296	--	50	12/89	STEPHANIE DE MONACO (GP) (1000) Multicolour	120 ⊡
P297	--	50	12/89	C.T.I.F. (GP) (1000) Multicolour	50 ⊡
P298	--	50	12/89	NEC '90 (GP) (?000) Multicolour	60 ⊡
P299	--	50	12/89	E.D.F. (SI) (1000) Multicolour	40 ⊡
P300	--	50	12/89	BENCKISER '90 (GP) (1000) Multicolour	25 ⊡
P301	--	50	12/89	ULTRA PAMPERS (GP) (?000) Multicolour	20 ⊡
P302	--	50	12/89	HOPITAL LA ROSERAIE (GP) (1000) Multicolour	25 ⊡
P303	--	50	12/89	MUSEE ALBERT DEMARD (GP) (1000) Multicolour	25 ⊡
P304	--	50	12/89	LA BARILLA (GP) (1000) Multicolour	30 ⊡
P305	--	50	12/89	VAN GOGH (GP) (1000) Multicolour	25 ⊡
P306	--	50	12/89	20 ANS DE CARANAVA (GP) (1000) Multicolour	20 ⊡
P307	--	50	12/89	RHONE POULENC - LABO (GP) (1000) Multicolour	40 ⊡
P308	*P245*	50	1/90	BANCO EXTERIOR - FRANCE (SI IV Ag) (1000) Multicolour	40 ⊡
P309	*P246*	50	1/90	TELEPHONE - FIL DE LA VIE (SI) (????) Multicolour	30 ⊡
P310	--	50	1/90	OPEN de FOOTBALL - METZ (SI) (2000) Multicolour	13 ⊡
P311	--	50	1/90	SAMUWA - COUPE DU MOND FOOT (SI) (1000) Multicolour	20 ⊡
P312	--	50	1/90	SAMUWA - CHRISTOPHE COLOMB (SI) (1000) Multicolour	20 ⊡
P313	--	50	1/90	GUSTAVA MAHLER (??) (5000) Multicolour	15 ⊡
P314	--	50	1/90	GSI TECSI (GP) (1000) Multicolour	35 ⊡
P315	--	50	1/90	A.S. PTT METZ (SI) (2000) Multicolour	15 ⊡
P316	--	50	1/90	LE ST CLAIR (SI) (1000) Multicolour	20 ⊡
P317	--	50	1/90	FESTIVAL DE LA BANDE DESSINEE (GP) (1000) Multicolour	18 ⊡
P318	--	50	1/90	SATAS II (GP) (1000) Multicolour	30 ⊡
P319	--	50	1/90	GUYOT 'DECORATION' (GP) (50) Multicolour, Signed.	50 ⊡
P320	--	50	1/90	GUYOT 'DECORATION' (GP) (950) Multicolour, Not signed.	20 ⊡
P321	--	50	1/90	ONLY YOU (SI) (1000) Multicolour	40 ⊡
P322	--	50	1/90	AUGUSTE THOUARD (GP) (5000) Multicolour	20 ⊡

O. - OFFICIAL/SERVICE CARDS

Electronic service (maintenance) cards were manufactured by Schlumberger and Bull CP8. These
cards are PIN coded and have no set unit value.

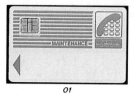

01

01	*01*	–	1984?	Green / white (SI II) Black text on reverse	--- ▯
02	*(01)*	–	1984?	Green / white (SI) Green text on reverse	--- ▯
03	*(01)*	–	1984?	Green / white (BU)	--- ▯

FRENCH POLYNESIA

Electronic or 'smart' cards manufactured by Schlumberger Industries of France were introduced
into French Polynesia during 1989. It is understood that there are eight telephones in Papeete,
three on Mururoa atol and one on Hao atol. Some cards are reported to ave been overprinted on
the reverse for use on Mururoa. Only definitives are known to have been issued so far. Control
numbers on the reverse are laser-punched and about 2.5mm high.

D1

Nº	Ill.	Units	Date	Description	Value
D1	*(D1)*	60	1889	Blue-green / white (71,000)	14.00 ▯
D2	*D1*	150	1989	Magenta / white (32,000)	14.00 ▯

Note. The above illustration is of a punched sample.

GABON

Magnetic cards are supplied to O.P.T. Gabon by Autelca of Switzerland. Only definitive cards have
appeared up to the present but there were changes of design and values during 1989. Some cards have
advertising on the reverse but, like those of the Netherlands, Turkey, etc., these have been listed as
definitives. Control numbers are in black and, like many Autelca cards, show at least three varieties
- 3mm 'reverse italics' with slashed '0', 3.75mm also with slashed '0' and 3.4mm with open '0'.

D1

D2

Nº	Ill.	Units	Date	Description	Value
D1	*D1*	F3100	1985	Blue, black / white (220,000)	6.00 ▯
D2	*(D1)*	F6200	1985	Yellow, black / white (90,000)	18.00 ▯

Nº	Ill.	Units	Date	Description	Value
D3	*D1*	F3100	1987	Blue, black / white, Advertising on reverse	4.00 U
D4	*(D1)*	F6200	1987	Yellow, black / white, Advertising on reverse	15.00 □

Note.   D3 has "MBOLO / notre métier : / les prix" in blue on the reverse while D4 has "SCORE / notre métier : / les prix" in yellow on the reverse.   The numbers of D1 and D2 printed are thought to incorporate those for D3 and D4.

Second Issue.   Design and values changed.

Nº	Ill.	Units	Date	Description		Value
D5	*(D2)*	F3250	2/89	Blue, black / white	(100,000)	3.00 □
D6	*D2*	F6500	7/89	Yellow, black / white		10.00 □

GERMANY — FEDERAL REPUBLIC

Deutsche Bundespost (DBP) ran parallel field trials of four different systems – one optical, two magnetic and one electronic (i.e. 'smart' cards) – before deciding to adopt an electronic system similar to that used in France. Each test employed 30 card-operated telephones. Optical cards, manufactured by Landis and Gyr in Switzerland, were used at **Frankfurt** airport and in and around the main railway station.   A magnetic system by Autelca, Switzerland, was field tested in **Goslar**, a holiday resort in the Harz Mountains.   A second magnetic system by Standard Electric Lorenz, Germany, was deployed in **Bamberg** and electronic or 'smart' cards, manufactured by GAO (Gesellschaft für Automation und Organisation mbH) for Siemens, both of Munich, West Germany, were introduced in the **Aachen** area and in the city of **Bonn**.   Subsequently slightly different cards, with the size and position of the contacts altered, were introduced for 'operational trials' at airports and main railway stations in sixteen major German cities and, more generally, in the Stuttgart area.   These have since been adopted nationally. Cards are now made by two manufacturers – Giesecke & Devrient GmbH of Munich, usually refered to as G&D, and Oldenbourg Datensysteme, also of Munich, refered to as ODS.   Besides the prepayment cards listed below there also exist 'Tele Karte' – smart, PIN-coded charge-transfer cards analogous to the French 'Carte Télécom' or Carte Pastel but these are, like their French equivilents, not listed.   An agreement has been reached with the French PTT that the two systems will eventually be compatible so that cards of each country can be used in the other.   It is understood that France Telecom will in due course change the location of the contact on French cards.   The four types of field-test cards have become known by their test locations and are therefore now prefixed 'F' for Frankfurt, 'G' for Goslar, 'B' for Bamberg and 'A' for Aachen/Bonn in the listings below.   The 'operational trial' cards have now become the standard cards of West Germany and are therefore no longer prefixed.

FC1

FD1

FS1

FO1

GC1

GD1

BC1

BD1

3S1 (reverse)

FRANKFURT (OPTICAL) CARDS (Landis and Gyr)

C – COMPLIMENTARY CARD

Nº	Ill.	Units	Date	Description	Value	
FC1	*FC1*	5	20/6/83	Red / silver (10,000)	40.00 ◻	30.00 ◻

FD – DEFINITIVE CARDS

FD1	*FD1*	45	20/6/83	Red / silver (100,000)	50.00 ◻	30.00 ◻
FD2	*(FD1)*	92	20/6/83	·· ·· ·· (27,800)	80.00 ◻	50.00 ◻

FS – SPECIAL CARD

Weldpostkongress (World Postal Congress), Hamburg, 18 June – 27 July, 1984.

FS1	*FS1*	92	18/6/84	Red / silver (9817)	200.00 ◻	120.00 ◻
FS2	–	40	1985	Red/silver, DEBIT-KARTE. 1.5mm band (94)	500.00 ◻	300.00 ◻
FS3	–	80	1985	Red/silver, DEBIT-KARTE. 1.5mm band (94)	500.00 ◻	300.00 ◻

Note 1.   1000 of FS1 were given to delegates at the Congress and 9000 sold in Frankfurt.

Note 2.   The status of FS2 and 3 is not clear but they seem to have been used at exhibitions.   A similar card bearing the word 'CREDIT' and no units was also printed at the same time (100).

FO – OFFICIAL/SERVICE CARD

FO1	*FO1*	(120)	20/6/83	Red / silver	--- ◻	300.00 ◻

FT – TEST CARDS

FT1	*(FO1)*	–	1983	Red / silver, "TEST-KARTE"	--- ◻	300.00 ◻

Note 1. In addition a red Landis and Gyr general 'phonocard' test card was used in Germany.

Note 2. The field-trial ended on 10 December, 1986.

Note 3. A very few trial cards with white bands exist but were not issued.

GOSLAR (MAGNETIC) CARDS (Autelca)

GC – COMPLIMENTARY CARD

GC1	*GC1*	5	23/10/84	Yellow, black / white (4000)	50.00 ◻

GD – DEFINITIVE CARDS

GD1	*GD1*	40	23/10/84	Yellow, black / white	50.00 ◻
GD2	*(GD1)*	80	23/10/84	·· ·· ·· ·· ·· (10,000)	25.00 ◻

Note 1.   There were no special service/test cards for Goslar.   General Autelca cards of the type illustrated under Nigeria and a similar card with 'SERVICE' in a long arrow were used.

Note 2.   The use of these cards finished in May/June 1989 with the introduction of the smart cards.

BAMBERG (MAGNETIC) CARDS (Copytex by Standard Electric Lorenz)

BC – COMPLIMENTARY CARD

BC1	*BC1*	5	12/2/85	Red, black / cream (≈13,000) (paper)	50.00 ◻

BD – DEFINITIVE CARDS

BD1	*BD1*	40	12/2/85	Red, black, grey / cream (paper)	50.00 ◻
BD1(a)				·· ·· ·· ·· / white (plastic)	70.00 ◻
BD2	*(BD1)*	80	12/2/85	·· ·· ·· ·· / cream (paper)	30.00 ◻
BD2(a)				·· ·· ·· ·· / white (plastic)	50.00 ◻

BS – SPECIAL CARD

International Federation of Telecommunications Engineers Conferance, 9 – 14 September, 1985.

№	Ill.	Units	Date	Description	Value
BS1	*BS1*	40	9/9/85	Red, black, grey / white (500)	300.00 ⬜

Note. The front of BS1 is exactly like that of BD1. The 500 cards were issued at the conference and were never available to the general public.

BO & BT – OFFICIAL/SERVICE AND TEST CARDS

BO1	*(BD1)*	100	1985	Red, black, grey / white, "Service"	300.00 ⬜
BT1	*(BD1)*	–	1985	Red, black, grey / white, "Test"	350.00 ⬜

AC1

AD1

AD2

AS1 (reverse)

D1

D1 (reverse)

D2 (reverse)

S1

S2

AACHEN/BONN (ELECTRONIC or 'SMART') CARDS (GAO)

AC – COMPLIMENTARY CARD

AC1	*AC1*	5	9/10/84	Silver / green (3,000) (silver contact)	50.00 ⬜
AC1(a)				(gold contact)	75.00 ⬜

AD – DEFINITIVE CARDS

AD1	*AD1*	20DM	1984	Black / green (Silver contact)	1000.00 ⬜
AD1(a)	*AD1*	20DM	1984	Black / green (Gold contact)	1000.00 ⬜

Note. Only a few of these cards were manufactured for early internal DBP tests and they were not issued to the public. They are very rare.

AD2	*AD2*	40	9/10/84	White / green (24,000) (silver contact)	50.00 ⬜
AD2(a)				(gold contact)	250.00 ⬜
AD3	*(AD2)*	80	9/10/84	Black / green (16,000) (silver contact)	25.00 ⬜
AD3(a)				(gold contact)	300.00 ⬜

Note 1. The use of these cards in Aachen started on 23 November, 1984, and ceased in Bonn on 10 December, 1986. Their use in Aachen ended in June 1987.

Note 2. The numbers of cards issued given above include both contact types. The numbers of silver and gold contact types are not known exactly but the silver contacts are much more common.

AS – SPECIAL CARD

International Federation of Telecommunications Engineers Conference, 9 – 14 September, 1985.

Nº	Ill.	Units	Date	Description	Value
AS1	*AS1*	40	9/9/85	White / green (500) (silver contact)	500.00 ◻

Note 1. The front of AS1 is exactly like that of AD2.

Note 2. The 500 cards were issued at the conference and were not available to the general public.

AO & AT – OFFICIAL/SERVICE AND TEST CARDS

| AO1 | *(AD1)* | (120) | 1985 | Black / green, "Service" | 300.00 ◻ |
| AT1 | *(AD1)* | – | 1985 | Black / green, "Statistik" | 350.00 ◻ |

STANDARD (including 'Operational Trial') CARDS

The first cards were made by Siemens and may be distinguished from the control number on the reverse which is at the top left. Cards have since been made by G&D or by ODS and have their controls on the reverse at top right. The earliest G&D cards had a matt circular area or disk on the reverse behind the contact but this has since been dropped. Cards by both manufacturers are laminated and those by G&D have a transparent center laminate (which looks dark) while those by ODS have a white center laminate which allows them to be distinguished easily with a magnifying glass. Since October, 1988, all German cards have carried a series code comprising the logo of the manufacturer, a series letter and number, the month and year of manufacture and the number produced. W 01 was accidently used twice so, to maintain the sequence, W 03 was not used. W 07 appeared before W 06. The modern German cards do not fit easily into the classifications used for most other countries in this book since there is no clear distinction between complimentary and advertising cards. Similarly the DBP catagories do not correspond to those used in this listing. Listed below are Definitive cards, Special cards which include the "P" (postal slogan cards on general sale) and "S" (other special or advertising cards on general sale) series, and what have been called Private cards which include the "K" series (bought and distributed by the customer), the "W" and "X" series (DBP advertising cards) and those earlier cards which carried no series letter but also promoted DBP services and were not on general sale.

D – DEFINITIVE CARDS

Nº	Ill.	Units	Date	Description	Value
D1	*D1*	12DM (40)	16/12/86	Red / white (control top left on reverse)	60.00 ◻
D2	*(D1)*	50DM(200)	16/12/86	Gold / white (control top left on reverse)	45.00 ◻
D3	*D1*	12DM (40)	1987	Red / white (black lettering on reverse)(5000)	250.00 ◻
D4	*D1*	12DM (40)	1987	Red / white (control top right on reverse)	5.00 ◻
D5	*(D1)*	50DM(200)	1987	Gold / white (control top right on reverse)	15.00 ◻
D6	*D1*	12DM (40)	1988	Red / white (no matt disk on reverse)	4.00 ◻
D7	*(D1)*	50DM(200)	1988	Gold / white (no matt disk on reverse)	12.50 ◻

Nº	Ill.	Units	Date	Colours (Front)	(Reverse)	Value
D8	*D1*	12DM/40	1989	Red / white	*D2* Multicoloured (14,000)	30.00 ◻
D9	*(D1)*	50DM/200	1988	Gold / white	*D2* Multicoloured (2000)	60.00 ◻

S – SPECIAL CARDS

Nº	Ill.	Units	Date	Colours (Front)	(Reverse)	Value
S1	*(S1)*	12DM/40	8/88	Multicolour (P01A)	-- Yellow, black/white (9,500)	7.00 ◻
S2	*S1*	12DM/40	8/88	"Solaic" contact	-- Yellow, black/white (20,500)	5.00 ◻
S3	*S2*	50DM/200	8/88	Multicolour (P01B)	-- Yellow, black/white (20,000)	20.00 ◻

PLEASE NOTE: ALL CARDS ARE THE PROPERTY OF THE PTT OR ADVERTISER WHICH COMMISSIONS THEM AND CAN NOT BE SUPPLIED TO COLLECTORS BY THE MANUFACTURERS. Those wishing to order German cards directly from the DBP should write to: Telefonkarten-Versandstelle, Fernmeldeamt 2, Postfach 10 00 12, D-8500 Nürnberg 1. Federal Republic of Germany.

S3

S4

S5

S6

S7

S8

S9

S10

S11

№	Ill.	Units	Date	Colours (Front)	(Reverse)		Value
S4	(S3)	12DM/40	9/88	Brown, white (S01A)	--	Brown / white TÜV (12,000)	15.00 ☐
S5	(S3)	12DM/40	9/88	"Solaic" contact	--	Brown / white TÜV (18,000)	6.00 ☐
S6	S3	50DM/200	9/88	Brown, white (S01B)	--	Brown / white TÜV (20,000)	25.00 ☐
S7	S4	50DM/200	9/89	"Solaic" cont. (S01C)	--	Brown / white TÜV (12,000)	18.00 ☐
S8	(S5)	12DM/40	1/89	Multicolour (S02A)	--	Multicolour HOECHST FAX (86,000)	10.00 ☐
S9	S5	12DM/40	1/89	"Solaic" contact	--	Multicolour HOECHST FAX (3000)	45.00 ☐
S10	(S6)	50DM/200	1/89	Multicolour (S02B)	--	Multicolour HOECHST FAX (57,600)	12.00 ☐
S11	S6	50DM/200	1/89	"Solaic" contact	--	Multicolour HOECHST FAX (8400)	25.00 ☐
S12	(S5)	12DM/40	1/89	Multicolour (S02C)	--	Multicol. HOECHST FOLIEN (89,000)	5.00 ☐
S13	(S6)	50DM/200	1/89	Multicolour (S02D)	--	Multicol. HOECHST FOLIEN (66,000)	15.00 ☐

Note 1.   The alternative contact type refered to as "Solaic" above is the same as that called Type VI and illustrated under Solaic cards in the section on France (page 49).   All those with a Solaic type contact (refered to as Type II in Germany) have been made by ODS.

Note 2.   German specialist collectors, like their French and British counterparts, also often distinguish between control numbers with different numbers of digits (7, 11, 12).

№	Ill.	Units	Date	Colours (Front)	(Reverse)		Value
S14	S7	12DM/40	2/89	Multicolour (P02A)	--	White/blue, SERVICE 130 (150,000)	8.00 ☐
S15	S8	50DM/200	2/89	Multicolour (P02B)	--	White/blue, TEL. AUSLAND (100,000)	15.00 ☐
S16	S9	50DM/200	4/89	Multicolour (S03)	--	Black/white, SALZBURGER (400,000)	15.00 ☐
S17	S10	12DM/40	9/89	Multicolour (P03A)	--	White/blue, TEL. SERVICES (150,000)	8.00 ☐
S18	(S10)	50DM/200	9/89	Multicolour (P03B)	--	White/blue, TEL. SERVICES (100,000)	10.00 ☐
S19	S11	12DM/40	11/89	Multicolour (P04)	--	Black/white, TELEKOM (300,000)	5.00 ☐
S20	S11	12DM/40	11/89	"Solaic" cont. (P04)	--	Black/white, TELEKOM (???????)	5.00 ☐

PRIVATE CARDS

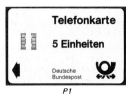
P1

P2 (reverse)

P3 (reverse)

P4 (reverse)

P5 (reverse)

P6 (reverse)

P7 (reverse)

P8 (reverse)

P9 (reverse)

P10 (reverse)

P11

P12 (reverse)

P13 (reverse)

P14 (reverse)

P15

№	Ill.	Units	Date	Colours (Front)		(Reverse)		Value
P1	*P1*	5	16/12/86	Black / white	*P2*	Gold / white, Contr. left	(????)	25.00 ▢
P2	*P1*	5	1987	Black / white	*P3*	Black / white, CeBIT'87	(3400)	30.00 ▢
P3	*P1*	5	1987	Black / white	*P4*	Black / white, Control right	(????)	45.00 ▢
P3(a)					*P4*	Control top left	(????)	100.00 ▢
P4	*P1*	5	1987	Black / white	--	B/w, Überreicht..PTZ Referat	(200)	350.00 ▢
P5	*P1*	5	1987	Black / white	--	B/w, Überreicht..PTZ Einkauf	(200)	350.00 ▢
P6	*D1*	40	1987	Red / white	*P5*	Red / white	(1000)	60.00 ▢
P7	*P1*	5	1988	Black / white	*(P3)*	Black / white, CeBIT'88	(4000)	70.00 ▢
P8	*P1*	5	1988	Black / white	*P6*	Black, red / white	(6000)	35.00 ▢
P9	*P1*	5	1988	Black / white	*P7*	White / black, IVA88	(1000)	50.00 ▢
P10	*P1*	5	1988	Black / white	*P8*	Multicolour (matt disk)	(1000)	45.00 ▢
P11	*P1*	5	1988	Black / white	*P8*	·· (no matt disk)	(1000)	45.00 ▢
P12	*P1*	5	1988	Black / white	*P9*	Black, red / white, RICOH	(2000)	60.00 ▢
P13	*P1*	5	1988	Black / white	*P10*	Red, black/white, TELENORMA I	(1500)	70.00 ▢
P14	*P11*	5	1988	Multicolour	*P4*	Black / white	(8700)	60.00 ▢
P15	*P1*	5	1988	Black / white	*P12*	Multicolour G&D I	(800)	80.00 ▢
P16	*P1*	5	1988	Black / white	*P13*	Multicolour G&D II	(1000)	65.00 ▢
P17	*P1*	5	1988	Black / white	*P14*	Multicolour ODS I	(1000)	75.00 ▢

P16(reverse)

P17(reverse)

P19

P20(reverse)

P21(reverse)

P22

P23

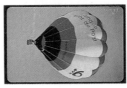

P24(reverse)

P25

P26

P27

P28

P29

P30

P31

№	Ill.	Units	Date	Colours (Front)		(Reverse)		Value
P18	*P15*	20	5/88	Green, black/white (K01A)	*P16*	Multicolour KRAFT KRÄUTER	(1500)	150.00 □
P19	*(P15)*	20	5/88	Red, black / white (K01B)	*P17*	Multicolour KRAFT TZATZIKI	(4500)	75.00 □
P20	*P19*	20	9/88	Multicolour	*P20*	Black/multicolour, ODS II	(1000)	75.00 □
P21	*P19*	20	9/88	Multicolour (X01A)	*P21*	Multicolour POSTREKLAME	(6060)	40.00 □
P22	*P22*	5	10/88	White / blue (W01)	--	Blue/white, BILDSCHIRMTEXT	(5000)	50.00 □
P23	*(P11)*	5	10/88	Multicolour (W01)	*P13*	Multicolour G&D III	(1000)	80.00 □
P24	*P23*	40	11/88	Black / blue (W02)	*P24*	Multicolour, MINISTERIAL I	(2000)	75.00 □
P25	*P25*	20	12/88	Blue / white (K02)	--	Blue / white, BUHL PAPIER	(1500)	90.00 □
P26	*P26*	20	12/88	Green / white (K03)	--	Green / white, PANORAMA	(1000)	75.00 □
P27	*P27*	20	12/88	Blue, black/white (K04A)	--	Black / white, FUNKSHAU	(1000)	75.00 □
P28	*P28*	20	12/88	Red, black/white (K04B)	--	Black / white, ELEKTRONIK	(1000)	75.00 □
P29	*P29*	5	2/89	Multicolour (W04)	--	Multicolour, ISDN/CeBit'89	(3000)	45.00 □
P30	*P30*	5	2/89	Yel., blk / white (W05)	--	Yel., black/white, PIEP	(10,000)	60.00 □
P31	*P31*	20	2/89	Red, black / white (K06)	--	Black / white, O&K	(2000)	60.00 □

P32

P33

P34

P35

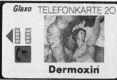

P36

P37

P38

P39 (reverse)

P40

P41

P42

P43

P44

P45

P46

№	Ill.	Units	Date	Colours (Front)		(Reverse)		Value
P32	*P32*	20	2/89	Blue, red / white	(K05)	--	Black, red/white, TELENORMA (10,000)	25.00 □
P33	*(P32)*	200	2/89	Blue, red / white	(K08)	--	Black, red/white, TELENORMA II (500)	100.00 □
P34	*P33*	40	2/89	Multicolour	(K07)	--	Black, etc. / white, KDD (1000)	75.00 □
P35	*P34*	40	2/89	Shades of blue	(K09)	--	Black, red/white, DG LEASING (2000)	60.00 □
P36	*P35*	20	3/89	Multicolour	(K10)	--	Shades of blue, FESTO (3000)	50.00 □
P37	*P36*	20	3/89	Multicolour	(K11)	--	Black, red/grey, DERMOXIN (10,000)	20.00 □
P38	*P37*	20	3/89	Multicolour	(K12)	--	Multicolour, EURO-MAGAZIN (1000)	70.00 □
P39	*P38*	40	3/89	Black / blue	(W07)	*(P24)*	Multicolour, MINISTERIAL II (2000)	60.00 □
P40	*(P11)*	5	4/89	Multicolour	(W06)	*P39*	Gold/dark blue, COMMUNICA (10,000)	20.00 □
P41	*P40*	40	4/89	Multicolour	(K13)	--	White, blue shades, SIEMENS (10,000)	20.00 □
P42	*P41*	20	5/89	Multicolour	(W08)	--	Blank, pale grey, ISDN II (5000)	40.00 □
P43	*P42*	40	5/89	Black, red / white	(K14)	--	White / red, TAKEDA PHARMA (2500)	30.00 □
P44	*(P42)*	200	5/89	Black, red / white	(K15)	--	White / red, TAKEDA PHARMA (500)	120.00 □
P45	*P43*	20	5/89	Black, red / white	(K16)	--	Black, red/white, SIEMENS II (2000)	60.00 □
P46	*P44*	20	6/89	Multicolour	(XA03)	--	Blk/yel., POSTREKLAME-IHNEN (1500)	50.00 □
P47	*P44*	20	6/89	Multicolour	(XB03)	--	Blk/yel., POSTREKLAME-65JÄHR. (500)	120.00 □
P48	*P45*	20	6/89	Blue / white	(K17)	--	Blue / white, OASIS-FORD (2000)	60.00 □
P49	*P46*	20	6/89	Black, red / white	(W09)	--	Multicolour, BONN IST 2000 (4000)	40.00 □

Note. P24 and P39 are Ministerial greeting cards. They differ only in the arrangement of the words below the signature and, of course, in the series numbers - W 02 and W 07 respectively.

P47

P48

P49

P50

P51

P52

P53

P54

P55

P56

P57

P58

P59

P60

P61

Nº	Ill.	Units	Date	Colours (Front)		(Reverse)		Value
P50	P47	20	6/89	Black, yellow, white	(W10)	--	Black / yellow, SPRACHBOX I (1500)	60.00 □
P51	P48	40	6/89	Multicolour	(W11)	--	White / blue, SPRACHBOX II (700)	100.00 □
P52	P49	20	6/89	Multicolour	(W12)	--	Black / white, HAMBURG KOMMT (3000)	40.00 □
P53	P50	20	6/89	Black / blue	(W13)	--	Blue, black, yel. DBP-NÜRNBERG (1000)	50.00 □
P54	P51	20	7/89	Multicolour	(XA04)	--	Black, yel. /white, 500Ja. POST (600)	120.00 □
P55	(P51)	200	7/89	Multicolour	(XB04)	--	Black, yel. /white, 500Ja. POST (400)	150.00 □
P56	(P41)	20	7/89	As P42, 'Solaic' C.	(W14)	--	Plain grey, ISDN III (10,000)	30.00 □
P57	P52	20	7/89	Multicolour	(W15)[1]	--	Black/grey, PERSPEKTIVEN (10,000)	30.00 □
P58	(P36)	20	7/89	As P37, 'Solaic' C.	(K18)	--	As P37, GLAXO DERMOXIN (10,000)	25.00 □
P59	P53	40	7/89	Red, black / white	(K19)	--	Multicolour, MAXI (1000)	60.00 □
P60	P54	20	7/89	Multicolour	(K20)	--	Multicolour, TELENORMA III (2100)	40.00 □
P61	P55	20	7/89	Multicolour	(K22)	--	Black, red, etc. STAT. LOTTERIE (5000)	30.00 □
P62	P56	20	8/89	Black / yellow	(K21)	--	Black/white, SAMMLE T'KARTEN (1000)	60.00 □
P63	P57	40	8/89	Blue, black/white	(K23)	--	Black / white, THÜGA (2000)	50.00 □
P64	P58	20	9/89	Blue, black, p. blue	(K24)	--	As front. FINNAIR (4000)	25.00 □
P65	P59	20	9/89	Multicolour	(K28)	--	Black / white, ODS III (500)	125.00 □
P66	P60	20	10/89	Blue, white, grey	(K25)	--	White / blue, LUFTHANSA (10,000)	20.00 □
P67	P61	20	10/89	Gold / white	(K26)	--	Gold / white, CONTENTON (1200)	60.00 □

Note. P56 and P58 are the same as P42 and P37 but with 'Solaic' type contacts. P57 has, accidently, no series number but is in fact W 15.

P62

P63

P64 (reverse)

P65

P66 (reverse)

O1

Nº	Ill.	Units	Date	Colours (Front)		(Reverse)			Value
P68	*P62*	40	10/89	Black, pink, white	(W16)	-- Multicolour, F.G.MINISTRY	(2000)		50.00 ◻
P69	*P63*	40	11/89	Black / blue	(W17)	*P64* Multicolour, HELMUT RICKE	(5000)		30.00 ◻
P70	*(P65)*	20	11/89	Black / yellow	(W18A)	*P66* Multicolour, POST & BÜRO	(3000)		20.00 ◻
P71	*P65*	40	11/89	Black / white	(W18B)	--ᴸ White / red, T.OHNE MÜNZEN	(2000)		25.00 ◻

O - OFFICIAL/SERVICE CARD

Nº	Ill.	Units	Date	Description	Value
O1	*O1*	--	?/??	Red / grey (500)	150.00 ◻

General Note.   The prices suggested above can only be approximate and could well rise rapidly as the number of collectors increase and available stocks of rare cards are absorbed.

GHANA

Optical cards by Landis and Gyr have recently been introduced by Ghana P&T.

First issue.

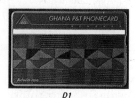

D1

D2

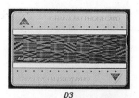

D3

Nº	Ill.	Units	Date	Description		Value	
D1	*D1*	60	1989	Multicolour (100,000) •		7.50 ◻	3.00 ◻
D2	*D2*	120	1989	Multicolour (80,000)		15.00 ◻	5.00 ◻
D3	*D3*	240	1989	Multicolour (10,000)		25.00 ◻	10.00 ◻

Note.   These designs show traditional weaving patterns.

GIBRALTAR

Gibraltar Telephone has recently introduced optical cards by Landis and Gyr, Switzerland.

First Issue.

D1

Nº	Ill.	Units	Date	Description	Value	
D1	*D1*	40	1989	Yellow, white / silver (10,000)	8.00 ☐	3.00 ☐

GREAT BRITAIN

Following the privatisation of British Telecom and the ending of their monopoly, three telephone companies now operate payphone systems in the UK. Optical cards are manufactured by Landis and Gyr for British Telecom. Mercury Communications, a Cable and Wireless company, introduced payphones using GPT magnetic cards in London in 1988 and has since expanded to other major UK cities. A further company, International Payphones Ltd, introduced a second magnetic system using Autelca telephones and cards in January, 1990.

BRITISH TELECOM

Earlier types (control numbers on reverse begin with letter G) were manufactured in Switzerland. Since March, 1983, many cards have been made in the UK and control numbers on the reverse have begun with three numerals followed by a letter and serial number. The first of the three numerals before the letter in the control number is the year in the 1980s and the second two the month of manufacture. Thus '05' is May and '12' is December. The '0' may be substituted by any even number and the '1' by any odd number so '25' or '45' would also be May and '32' or '52' would also be December. 999 and 998 controls are arbitrarily used for very short runs – for some special cards like the 50,000,000th and also for ordinary cards made to replace defective cards and complete a batch. The latter are rare. UK-made cards can generally be distinguished from Swiss-made cards in that the former have the optical strip set into a shallow trough, often with ridges on either side, while the latter do not and the surface is thus flat and smooth. Cards are found with long or short optical tracks. The long tracks extend into the margins. There is a gradual change from short to long track but no particular pattern to their occurrence. The unit was originally £0.05 but it was increased after a short period to £0.10. The complimentary cards, of initially 10 and later 5 units, are given out by British Telecom to introduce new customers to the system and are also extensively used by British Telecom staff for official purposes. The issue of advertising cards began at the end of 1986 and special or commemorative cards first appeared in 1987.

C1

C2

C3

C4

C5

D1

GREAT BRITAIN

C - COMPLIMENTARY CARDS

№	Ill.	Units	Date	Description	Value	
C1	*C1*	5	11/85	Green / silver (1,600,000)	4.00 ☐	2.00 ☐
C2	*C2*	5	1/86	·· ·· ·· ·· (3,100,000)	1.00 ☐	0.50 ☐

Note 1. The 10 unit 'Cardphone' card, D1 below, was in fact mainly used as a complimentary but has been listed as a definitive since it clearly falls into the 'Cardphone' series. The unit was then 5p.

Note 2. A further printing of C1, after the printing of C2, has been reported but does not appear in Landis and Gyr's records and no copy of C1 dated after January, 1986, has been seen.

C3	*C3*	5	1/86	COMPANY MESSAGE, Green, blue / silver (5000)	50.00 ☐	20.00 ☐
C4	*C4*	5	9/87	LANDIS & GYR - 75 YRS, Green / silver (9000)	75.00 ☐	35.00 ☐
C5	*C5*	5	1/90	Green / silver, Notched	1.00 ☐	0.50 ☐

Note. C3 was issued, initially at a conference in Brighton, as a sample to demonstrate the advertising potential. C4 celebrated 75 years of Landis and Gyr's trading in the UK. Both were issued before cards were widely collected in the UK and few seem to have survived.

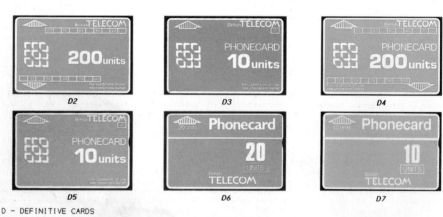

D - DEFINITIVE CARDS

First (Cardphone) Series.

№	Ill.	Units	Date	Description	Value	
D1	*D1*	10	1981	Green / silver (50,000)	45.00 ☐	15.00 ☐
D4	*(D1)*	40	7/81	·· ·· ·· ·· (2,635,000)	5.00 ☐	1.50 ☐
D5	*(D1)*	100	1983	·· ·· ·· ·· (552,000)	12.00 ☐	3.50 ☐
D6	*D2*	200	7/81	·· ·· ·· ·· (481,000)	24.00 ☐	6.00 ☐
D6(a)				Control on inverted card (incl. above)	30.00 ☐	10.00 ☐

Note 1. The 20 and 30 unit cardphone cards listed as D2 and D3 in the first edition are no longer listed. Neither appears in the production records of Landis and Gyr although sample or trial copies of a 30 unit card certainly exist.

Note 2. In the case of D6(a) above and D11(a) below, the control has been applied to an inverted card, i.e. it appears inverted in the top left corner of the reverse rather than the right way up in the bottom right corner as was usual at that time, whereas in the case of most later cards of Great Britain inverted controls are in the correct position but upside down. Many UK cards over the last two years have had inverted controls due to a change in the control cutting dies.

Note 3. A trial version of D6 with a 2mm white band over the optical strip is known to exist.

Second (Phonecard) Series.

№	Ill.	Units	Date	Description	Value	
D7	*D3*	10	6/84	Green / silver (long track) (10,759,000)	2.50 ☐	0.50 ☐
D7(a)				·· ·· ·· ·· (short track)	6.00 ☐	4.00 ☐
D8	*(D3)*	20	4/85	·· ·· ·· ·· (long track) (9,935,000)	3.50 ☐	0.60 ☐
D8(a)				·· ·· ·· ·· (short track)	8.00 ☐	4.00 ☐
D9	*(D3)*	40	6/84	·· ·· ·· ·· (short track) (7,638,000)	8.00 ☐	2.00 ☐
D10	*(D3)*	100	6/84	·· ·· ·· ·· (long track) (2,423,000)	15.00 ☐	4.00 ☐
D10(a)				·· ·· ·· ·· (short track)	15.00 ☐	4.00 ☐
D11	*D4*	200	6/84	·· ·· ·· ·· (916,000)	25.00 ☐	12.00 ☐
D11(a)				Control on inverted card	40.00 ☐	20.00 ☐

Third (Notched) Series.

№	Ill.	Units	Date	Description	Value	
D12	*D5*	10	10/87	Green / silver	1.20 ☐	0.30 ☐
D12(a)				Control **not** inverted	5.00 ☐	1.00 ☐
D12(b)				Control **missing**	100.00 ☐	50.00 ☐
D13	*(D5)*	20	10/87	·· ·· ·· ··	2.40 ☐	0.60 ☐
D13(a)				Control **not** inverted	4.00 ☐	1.50 ☐
D13(b)				Control missing	50.00 ☐	25.00 ☐
D13A	*(D5)*	40	10/87	·· ·· ·· ··	4.50 ☐	0.60 ☐
D13A(a)				Control **not** inverted	5.00 ☐	1.00 ☐
D13A(b)				Control missing	50.00 ☐	25.00 ☐
D13B	*(D5)*	100	10/87	·· ·· ·· ··	12.00 ☐	3.00 ☐
D13B(a)				Control missing	75.00 ☐	50.00 ☐

Note. Inverted controls are normal for this series. Missing controls, which have now been found on all four above values, are very rare and are thought to be due to a machine malfunction. More generally Landis and Gyr cards without controls are often 'specimens'; they may never have been encoded and may even have no optical strip at all. One case of two controls, side by side, on one card and a few double strikes have been reported.

Fourth Series.

№	Ill.	Units	Date	Description	Value	
D14	*(D6)*	10	5/88	Green / silver (29,885)	10.00 ☐	4.00 ☐
D15	*D6*	20	5/88	·· ·· ·· ·· (29,179)	15.00 ☐	5.00 ☐
D16	*D7*	10	2/89	Green / silver (500,000)	3.00 ☐	1.00 ☐
D16(a)				Control **not** inverted	5.00 ☐	2.00 ☐

Note. D14 and D15 were trials for a new design and were manufactured in Switzerland. The control numbers on them are not inverted and do not follow the normal UK pattern. Both D14 and D15 are already scarce. D16 was manufactured later, in the UK, and differs from D14 in the length of the word 'Phonecard' and, most noticably, in that the horizontal line across the card is 2mm wide while those on D14 and D15 are 1mm wide; its controls are normally inverted and of the usual UK type. It is relatively common. It is perhaps debatable whether D14 to D16 should be regarded as a new series. Third series cards are still current but are being replaced by the fifth series cards below at the time of writing. Two cards, similar to D13B but with a white band over the optical track, have been reported; the status of these is unclear but they may have been engineering trial cards.

Fifth (Offset) Series.

№	Ill.	Units	Date	Description	Value	
D17	*(D8)*	10	2/90	Green, white / silver	1.50 ☐	0.50 ☐
D17(a)				Control missing	50.00 ☐	35.00 ☐
D18	*(D8)*	20	2/90	Green, white / silver	2.50 ☐	0.75 ☐
D18(a)				Control missing	50.00 ☐	35.00 ☐
D20	*D8*	100	2/90	Green, white / silver	11.00 ☐	1.50 ☐
D20(a)				Control missing	50.00 ☐	35.00 ☐
D21	*(D8)*	200	3/90?	Green, white / silver	22.00 ☐	4.00 ☐

Note. D19, the 40 unit card, is not yet being printed but will no doubt appear eventually. This series is offset-printed apart from the green band over the optical strip which is silk-screened. The first copies to be found lacked controls and were probably engineering trial cards. D21 is being printed at the time of writing but may not be generally issued (except to collectors) until stocks of D11 are exhausted.

S - SPECIAL/COMMEMORATIVE CARDS

№	Ill.	Units	Date	Description	Value	
S1	*(S1)*	10	1/7/87	MUIRFIELD (GOLF), Green / silver (6000)	350.00 ☐	200.00 ☐
S2	*(S1)*	20	1/7/87	·· ·· ·· ·· ·· ·· ·· ·· (5000)	350.00 ☐	200.00 ☐
S3	*S1*	100	1/7/87	·· ·· ·· ·· ·· ·· ·· ·· (900)	1000.00 ☐	300.00 ☐
S4	*S2*	40	4/11/87	LONDON CHALLANGE, Black, white, green (500)	1000.00 ☐	500.00 ☐

Note. The British Telecom London Challenge card was issued in connection with a joint initiative between British Telecom and the Student Industrial Society to promote the latter. Very few were sold on that occasion and others were disposed of in connection with Live Aid, a charity event.

S5	*S3*	20	16/11/87	CHRISTMAS 1987, Multicolour (100,000)	6.00 ☐	4.00 ☐
S5(a)				Control inverted	10.00 ☐	6.00 ☐

Note. S5 was made in Switzerland.

S6	*S4*	40	18/1/88	VALENTINE'S DAY 1988, Multicolour (250,000)	10.00 ☐	5.00 ☐

№	Ill.	Units	Date	Description		Value	
S7	*S5*	20	7/88	EDINBURGH FESTIVAL 1988, Multicolour (30,000)		15.00 ☐	4.00 ☐
S8	*(S5)*	40	7/88	·· ·· ·· ·· ·· ·· ·· ·· ·· (15,000)		8.00 ☐	6.00 ☐
S9	*(S5)*	100	7/88	·· ·· ·· ·· ·· ·· ·· ·· ·· (8,000)		17.50 ☐	12.00 ☐
S10	*S6*	40	10/88	FIFTY MILLIONTH, Blue, green / gold (600)		500.00 ☐	400.00 ☐

Note. This rare card commemorated the production of 50,000,000 Landis and Gyr cards in the UK. They were given to BT officials and journalists at the celebration. About half were in leather wallets.

№	Ill.	Units	Date	Description		Value	
S11	*S7*	20	10/88	CHRISTMAS 1988, Multicolour (1,500,700)		6.00 ☐	2.00 ☐
S11(a)				Deeper shade of blue		8.00 ☐	3.00 ☐
S11(b)				Control misplaced to left		10.00 ☐	4.00 ☐
S11(c)				Control missing		35.00 ☐	25.00 ☐
S12	*S8*	40	10/88	·· ·· ·· ·· ·· ·· ·· (750,000)		6.00 ☐	2.00 ☐
S12(a)				Control inverted		10.00 ☐	5.00 ☐

Note. S11 was manufactured in the UK. The two shades of blue background are quite distinct and are accompanied by different shades of green. D11(b) is of the lighter shade and the displacement of the (inverted) control is about 15mm. D12 was manufactured in Switzerland. Most copies have inverted controls but non-inverted are not uncommon.

№	Ill.	Units	Date	Description		Value	
S13	*S9*	20	10/89	WINTER 1989, Multicolour (1,224,400)	·	3.00 ☐	1.00 ☐
S13(a)				Control not inverted		5.00 ☐	3.00 ☐
S13(b)				Control missing		75.00 ☐	50.00 ☐
S14	*S10*	40	10/89	WINTER 1989, Multicolour (365,800)		5.00 ☐	2.00 ☐
S14(a)				Control not inverted		12.00 ☐	4.00 ☐
S14(b)				Control missing		75.00 ☐	50.00 ☐
S15	*S11*	100	10/89	WINTER 1989, Multicolour (151,000)		12.00 ☐	4.00 ☐
S15(a)				Control not inverted		75.00 ☐	35.00 ☐
S15(b)				Control missing		75.00 ☐	50.00 ☐

Note 1. 600 of S14 and 600 of D15 were manufactured in Switzerland. These can in theory be distinguished by the presence of ridges above and below the optical track on UK-made cards and their absence on Swiss-made cards. There are marked differences in shade in the two lower values the blue being much stronger some than in others. There are also differences in the surface textures. Some copies of D15 have the 'British / TELECOM' offset on the reverse. Cards with 999 (followed by a letter) controls can be found for all three values. These are short-run cards made to make up for any rejected cards in a batch and are rare.

№	Ill.	Units	Date	Description		Value	
S16	*S12*	20	2/89	FORTH BRIDGE CENTENARY, Multicolour (50,000)		3.00 ☐	1.50 ☐
S17	*S13*	40	2/89	FORTH BRIDGE CENTENARY, Sepia, green (25,000)		5.00 ☐	2.50 ☐

A2

A3

A4

A5

A6

A7

A - ADVERTISING CARDS

№	Ill.	Units	Date	Description		Value	
A1	*A1*	10	1/12/86	GRAHAM'S, Multicolour (15,000)		300.00 ☐	100.00 ☐
A2	*A2*	10	1987	MENTADENT, Multicolour (Swiss-made) (50,000)		25.00 ☐	15.00 ☐
A2A	*(A2)*	10	1988	MENTADENT, Notch added (Swiss-made) (60,000)		3.50 ☐	2.50 ☐
A2A(a)				Control not inverted		5.00 ☐	4.00 ☐

Note. A1 has been reported with three different widths of strip (*not* band) as seen in the margins at the end of the green band - 3.2mm, 3.6mm and 4.2mm.

A8   A9   A10

A11   A12   A13

A14   A15   01

№	Ill.	Units	Date	Description	Value	
A3	A3	10	1987	TREBOR, Green / silver (26,700)	100.00 ☐	30.00 ☐
A4	A4	10	11/87	BIRD'S, Green / silver (5000)	45.00 ☐	15.00 ☐
A5	A5	10	2/88	GATEWAY, Black, green / silver (30,000)	35.00 ☐	20.00 ☐
A6	A6	5	3/88	PERSIL, Multicolour (630,990)	3.00 ☐	2.50 ☐
A6(a)				·· ·· ·· ·· Control not inverted	4.00 ☐	3.00 ☐
A6(b)				·· ·· ·· ·· Darker blue	6.00 ☐	4.00 ☐

Note. A version of A6 without the white box round the logo exists as a specimen and a few may have been issued. A6, even when sealed, often has a scrape in the margin by the 'd' in Phonecard.

| A7 | A7 | 5 | 3/88 | BROOK BOND, Yellow, red, green / silver (250,000) | 10.00 ☐ | 4.00 ☐ |
| A8 | A8 | 10 | 3/88 | ·· ·· ·· ·· ·· ·· ·· ·· ·· (45,550) | 25.00 ☐ | 6.00 ☐ |

Note. A7 and A8 were manufactured in Switzerland. A7 shows two distinct shades of red and a tendency to colour misplacement of either red or yellow.

A9	A9	10	4/88	PALMOLIVE, Blue, white, magenta / silver (30,000)	5.00 ☐	3.50 ☐
A10	A10	10	5/88	CASTLEMAINE, Multicolour (20,000)	17.00 ☐	10.00 ☐
A11	A11	40	5/88	·· ·· ·· ·· ·· ·· (10,000)	25.00 ☐	12.00 ☐
A12	–	20	7/88	GLAXO, Blue, green / silver (52,600)	20.00 ☐	8.00 ☐
A13	A12	40	8/88	3i, Blue, black, yellow, green / silver (5500)	150.00 ☐	75.00 ☐
A14	A13	10	10/89	LANDIS & GYR – DFS, Green / silver (400)	200.00 ☐	150.00 ☐
A15	(A13)	40	10/89	·· ·· ·· ·· ·· Green / silver (50)	750.00 ☐	300.00 ☐

Note. For reasons connected with the laws on the advertising of pharmacuticals in the UK it is unfortunately not possible to illustrate the Glaxo card, A12.

| A16 | A14 | 20 | 11/89 | WILTSHIER, Blue, red, white, green/silver (11,100) | 35.00 ☐ | 20.00 ☐ |
| A17 | A15 | 5 | 11/89 | SIGMAGYR, Multicolour (5,000) | 45.00 ☐ | 25.00 ☐ |

0 - OFFICIAL/SERVICE CARDS

01	01	(200)	1983?	Green / silver (short track)	---	50.00 ☐
02	(01)	(200)	1986?	Green / silver (long track)	---	35.00 ☐
03	(01)	(200)	1989	Green / silver - Notched	---	20.00 ☐

T - TEST CARDS

T1	*T1*	—	1983?	Green / silver		---	300.00 ☐
T2	*(T2)*	—	?	Green / matt silver		---	200.00 ☐
T3	*T2*	—	?	Green / polished silver		---	40.00 ☐

Note. The printed numbers on T2 and T3 and the manuscript numbers on T1 refer to settings of the telephones being tested and differ from card to card. Like the Service cards they are not available to the general public in an unused condition and no unused price is therefore given.

General Note: In addition to the above, there exist a number of private cards, essentially visiting cards, bearing the names of specific individuals. These are not generally available and are not therefore listed.

MERCURY COMMUNICATIONS

Mercury Communications Ltd launched its payphone business on 27 July, 1988, with the opening of 26 call boxes at Waterloo Station in London with one complimentary card, three definitive cards and three special cards. The service has since spread throughout London and to other major cities in the UK. They are denominated in UK currency rather than units and have almost invisible control numbers on the reverse. The cards are manufactured by GPT, previously Plessey, UK, and are prefixed 'M' in the listings below. At the time of writing it is not possible to distinguish used from unused cards so only a single value is given. A new technology to indicate the number of units used may be introduced soon. Mercury cards are classified as Definitives and Specials (both on sale generally) and Private issues which include advertising cards and other very limited issues not sold generally although all are on sale through Stanley Gibbons for the Mercury Collectors Club.

C - COMPLIMENTARY CARDS

№	Ill.	Units	Date	Description	Value
MC1	*MC1*	(£0.40)	27/7/88	Black, blue, silver, shades of metallic grey (27,000)	10.00 ▯
MC2	*MC2*	(£0.40)	6/89	Multicolour (100,000)	1.00 ▯

MD - DEFINITIVE CARDS

Nº	Ill.	Units	Date	Description	Value
MD1	(MD1)	£2	27/7/88	Black, blue, shades of metallic bronze (130,000)	2.50 ☐
MD1(a)				Black, blue, shades of metallic copper (incl. above)	2.50 ☐
MD2	(MD1)	£4	27/7/88	Black, blue, shades of metallic silver (38,185)	5.00 ☐
MD3	MD1	£10	27/7/88	Black, blue, shades of metallic gold (14,000)	12.00 ☐

MS - SPECIAL / COMMEMORATIVE CARDS

Nº	Ill.	Units	Date	Description	Value
MS1	MS1	£2	27/7/88	FIRST ISSUE, Multicoloured (5000)	10.00 ☐
MS2	MS2	£4	27/7/88	·· ·· ·· ·· ·· ·· ·· (5000)	15.00 ☐
MS3	MS3	£10	27/7/88	·· ·· ·· ·· ·· ·· ·· (5000)	25.00 ☐
MS4	MS4	£5	9/88	WATERLOO CARD, Multicoloured (150,000)	5.00 ☐
MS5	MS5	£2	10/88	CHRISTMAS 1988, Multicoloured (85,000)	4.00 ☐
MS6	MS6	£4	10/88	·· ·· ·· ·· ·· ·· ·· (34,000)	6.00 ☐
MS7	MS7	£10	10/88	·· ·· ·· ·· ·· ·· ·· (17,000)	15.00 ☐
MS8	MS8	£2	5/89	LONDON, Multicoloured (741,500)	2.50 ☐
MS9	MS9	£4	5/89	·· ·· ·· ·· ·· ·· (31,031)	5.00 ☐
MS10	MS10	£10	5/88	·· ·· ·· ·· ·· ·· (6000)	40.00 ☐
MS11	MS11	£5	6/89	BIRMINGHAM, Multicoloured (5000)	8.00 ☐
MS12	MS12	£5	6/89	BRISTOL ·· ·· ·· (5000)	8.00 ☐
MS13	MS13	£5	6/89	EDINBURGH ·· ·· ·· (5000)	8.00 ☐
MS14	MS14	£5	6/89	MANCHESTER ·· ·· ·· (5000)	8.00 ☐
MS15	MS15	£5	6/89	GLASGOW TOWN HALL, ·· (5000)	8.00 ☐

Note. The above series was issued to mark the introduction of Mercury payphones in the named cities. MS15 was inscribed "Glasgow Town Hall" instead of 'Glasgow City Chambers' in error and a replacement may be issued.

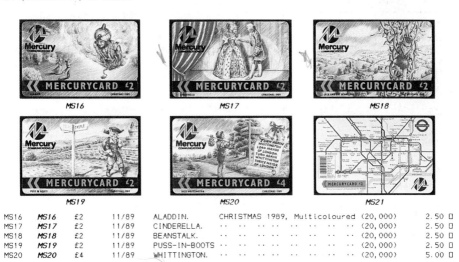

MS16 MS17 MS18

MS19 MS20 MS21

Nº	Ill.	Units	Date	Description	Value
MS16	MS16	£2	11/89	ALADDIN. CHRISTMAS 1989, Multicoloured (20,000)	2.50 ☐
MS17	MS17	£2	11/89	CINDERELLA. ·· ·· ·· ·· ·· ·· ·· ·· (20,000)	2.50 ☐
MS18	MS18	£2	11/89	BEANSTALK. ·· ·· ·· ·· ·· ·· ·· ·· (20,000)	2.50 ☐
MS19	MS19	£2	11/89	PUSS-IN-BOOTS ·· ·· ·· ·· ·· ·· ·· ·· (20,000)	2.50 ☐
MS20	MS20	£4	11/89	WHITTINGTON. ·· ·· ·· ·· ·· ·· ·· ·· (20,000)	5.00 ☐
MS21	MS21	£2	2/90	MAP OF UNDERGROUND, Multicoloured (10,000)	2.50 ☐

MP - PRIVATE CARDS

№	Ill.	Units	Date	Description	Value
MP1	*MP1*	£2	6/89	NETWORKS 89, Black, blue / white (800)	100.00 □
MP2	*MP2*	£2	9/89	SPIRIT OF ADVENTURE, Multicoloured (500)	200.00 □
MP3	*MP3*	£2	9/89	SIR ERIC SHARP, Multicoloured (1500)	35.00 □
MP4	*MP4*	£2	9/89	INN ON THE PARK, Silver, etc./cream, Large notch	5.00 □
MP5	*(MP4)*	£2	9/89	INN ON THE PARK, ·· ·· (500) Small notch, (15 MER..)	200.00 □
MP5(a)		£2	1/90	Small notch, Control 17 MER......	3.00 □
MP6	*(MP4)*	£10	2/90	INN ON THE PARK, Gold, etc /cream, Small notch	12.00 □

Note. Where no number of cards issued is given, as in the cases of MP4 and MP6 above and MP 16, 17 and 18 below, it is normally because these are continuing issues which will be reordered as required and it will only be possible to give a total number when the design is discontinued. They are, in effect, 'private definitives'.

№	Ill.	Units	Date	Description		Value
MP7	*(MP5)*	£2	10/89	ORIENT EXPRESS, Multicoloured, Large notch (1000)		150.00 ☐
MP8	*MP5*	£2	10/89	ORIENT EXPRESS, Multicoloured, Small notch (1050)		35.00 ☐
MP9	*(MP6)*	£0.50	10/89	ABRAXAS. Multicolour. Large notch (600)		95.00 ☐
MP10	*MP6*	£0.50	10/89	ABRAXAS. Multicolour. Small notch (1300)		25.00 ☐
MP10(a)			4/90	Small notch, Tel. 071 387 5599 (3500)		2.50 ☐
MP11	*MP7*	£2	10/89	DOCKLANDS TELECOMS CENTRE, Multicoloured	(1525)	25.00 ☐
MP12	*MS8*	£1	11/89	IT DIRECTION, Red, grey, etc. / white	(2003)	20.00 ☐
MP13	*MP9*	£2	11/89	HARBOUR SCENE, UK-FRANCE CABLE	(1589)	25.00 ☐
MP14	*MP10*	£2	11/89	VESSELS CLOSE HAULED, UK-NETHERLANDS CABLE.	(1428)	25.00 ☐
MP15	*MP11*	£2	11/89	GREAT EASTERN, Multicoloured	(1964)	25.00 ☐
MP16	*MP12*	£2	1/90	HARRODS, Multicoloured		3.00 ☐
MP16(a)				Gold printed on both sides		75.00 ☐
MP17	*MP13*	£2	1/90	SWALLOW HOTELS, Multicoloured		3.00 ☐
MP18	*MP14*	£10	1/90	SWALLOW HOTELS, Multicoloured, Large notch		12.00 ☐
MP18(a)				Small notch		12.00 ☐
MP19	*MP15*	£1	2/90	BROADGATE, Multicoloured (6000)		10.00 ☐
MP19(a)				Silver printed on both sides		40.00 ☐
MP20	--	£0.50	2/90	NatWest, Multicoloured (1000) (Illustration forbidden)		15.00 ☐
MP21	*MP16*	£2	3/90	ManuLife, Multicoloured (1300) Tel. No. 01 256 5858		2.50 ☐
MP22	*(MP16)*	£2	3/90	ManuLife, Multicoloured (1700) Tel. No. 0276 51888		2.50 ☐
MP23	*MP17*	£0.50	3/90	STANLEY GIBBONS - 150 YEARS, Black / Gold (6000)		1.00 ☐
MP24	*MP18*	£0.50	3/90	SPACE MANAGEMENT SERVICES, Multicoloured (?000)		1.00 ☐

MP19

MP20

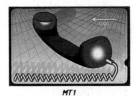

MT1

MP25	*MP19*	£0.50	3/90	PARAGON COMMUNICATIONS, Black, blue / white	(3000)	1.00 ☐
MP26	*(MP20)*	£0.50	3/90	BRIAN REEVES, Black / gold, Tel. 01 836 2391	(3500)	2.50 ☐
MP27	*MP20*	£0.50	3/90	BRIAN REEVES, Black / gold, Tel. 071 836 2391	(4500)	2.50 ☐
MP28	*(MP20)*	£0.50	3/90	BRIAN REEVES, Black / gold, Tel. 071 836 3780	(4500)	2.50 ☐

MT - TEST CARD

MT1	*MT1*	1000	1986?	Red, blue, white	35.00 ☐

Note. These cards, although the standard test cards for GPT systems, also formed the basis of the China (Shanghai) and Canadian trial cards and for the Irish 'Cork card'.

MPT - MERCURY PAYTELCO CARDS

SHELL First Series

MPT1	*MPT1*	£0.50	1/90	COMPLIMENTARY. Multicoloured	(7625)	2.00 ☐
MPT2	*MPT2*	£2	1/90	Multicoloured	(33,450)	2.50 ☐
MPT3	*(MPT1)*	£4	1/90	Multicoloured	(9275)	5.00 ☐
MPT4	*MPT3*	£10	1/90	Multicoloured	(26,650)	12.00 ☐

SHELL Second Series

MPT5	*MPT4*	£2	3/90	Multicoloured	2.50 ☐
MPT6	*MPT5*	£4	3/90	Multicoloured	5.00 ☐
MPT7	*MPT6*	£10	3/90	Multicoloured	12.00 ☐

MPT1

MPT2

MPT3

MPT4

MPT5

MPT6

MPT7

MPT8

MPT9

MPT10

MPT11

MPT12

MPT13

IC1

IC1 (reverse)

BOOTS

№	Ill.	Units	Date	Description	Value
MPT8	*MPT7*	£2	3/90	MAKING FACES, Multicoloured (?000)	2.50 ☐
MPT9	*MPT8*	£2	3/90	LUNCHTIME FOODS, Multicoloured (?000)	2.50 ☐
MPT10	*MPT9*	£2	3/90	NAPPY SERVICE, Multicoloured (?000)	2.50 ☐
MPT11	*MPT10*	£2	3/90	FILM PROCESSING, Multicoloured (?000)	2.50 ☐
MPT12	*MPT11*	£4	3/90	№ 7, Multicoloured (?000)	5.00 ☐
MPT13	*MPT12*	£10	3/90	OPTICIANS, Multicoloured (?000)	12.00 ☐

TRUSTHOUSE FORTE

MPT14	*MPT13*	£2	3/90	TRAVELODGE, Multicoloured (?000)	2.50 ☐

INTERNATIONAL PAYPHONES LIMITED

IPL was due to begin operation in the UK in January, 1990, with the instalation of telephones n five hospitals and a shopping precinct. Cards are produced by Autelca, Switzerland. The unit is £0.10. The cards are given 'I' prefixes below.

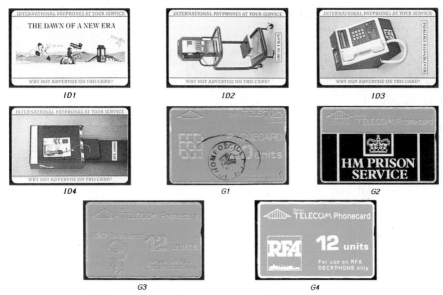

ID1　*ID2*　*ID3*

ID4　*G1*　*G2*

G3　*G4*

IC - COMPLIMENTARY CARD

IC1	*IC1*	(20)	11/89	Multicolour (?00) Reverse as *IC1 (reverse)*	50.00 ☐

ID - DEFINITIVE CARDS

ID1	*ID1*	20	11/89	Multicolour (?000)	2.50 ☐
ID2	*ID2*	20	11/89	Multicolour (?000)	2.50 ☐
ID3	*ID3*	20	11/89	Multicolour (?000)	2.50 ☐
ID4	*ID4*	20	11/89	Multicolour (?000)	2.50 ☐

№	Ill.	Units	Date	Description		Value
ID5	*ID1*	50	11/89	Multicolour (?000)		6.00 ☐
ID6	*ID2*	50	11/89	Multicolour (?000)		6.00 ☐
ID7	*ID3*	50	11/89	Multicolour (?000)		6.00 ☐
ID8	*ID4*	50	11/89	Multicolour (?000)		6.00 ☐
ID9	*ID1*	100	11/89	Multicolour (?000)		11.50 ☐
ID10	*ID2*	100	11/89	Multicolour (?000)		11.50 ☐
ID11	*ID3*	100	11/89	Multicolour (?000)		11.50 ☐
ID12	*ID4*	100	11/89	Multicolour (?000)		11.50 ☐
ID13	*ID1*	150	11/89	Multicolour (?000)		17.00 ☐
ID14	*ID2*	150	11/89	Multicolour (?000)		17.00 ☐
ID15	*ID3*	150	11/89	Multicolour (?000)		17.00 ☐
ID16	*ID4*	150	11/89	Multicolour (?000)		17.00 ☐

Note. All values are found with all four face designs. The reverse is similar to *IC1 (reverse)* above but with the number of units shown in the top right corner below the magnetic band.

G - CLOSED USER GROUP CARDS

HM PRISON SERVICE Cards. These cards are for use only in prisons and are not encoded for use in normal BT telephones. They are to prevent the use of ordinary BT cards as an inflated currency in prisons. Previously standard BT 20 unit cards (D13) were hand-stamped locally to differentiate them from smuggled cards as in G1 below. Various Home Office hand-stamps have apparently been used and there is more research to be done on this subject. A hand-stamp has also been found on S13, the 20 unit 1989 Winter card, G2 below, and no doubt there are others. Care should be taken, however, since forgeries are known to exist.

№	Ill.	Units	Date	Description		Value	
G1	*G1*	20	1988	Black / Green / silver (D13) (?000)	--- ☐	15.00 ☐	
G2	--	20	1988	Black / Multicolour (S13) (?000)	--- ☐	20.00 ☐	
G3	*G2*	20	6/89	Dark blue, green / silver (65,000) '2' 2.6mm	--- ☐	15.00 ☐	
G4	*(G2)*	20	11/89	Dark blue, green / silver (76,000) '2' 3.1mm	--- ☐	15.00 ☐	

INMARSAT Cards. These cards are for use on ships through the International Maritime Satellite communication system. Units are expensive which is why the cards carry only 12 of them. P&O is a shipping and ferry company while RFA stands for the Royal Fleet Auxiliary.

№	Ill.	Units	Date	Description		Value	
G5	*G3*	12	7/89	P&O, Green / silver (5000)	35.00 ☐	10.00 ☐	
G6	*G4*	12	1/90?	RFA, Green / silver (5000)	35.00 ☐	10.00 ☐	

Note. A standard £2 BT phonecard is reported to have been overprinted with the compliments of British Airways and their logo on the reverse for an executive function in, it is thought, 1986. No further details are known at present but it must be rare. Other private overprints are known.

OFFSHORE OIL AND GAS RIGS (PLATFORMS)

Currently seven companies operating in the North Sea have card-operated telephones installed for the private use of their employees, six using optical cards made by Landis and Gyr (UK) and one, British Petroleum, using magnetic cards produced by GPT, UK. These were given the prefix 'R' in the first edition of this book and, because many collectors regard these cards as a self-contained group, it has been decided to retain this although strictly speaking they form a subset of Closed User Group cards.

R1

R2

R3

R4

R5

R6

R7

R8

R9

Nº	Ill.	Units	Date	Description		Value	
R1	*R1*	40	1984	BRITISH GAS: Green / silver	(51,200)	15.00 ☐	10.00 ☐
R1A	*(R1)*	40	7/89	Notched	(20,000)	7.00 ☐	5.00 ☐
R1A(a)				Notch on left edge		75.00 ☐	50.00 ☐
R2	*R2*	40	1984	BRITOIL : Green / silver	(119,200)	8.00 ☐	6.00 ☐
R2A	*(R2)*	40	1989	Notched	(36,000)	6.00 ☐	4.00 ☐
R3	*R3*	60	1985	SHELL EXPRO: Red, etc., (1.5mm band)	(48,000)	25.00 ☐	20.00 ☐
R3A	*(R3)*	60	1987?	2mm white band	(290,000)	20.00 ☐	8.00 ☐
R3B	*(R3)*	60	1988?	4mm white band	(200,000)	15.00 ☐	7.00 ☐
R3C	*(R3)*	60	6/88	3mm white band	(50,000)	8.00 ☐	5.00 ☐
R3D	*(R3)*	60	2/89	3mm white band, notched	(190,000)	8.00 ☐	5.00 ☐
R3E	*R8*	120	9/89	Green, no band, notched		14.00 ☐	4.00 ☐
R4	*R4*	100	2/87	BRITISH PETROLEUM: Multicolour	(40,000)		8.00 ☐
R4A	*(R4)*			With control number	(51,025)		5.00 ☐
R4B	*R9*	40	2/90	Landis and Gyr card. Green / silver		8.00 ☐	4.00 ☐
R5	*R5*	60	1986?	SUN OIL Co. Ltd: Green / silver	(30,000)	10.00 ☐	6.00 ☐
R6	*R6*	100	8/88	MARATHON : Green / silver	(15,000)	15.00 ☐	10.00 ☐
R6A	*(R6)*	50	10/88	Notched	(30,000)	7.00 ☐	5.00 ☐
R6B	*(R6)*	100	10/88	Notched	(15,000)	12.00 ☐	8.00 ☐
R7	*R7*	(40)	1988	AMERADA HESS: Green, silver / silver	(30.000)	6.00 ☐	4.00 ☐

Note: All the above cards are by Landis and Gyr except for R4 which was supplied by GPT.

P - PRIVATE/PROMOTIONAL CARDS

The cards below, issued by GPT, UK, have been used at conferences and exhibitions in the UK and subsequently elsewhere.

P1

P2

P3

P4

P5

№	Ill.	Units	Date	Description	Value
P1	*P1*	1000	6/87	ROVER, Multicoloured (1500)	50.00 ☐
P2	*P2*	1000	6/87	BUCKINGHAM PALACE, Multicoloured (1500)	50.00 ☐
P2(a)	*P2*	1000	16/3/87	·· ·· (?00) Reverse-"Press luncheon, Ritz Hotel," etc.	75.00 ☐
P3	*P3*	1000	6/87	Multicoloured (1500)	50.00 ☐
P4	*P4*	(1000)	6/87	Blue, yellow, black, white (?000)	50.00 ☐
P5	*P5*	1000	1989	LIVERPOOL F.C., Multicoloured (?000)	50.00 ☐

Note: The above cards are encoded with 1000 units of £0.10; i.e. they are £100 cards. Most are also seen without inscription; these are samples or essays and probably not encoded. The cards do not normally bear control numbers.

GENERAL NOTE. I have attempted in this book to include all major varieties of UK Landis and Gyr cards but there are many other minor varieties of interest to the specialist. A group of UK specialists is currently compiling a listing of all known varieties. Those interested sould write to Mr. Peter Harradine, 61 Elford Close, Kidbrook, London, SE3 9YW, UK enclosing, if possible, a stamped and addressed envelope.

GREECE

Magnetic cards, supplied by Plessey, UK, underwent field trials in Athens. Only the two definitive cards illustrated below have so far been issued.

D1

D2

№	Ill.	Units	Date	Description	Value
D1	*D1*	100	1987	Yellow, black (10,000)	25.00 ☐
D2	*D2*	100	1987	Yellow, red, black (10,000)	25.00 ☐

Note. D1 shows the Parthenon in Athens and D2 a windmill on Mikonos.

GRENADA

Magnetic cards by GPT (UK) are about to be introduced.

First Issue.

D1

№	Ill.	Units	Date	Description		Value
D1	*D1*	EC$5.40	1989	Multicolour	(1000)	30.00 ☐
D2	*(D1)*	EC$10	1989	Multicolour	(16,233)	10.00 ☐
D3	*(D1)*	EC$20	1989	Multicolour	(6666)	15.00 ☐
D4	*(D1)*	EC$40	1989	Multicolour	(2441)	20.00 ☐

Note 1.   D1 is included in the Cable and Wireless collectors pack of British West Indies cards (see under Promotional Cards at the end of this book).   Further printings of the two higher values with different pictures are expected in mid-1990.

Note 2.   A small number of higher value cards were accidently encoded with EC$5.4 but these can only be identified with the help of a payphone in Grenada.

HONG KONG

Twelve Autelca payphones were installed for field trials in 1983 and over 100 more have been installed since then.

| *D1* | *D2* | *D3* |

First Issue (Field Trial Cards)

№	Ill.	Units	Date	Description		Value
D1	*(D1)*	HK$25	3/84	Red, black / white	(63,000)	15.00 ☐
D2	*D1*	HK$100	3/84	·· ·· ·· ·· ··	(140,000)	10.00 ☐

Second Issue.

D3	*D2*	HK$50	9/85	Black / white	(200,000)	4.00 ☐
D4	*(D2)*	HK$100	9/85	·· ·· ··	(134,000)	7.50 ☐
D5	*(D2)*	HK$250	9/85	·· ·· ··	(22,000)	15.00 ☐

Third Issue.   Wording changed.

D6	*D3*	HK$50	10/86	Black / white	(938,000)	2.00 ☐
D7	*(D3)*	HK$100	10/86	·· ·· ··	(610,000)	4.00 ☐
D8	*(D3)*	HK$250	10/86	·· ·· ··	(42,000)	10.00 ☐

Introducing
the new collector series of
Hong Kong Telephone Phonecards

Hong Kong Telephone have introduced a new set of phonecards depicting typical Hong Kong scenery and tourist attractions. Ten pictures of a lion dance, a dragon boat race, a Chinese junk and various mountain and harbour scenes are colourfully reproduced on the phonecards.

Join our "Phonecard Collectors' Club" for special offers, news and notification of future card issues. To register for the Collectors' Club or to order your phonecards, write or fax to:

Hong Kong Telephone
Regulated Voice Services
GPO Box 479 Hong Kong
Fax: + 852 824 1855
Tel : + 852 808 3838

For further details of cards see the entry for Hong Kong.

Orders may also be placed through Stanley Gibbons.

I wish to order the following Collector Phonecards:-

Item No.	Please indicate number required				
	HK$50	HK$100	HK$250	set	HK$ Amount
1 Victoria Harbour Night Scene					
2 Central Skyline Backdrop for Junk					
3 Peak Tram					
4 Repulse Bay Pagoda					
5 10,000 Buddhas Temple					
6 Causeway Bay at Dusk					
7 Tsim Sha Tsui Clock Tower					
8 Dragon Boat Festival					
9 Tin Hau Festival Boats					
10 Lion Dance – Lunar New Year					
11 Red card trial series *	@ HK $125 per set				
12 Black & white 1st series *	@ HK $400 per set				
13 Black & white 2nd series *	@ HK $400 per set				
14 Hong Kong Skyline 3rd series					
15 Hong Kong 1990 Rugby Invitation Sevens series*	@ HK $350 per set				
For orders under HK$1200 please add registered post handling charge					10.00
* Limited stock				Total	

I enclose a bank draft/ postal order no. _____ made payable to
Hong Kong Telephone Co Ltd

For office use
Auth. Code No.

I wish to pay by ☐ **VISA** ☐ MasterCard ☐ (AMERICAN EXPRESS) ☐ Diners Club International* ☐ JCB

Card Number ☐☐☐☐ ☐☐☐☐ ☐☐☐☐ ☐☐☐☐

Expiry Date ☐☐☐☐

Signature _____

Name _____   Contact Tel. No. _____

Mailing Address _____

_____ Postcode_____   Date _____

Hongkong Telephone

D4

D4 (reverse)

S1

S2

S3

S4

S5

S6

S7

S8

S9

S10

№	Ill.	Units	Date	Description	Value
D9	**D4**	HK$50	1/89	Black, red / white (385,000) Reverse as **D4 (reverse)**	2.00 ☐
D10	**(D4)**	HK$100	1/89	·· ·· ·· ·· ·· (307,000) ·· ·· ·· ·· ·· ··	3.50 ☐
D11	**(D4)**	HK$250	1/89	·· ·· ·· ·· ·· (47,000) ·· ·· ·· ·· ·· ··	6.00 ☐

S - SPECIAL CARDS

№	Ill.	Units	Date	Description	Value
S1	**S1**	$50	2/90	VICTORIA HARBOUR, Multicolour (?,000)	3.00 ☐
S2	**S1**	$100	2/90	VICTORIA HARBOUR, Multicolour (?,000)	5.00 ☐
S3	**S1**	$250	2/90	VICTORIA HARBOUR, Multicolour (?,000)	10.00 ☐
S4	**S2**	$50	2/90	CENTRAL SKYLINE, Multicolour (?,000)	3.00 ☐
S5	**S2**	$100	2/90	CENTRAL SKYLINE, Multicolour (?,000)	5.00 ☐
S6	**S2**	$250	2/90	CENTRAL SKYLINE, Multicolour (?,000)	10.00 ☐
S7	**S3**	$50	2/90	PEAK TRAM, Multicolour (?,000)	3.00 ☐
S8	**S3**	$100	2/90	PEAK TRAM, Multicolour (?,000)	5.00 ☐
S9	**S3**	$250	2/90	PEAK TRAM, Multicolour (?,000)	10.00 ☐
S10	**S4**	$50	2/90	REPULSE BAY PAGODA, Multicolour (?,000)	3.00 ☐
S11	**S4**	$100	2/90	REPULSE BAY PAGODA, Multicolour (?,000)	5.00 ☐
S12	**S4**	$250	2/90	REPULSE BAY PAGODA, Multicolour (?,000)	10.00 ☐
S13	**S5**	$50	2/90	10,000 BUDDHAS TEMPLE, Multicolour (?,000)	3.00 ☐
S14	**S5**	$100	2/90	10,000 BUDDHAS TEMPLE, Multicolour (?,000)	5.00 ☐
S15	**S5**	$250	2/90	10,000 BUDDHAS TEMPLE, Multicolour (?,000)	10.00 ☐
S16	**S6**	$50	2/90	CAUSEWAY BAY, Multicolour (?,000)	3.00 ☐
S17	**S6**	$100	2/90	CAUSEWAY BAY, Multicolour (?,000)	5.00 ☐
S18	**S6**	$250	2/90	CAUSEWAY BAY, Multicolour (?,000)	10.00 ☐

№	Ill.	Units	Date	Description	Value
S19	*S7*	$50	2/90	TSIM SHA TSUI CLOCK TOWER, Multicolour (?,000)	3.00 ☐
S20	*S7*	$100	2/90	TSIM SHA TSUI CLOCK TOWER, Multicolour (?,000)	5.00 ☐
S21	*S7*	$250	2/90	TSIM SHA TSUI CLOCK TOWER, Multicolour (?,000)	10.00 ☐
S22	*S8*	$50	2/90	DRAGON BOAT FESTIVAL, Multicolour (?,000)	3.00 ☐
S23	*S8*	$100	2/90	DRAGON BOAT FESTIVAL, Multicolour (?,000)	5.00 ☐
S24	*S8*	$250	2/90	DRAGON BOAT FESTIVAL, Multicolour (?,000)	10.00 ☐
S25	*S9*	$50	2/90	TIN HAU FESTIVAL BOATS, Multicolour (?,000)	3.00 ☐
S26	*S9*	$100	2/90	TIN HAU FESTIVAL BOATS, Multicolour (?,000)	5.00 ☐
S27	*S9*	$250	2/90	TIN HAU FESTIVAL BOATS, Multicolour (?,000)	10.00 ☐
S28	*S10*	$50	2/90	LION DANCE, Multicolour (?,000)	3.00 ☐
S29	*S10*	$100	2/90	LION DANCE, Multicolour (?,000)	5.00 ☐
S30	*S10*	$250	2/90	LION DANCE, Multicolour (?,000)	10.00 ☐

Note. The above illustrations are of the reverse of the cards. The fronts are as *D4* above except that the 'HK$' before the value has been omitted.

1990 CATHAY PACIFIC - HONG KONG BANK INVITATION SEVENS (Rugby Football)

№	Ill.	Units	Date	Description	Value
S31	–	$50	4/90	AMERICAN EAGLES v TONGA, Multicolour (1500)	8.00 ☐
S32	–	$50	4/90	AUSTRALIA v BARBARIANS (BRITISH ISLES), Multicolour (1500)	8.00 ☐
S33	–	$50	4/90	BAHRAIN v NETHERLANDS, Multicolour (1500)	8.00 ☐
S34	–	$50	4/90	FIJI v NEW ZEALAND, Multicolour (1500)	8.00 ☐
S35	–	$50	4/90	ITALY v THAILAND, Multicolour (1500)	8.00 ☐
S36	–	$50	4/90	JAPAN v PAPUA NEW GUINEA, Multicolour (1500)	8.00 ☐
S37	–	$50	4/90	KWONG HUA TAIPEI v SRI LANKA, Multicolour (1500)	8.00 ☐

Note. Information on the above cards was, unfortunately, too late to allow illustrations to be included. All show action scenes from the seven-a-side rugby matches on the reverse and are as S1 to S30 on the fronts. S31 to S37 were printed in Hong Kong on blanks supplied by Autelca.

Limited stocks of mint earlier cards and current mint cards are available at face value from: Special Services Division,/ Hong Kong Telephone,/ GPO Box 479,/ Hong Kong. Telephone 808 2291 or Fax 824 1117. Sterling or US dollar cheque or international money order. Add £1 or equivalent for postage on orders up to £100; postage free for larger orders. Price list on request. Hong Kong Telephone also offer some used cards at HK$20 each. All cards are offered subject to availability.

ICELAND

Optical cards by Landis and Gyr, Switzerland, were introduced in 1986. Only definitive cards have been issued. Initially these were in non-metallic paint while later specimens were in a metallic paint. This seems to have been a change within the single printing.

D1

№	Ill.	Units	Date	Description	Value	
D1	*D1*	100	1/86	Deep magenta, white / silver (100,000)	10.00 ☐	6.00 ☐
D2	*(D1)*	100	1/86	Deep metallic magenta, white/silver (incl.)	8.00 ☐	4.00 ☐

INDONESIA

Cards are supplied by Tamura, Japan.

D1   S1

D - DEFINITIVE CARDS

Nº	Ill.	Units	Date	Description	Value
D1	*D1*	20	1989?	Multicolour (?000)	4.00 ☐
D2	*(D1)*	80	1989?	Multicolour (?000)	8.00 ☐
D3	*(D1)*	140	1989?	Multicolour (?000)	12.00 ☐
D4	*(D1)*	280	1989?	Multicolour (?000)	15.00 ☐

S - SPECIAL CARD

Nº	Ill.	Units	Date	Description	Value
S1	*S1*	140	1989?	Multicolour (?000)	4.00 ☐

Note. The above card was bought at Jarkarta airport in February, 1990. It appears to be a new year card.

IRELAND

Telecom Eireann is currently carrying out field trials of three different systems in different cities. The GPT cards listed in the first edition of this book are still being used in the Dublin area. Cards and telephones by Autelca are in use in Limerick while the use of Landis and Gyr cards has recently begun in Galway. It is understood that Schlumberger and Gemplus smart cards will be introduced in the summer of 1990. The trial cards are designated 'D' for Dublin, 'L' for Limerick and 'G' for Galway. The French smart cards have no prefix.

DD1   DS1   DS2

DD - DUBLIN DEFINITIVE CARDS

Nº	Ill.	Units	Date	Description	Value
DD1	*(DD1)*	5	1987	Blue, deep blue, ochre / white (4570)	2.00 ☐
DD2	*(DD1)*	10	1987	·· ·· ·· ·· ·· ·· ·· ·· (53,946)	2.50 ☐
DD3	*(DD1)*	20	1987	·· ·· ·· ·· ·· ·· ·· ·· (49,135)	4.00 ☐
DD4	*(DD1)*	50	1987	·· ·· ·· ·· ·· ·· ·· ·· (16,959)	10.00 ☐
DD5	*DD1*	100	1987	·· ·· ·· ·· ·· ·· ·· ·· (4249)	20.00 ☐

DS - DUBLIN SPECIAL CARDS

Nº	Ill.	Units	Date	Description	Value
DS1	*DS1*	10	1988	DUBLIN MILLENNIUM. Multicolour. (10,000)	10.00 ☐
DS2	*DS2*	100	24/10/88	FITCE, CORK. Blue, red, white. (960)	150.00 ☐

Note. The FITCE (Federation of International Telecommunication Engineers) cards were mostly handed out to the 600 delegates at their conference in Cork on 24 October, 1988. The others were later sold in Dublin.

DL 1   SL 1   DG1

DL - LIMERICK DEFINITIVE CARDS

№	Ill.	Units	Date	Description		Value
DL1	*(DL1)*	5	02/89	Blue, green, black / white	(5500)	5.00 ☐
DL2	*(DL1)*	10	02/89	·· ·· ·· ·· ·· ·· ··	(35,500)	4.50 ☐
DL3	*(DL1)*	20	02/89	·· ·· ·· ·· ·· ·· ··	(15,500)	20.00 ☐
DL4	*DL1*	50	02/89	·· ·· ·· ·· ·· ·· ··	(3250)	35.00 ☐
DL5	*(DL1)*	100	02/89	·· ·· ·· ·· ·· ·· ··	(1100)	30.00 ☐

SL - LIMERICK SPECIAL CARDS

SL1	*SL1*	20	21/4/89	IRISH MANAGEMENT INSTITUTE 89, As DL1	(250)	130.00 ☐
SL2	*(SL1)*	50	21/4/89	IRISH MANAGEMENT INSTITUTE 89, As DL1	(750)	80.00 ☐

DG - GALWAY DEFINITIVE CARDS

DG1	*(DG1)*	5	25/7/89	Dark blue / white	(5000)		2.00 ☐	2.00 ☐
DG2	*(DG1)*	10	25/7/89	·· ·· ·· ··	(10,000)	2.50 ☐	1.50 ☐
DG3	*(DG1)*	20	25/7/89	·· ·· ·· ··	(10,000)	8.00 ☐	3.50 ☐
DG4	*(DG1)*	50	25/7/89	·· ·· ·· ··	(2000)	10.00 ☐	7.50 ☐
DG5	*DG1*	100	25/7/89	·· ·· ·· ··	(1000)	30.00 ☐	15.00 ☐

ELECTRONIC (SMART) CARDS

C1	--	5	4/90	COMPLIMENTARY, TEDDY BEAR, Multicolour (GP) (10,000)	10.00 ☐
D1	--	20	4/90	COTTAGE, Multicolour, (SI) (100,000)	2.50 ☐
D2	--	50	4/90	IRISH PRESIDENCY OF EEC, Multicolour, (GP) (50,000)	6.00 ☐
D3	--	100	4/90	ROCK OF CASHEL, Multicolour, (GP) (10,000)	12.00 ☐
S1	--	20	4/90	IRISH MANAGEMENT INSTITUTE 90, Multicolour, (SI) (1500)	8.00 ☐
S2	--	50	4/90	IRISH MANAGEMENT INSTITUTE 90, Multicolour, (SI) (1000)	10.00 ☐

Note. Illustrations of the electronic cards have not unfortunately become available in time to be included in this edition.

Note. Collectors may purchase cards from: Payphone Marketing, / Telecom Eireann, / 6-8 College Green, / DUBLIN 2, / Ireland.

THE PERFECT EXTENSION...
THE LIGHTHOUSE TELEPHONE CARD ALBUM

weichmacherfrei
free of chem. softeners
sans plastifiant

Telephone card
collecting is the hottest
new collectible on the market,
and LIGHTHOUSE albums will house
these attractive communication's cards
safely and clearly.
Suitable leaves, measuring 202 x 252 mm,
are made of clear view material, which is free of
chemical softeners. Two types are available:
1. clear view – for 8 cards, ref. no. H 4 TV
2. clear view with black background,
   double sided, for 16 cards, ref. no. FDC 1/4 TV
Both types represent the usual high quality of
LIGHTHOUSE products. They are interchangeable.
The ideal DE LUXE 4-ring binder/slip case combinations are:
a) for approx. 30 sheets, ref. no. DF/KF + colour
b) for approx. 60 sheets, ref. no. DG/KG + colour
Both binder/slip case combinations are available in red, blue, green, brown and black.
They are made of high grade leather grained vinyl.

ISLE OF MAN

The Isle of Man is a largish island in the Irish Sea midway between England and Ireland. It has its own internal laws passed by its own ancient Parliament and is not a member of the European Community. Manx Telecom is a seperate company but is owned by British Telecom. Optical telephone cards were manufactured by Landis and Gyr in the UK and could also be used in British Telecom telephones throughout the UK. Only the two definitive cards listed below were issued. They have been given the prefix 'O'. More recently the GPT magnetic system has been adopted. Some UK collectors are collecting the Isle of Man sets with matched control numbers.

1   OPTICAL CARDS (Landis and Gyr)

OD - DEFINITIVE CARDS

№	Ill.	Units	Date	Description		Value	
OD1	*OD1*	10	4/87	Green / silver (14,000)		5.00 ☐	2.00 ☐
OD2	*(OD1)*	20	4/87	·· ·· ·· ·· (13,600)		8.00 ☐	3.00 ☐

2   MAGNETIC CARDS (GPT)

D - DEFINITIVE CARDS

D1	*D1*	10	1/6/88	LAXEY WHEEL, Multicolour (14,000)	15.00 ☐
D2	*D2*	20	1/5/89	PEEL CASTLE, Multicolour (5707)	6.00 ☐
D3	*D3*	100	7/9/89	GROUND STATION, Multicolour (2339)	15.00 ☐
D4	*D4*	10	12/89	GREAT NORTH BEACH, Multicolour (12,000)	2.00 ☐
D5	*D5*	20	12/89	CASTLE RUSHEN, Multicolour (12,000)	4.00 ☐
D6	*D6*	30	12/89	PORT ST. MARY, Multicolour (12,000)	6.00 ☐

S - SPECIAL/COMMEMORATIVE CARDS

S1	*S1*	10	1/6/88	TT RACERS 1st SERIES, Multicolour (#3) (6000)	18.00 ☐
S2	*S2*	20	1/6/88	TT RACERS 1st SERIES, Multicolour (#2) (6000)	20.00 ☐
S3	*S3*	20	1/6/88	TT RACERS 1st SERIES, Multicolour (#4) (6000)	20.00 ☐
S4	*S4*	30	1/6/88	TT RACERS 1st SERIES, Multicolour (#1) (6000)	25.00 ☐

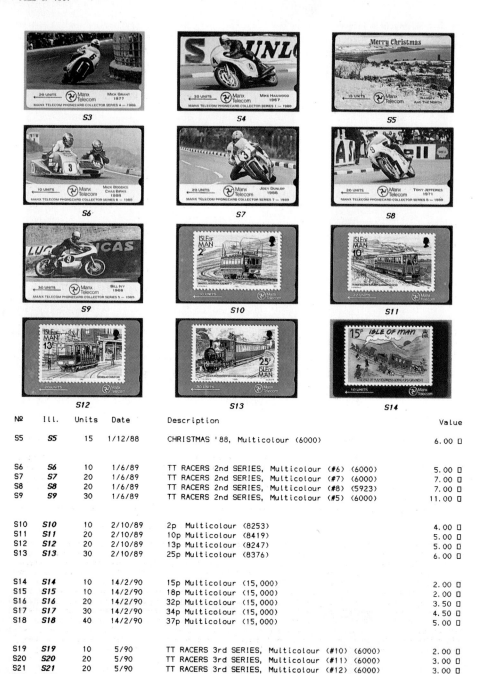

№	Ill.	Units	Date	Description	Value
S5	*S5*	15	1/12/88	CHRISTMAS '88, Multicolour (6000)	6.00 ☐
S6	*S6*	10	1/6/89	TT RACERS 2nd SERIES, Multicolour (#6) (6000)	5.00 ☐
S7	*S7*	20	1/6/89	TT RACERS 2nd SERIES, Multicolour (#7) (6000)	7.00 ☐
S8	*S8*	20	1/6/89	TT RACERS 2nd SERIES, Multicolour (#8) (5923)	7.00 ☐
S9	*S9*	30	1/6/89	TT RACERS 2nd SERIES, Multicolour (#5) (6000)	11.00 ☐
S10	*S10*	10	2/10/89	2p Multicolour (8253)	4.00 ☐
S11	*S11*	20	2/10/89	10p Multicolour (8419)	5.00 ☐
S12	*S12*	20	2/10/89	13p Multicolour (8247)	5.00 ☐
S13	*S13*	30	2/10/89	25p Multicolour (8376)	6.00 ☐
S14	*S14*	10	14/2/90	15p Multicolour (15,000)	2.00 ☐
S15	*S15*	10	14/2/90	18p Multicolour (15,000)	2.00 ☐
S16	*S16*	20	14/2/90	32p Multicolour (15,000)	3.50 ☐
S17	*S17*	30	14/2/90	34p Multicolour (15,000)	4.50 ☐
S18	*S18*	40	14/2/90	37p Multicolour (15,000)	5.00 ☐
S19	*S19*	10	5/90	TT RACERS 3rd SERIES, Multicolour (#10) (6000)	2.00 ☐
S20	*S20*	20	5/90	TT RACERS 3rd SERIES, Multicolour (#11) (6000)	3.00 ☐
S21	*S21*	20	5/90	TT RACERS 3rd SERIES, Multicolour (#12) (6000)	3.00 ☐
S22	*S22*	30	5/90	TT RACERS 3rd SERIES, Brown, black, white (#9) (6000)	4.00 ☐

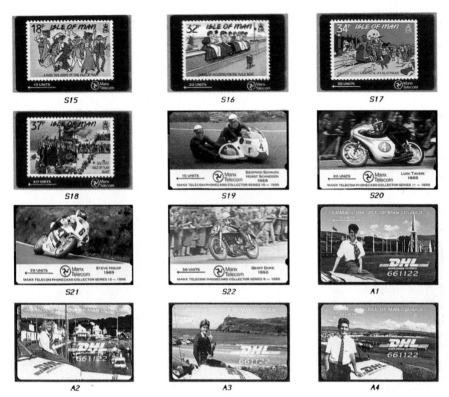

A - ADVERTISING CARDS

Nº	Ill.	Units	Date	Description	Value
A1	*A1*	10	9/12/89	DHL – EMMA, Multicolour (1500)	25.00 ☐
A2	*A2*	10	9/12/89	DHL – AMANDA, Multicolour (1500)	25.00 ☐
A3	*A3*	10	9/12/89	DHL – JACKIE, Multicolour (1500)	25.00 ☐
A4	*A4*	10	9/12/89	DHL – MARK, Multicolour (1500)	25.00 ☐

ITALY

Italy seems to have been one of the first countries to introduce card-operated payphones for public use. The first payphones were manufactured by Sida SpA of Montichiari and the cards by Pikappa under licence. Payphones are now manufactured in Italy by Urmet, SpA, of Turin and magnetically encoded cards are manufactured under licence by Pikappa and Mantegazza, both of Milan, and by Technicard/Polaroid of Arcisate. Two different systems, listed separately below, have been in use and their periods have overlapped. Some are of thin plastic-coated paper-board while others are of PVC. In both cases one corner of the card must be broken off along a perforated line before it will fit into the telephone. Unused cards are thus easily recognised. The cards, whether of thin card-board or plastic, need to be flexible because they are put into the telephone through one slot and ejected through another being bent within the machine en route. The values are in Italian Lire. Much new information has been obtained since the first edition of this book and it has been necessary to change the numbering system completely to accomodate it

DEFINITIVE CARDS

TYPE I. (VERTICAL CARDS)

Cards of this type ceased to be used at the end of 1988. Although, as in all Italian public cards, the corners have to be detatched before use, the magnetic band crosses the shorter dimension of the card at right angles to those on the later Type II cards. These seem to have the distinction of having been the first national PTT cards in use in the world. All of these cards are scarce because the telephones using them retained fully used cards. All used cards should therefore have some units remaining on them (unless they leaked from the checking office). As for all Italian cards, it has not been possible to obtain reliable dates of issue but most have a date of printing on them. Dates given are the earliest seen for that design. All were made by Pikappa and are given 'DV' numbers below.

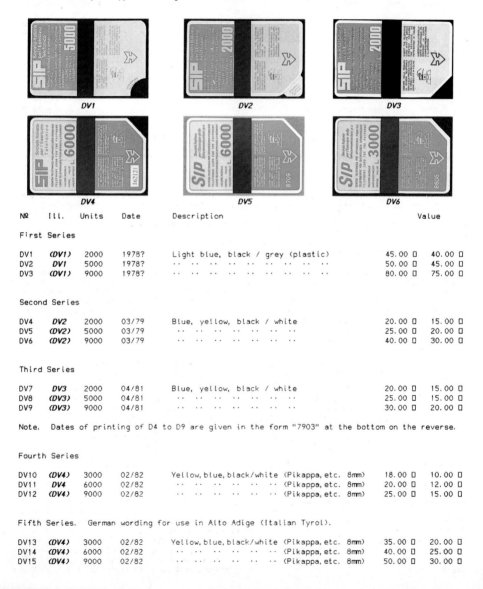

№	Ill.	Units	Date	Description	Value	

First Series

№	Ill.	Units	Date	Description	Value	
DV1	*(DV1)*	2000	1978?	Light blue, black / grey (plastic)	45.00 ▢	40.00 ▢
DV2	*DV1*	5000	1978?	" " " " " " " "	50.00 ▢	45.00 ▢
DV3	*(DV1)*	9000	1978?	" " " " " " " "	80.00 ▢	75.00 ▢

Second Series

DV4	*DV2*	2000	03/79	Blue, yellow, black / white	20.00 ▢	15.00 ▢
DV5	*(DV2)*	5000	03/79	" " " " " " " "	25.00 ▢	20.00 ▢
DV6	*(DV2)*	9000	03/79	" " " " " " " "	40.00 ▢	30.00 ▢

Third Series

DV7	*DV3*	2000	04/81	Blue, yellow, black / white	20.00 ▢	15.00 ▢
DV8	*(DV3)*	5000	04/81	" " " " " " " "	25.00 ▢	15.00 ▢
DV9	*(DV3)*	9000	04/81	" " " " " " " "	30.00 ▢	20.00 ▢

Note. Dates of printing of D4 to D9 are given in the form "7903" at the bottom on the reverse.

Fourth Series

DV10	*(DV4)*	3000	02/82	Yellow, blue, black/white (Pikappa, etc. 8mm)	18.00 ▢	10.00 ▢
DV11	*DV4*	6000	02/82	" " " " " " " (Pikappa, etc. 8mm)	20.00 ▢	12.00 ▢
DV12	*(DV4)*	9000	02/82	" " " " " " " (Pikappa, etc. 8mm)	25.00 ▢	15.00 ▢

Fifth Series. German wording for use in Alto Adige (Italian Tyrol).

DV13	*(DV4)*	3000	02/82	Yellow, blue, black/white (Pikappa, etc. 8mm)	35.00 ▢	20.00 ▢
DV14	*(DV4)*	6000	02/82	" " " " " " " (Pikappa, etc. 8mm)	40.00 ▢	25.00 ▢
DV15	*(DV4)*	9000	02/82	" " " " " " " (Pikappa, etc. 8mm)	50.00 ▢	30.00 ▢

Sixth Series

№	Ill.	Units	Date	Description	Value	
DV16	*(DV4)*	3000	02/85	Yellow, blue, black/white (Pikappa, etc. 15mm)	10.00 ☐	8.00 ☐
DV17	*(DV4)*	6000	03/85	·· ·· ·· ·· ·· ·· (Pikappa, etc. 15mm)	15.00 ☐	10.00 ☐
DV18	*(DV4)*	9000	02/85	·· ·· ·· ·· ·· ·· (Pikappa, etc. 15mm)	20.00 ☐	12.00 ☐

Seventh Series. As above but with German text for use in Alto Adige (Italian Tyrol).

DV19	*(DV4)*	3000	02/85	Yellow, blue, black/white (Pikappa, etc. 15mm)	20.00 ☐	15.00 ☐
DV20	*(DV4)*	6000	03/85	·· ·· ·· ·· ·· ·· (Pikappa, etc. 15mm)	30.00 ☐	20.00 ☐
DV21	*(DV4)*	9000	02/85	·· ·· ·· ·· ·· ·· (Pikappa, etc. 15mm)	40.00 ☐	25.00 ☐

Note. Dates of printing of D10 to D21 are given in the form "8504" at the bottom on the reverse. On D10-15, 'pikappa srl-mastate-mi' measures 8mm; on D16-21, it measures 15mm. The magnetic band is brown on the fourth and fifth series and black on the sixth and seventh. The existance of the two 9000 values, DV18 and DV24 below is assumed. They have not been seen.

Eighth Series

DV22	*(DV5)*	3000	05/86	Yellow, blue, black / white	7.50 ☐	4.00 ☐
DV23	*DV5*	6000	05/86	·· ·· ·· ·· ·· ·· ··	10.00 ☐	6.00 ☐
DV24	*(DV5)*	9000	05/86	·· ·· ·· ·· ·· ·· ··	15.00 ☐	8.00 ☐

Ninth Series. German text for use in Alto Adige (the Italian Tyrol).

DV25	*DV6*	3000	05/86	Yellow, blue, black / white	15.00 ☐	8.00 ☐
DV26	*(DV6)*	6000	??/86	·· ·· ·· ·· ·· ·· ··	20.00 ☐	12.00 ☐
DV27	*(DV6)*	9000	??/86	·· ·· ·· ·· ·· ·· ··	30.00 ☐	20.00 ☐

Note. In D25 to D27 the three lines of text below 'SIP' at the top are in Italian, German and English. In D22 to D24 they are in Italian, English and French.

General Note. Minor shade differences can be found on all the above cards.

TYPE II. (HORIZONTAL CARDS)

The two 'horizontal' series, the so-called red and blue series, were used in parallel with the above vertical series up to the end of 1988 when the vertical cards were discontinued. The red series cards, given 'DR' numbers below, were all apparantly made by Mantegazza, although the name appears on only one type. All are on plastic-coated paper. The blue series, given simple 'C' and 'D' numbers below, were made by all three manufacturers mentioned in the introduction and, for the definitive cards, are listed separately under their manufacturers. The Special cards form a single series by two manufacturers and are listed together. The first advertising card appeared in January, 1990.

DR1

DR2

Red Series

First Red Series

DR1	*DR1*	L5000	1986	Red, black, grey, red / white (02+5 fig. control)	5.00 ☐	3.00 ☐
DR1(a)				(6 fig. control)	6.00 ☐	3.50 ☐
DR1(b)				(only letters in control)	10.00 ☐	6.00 ☐
DR1(c)				(letters and numbers in control)	6.00 ☐	3.50 ☐
DR2	*(DR1)*	L10,000	1986	·· ·· ·· ·· ·· ·· ·· (04+5 fig. control)	10.00 ☐	5.00 ☐
DR2(a)				(6 fig. control)	12.00 ☐	6.00 ☐
DR2(b)				(only letters in control)	20.00 ☐	10.00 ☐
DR2(c)				(letters and numbers in control)	12.00 ☐	6.00 ☐

Second Red Series (German added for Alto Adige (Italian Tyrol)- 8 letters/numbers in control)

Nº	Ill.	Units	Date	Description		Value	
DR3	(DR1)	L5000	1986	Red, black, grey, red / white (German text added)	15.00 ◻		10.00 ◻
DR4	(DR1)	L10,000	1986	·· ·· ·· ·· ·· ·· ·· (German text added)	20.00 ◻		15.00 ◻

Third Red Series (* added)

DR5	DR2	L5000	1987?	Red, black, grey, red / white (*, letters only)	6.00 ◻		3.00 ◻
DR5(a)				(*, letters and numbers in control)	10.00 ◻		5.00 ◻
DR6	(DR2)	L10,000	1987?	·· ·· ·· ·· ·· ·· ·· (*, letters only)	10.00 ◻		5.00 ◻
DR6(a)				(*, letters and numbers in control)	15.00 ◻		7.50 ◻

Fourth Red Series (No Control, no *)

DR7	(DR1)	L5000	1987?	Red, black, grey, red / white (no control number)	8.00 ◻		5.00 ◻
DR8	(DR1)	L10,000	1987?	·· ·· ·· ·· ·· ·· ·· (no control number)	12.00 ◻		7.00 ◻

Fifth Red Series (No Control. 'Mantegazza' added at bottom-left on reverse)

DR9	(DR1)	L5000	1988?	Red, black, grey, red / white (Mantegazza added)	6.00 ◻		3.00 ◻
DR10	(DR1)	L10,000	1988?	·· ·· ·· ·· ·· ·· ·· (Mantegazza added)	10.00 ◻		5.00 ◻

Blue Series

All cards of these series bear a 'validity date' and it is these dates which are given below. Many of the issues show shade variations in all three colours, especially the red which can vary from scarlet to orange. Other varieties include long and short logos on the reverse and, in the control space, controls or lack of them, braille and bar-codes. The three manufacturers are indicated by M for Mantegazza, P for Pikappa and T for Technicard (or Polaroid/Technicard).

MD1

MD1 (reverse)

MD2

M - Mantegazza Cards

First Series. 10mm black strip. No control.

MD1	(MD1)	L5000	31/12/89	Blue, black, grey, red / white	3.00 ◻	2.00 ◻
MD2	(MD1)	L10,000	31/12/89	·· ·· ·· ·· ·· ·· ·· ··	8.00 ◻	3.00 ◻

Note. The card with a 6.5mm black magnetic strip (i.e. the strip used on the red series) shown in the first edition of this book is now thought to have been a trial and has been excluded.

Second Series. Text in Both Italian and German for use in Alto Adige (Italian Tyrol).

MD3	MD2	L5000	31/12/89	Blue, black, grey, red / white	8.00 ◻	5.00 ◻
MD4	(MD2)	L10,000	31/12/89	·· ·· ·· ·· ·· ·· ··	10.00 ◻	7.00 ◻

Note. The reverse is similar to MD2(reverse) but in both languages.

Third Series. Valid to 31 December, 1990.

MD5	(MD1)	L5000	31/12/90	Blue, black, grey, red / white	3.00 ◻	1.00 ◻
MD6	(MD1)	L10,000	31/12/90	·· ·· ·· ·· ·· ·· ·· ··	7.00 ◻	2.00 ◻

Fourth Series. Text in both Italian and German.

MD7	(MD2)	L5000	31/12/90	Blue, black, grey, red / white	8.00 ◻	4.00 ◻
MD8	(MD2)	L10,000	31/12/90	·· ·· ·· ·· ·· ·· ·· ··	12.00 ◻	6.00 ◻

P - Pikappa Cards

All blue series Pikappa cards are of plastic with, in most cases, a design of SIP and logo embossed onto the upper section of the card. The maker's name is, as usual, at the extreme right on the reverse. Some cards have 'PAT PEN' (Patent Pending) incised almost invisibly below the logo on the front. Some have the value of the card in Braille in the ~~~~~ box a)ttom~ ~~t.

PC1

PD1

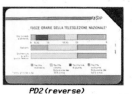

PD2(reverse)

PC - PIKAPPA COMPLIMENTARY CARDS

№	Ill.	Units	Date	Description	Value	
PC1	*PC1*	10	1987?	Blue, black, grey, red / white	15.00 ▢	8.00 ▢
PC2	*(PC1)*	5	1987?	Braille. Black control, PAT PEN, (Note 1)	25.00 ▢	15.00 ▢
PC3	*(PC1)*	10	1988?	Braille, No control, PAT PEN	10.00 ▢	6.00 ▢
PC4	*(PC1)*	10	1988?	Braille, No control, No PAT PEN	10.00 ▢	6.00 ▢

Note 1. PC2 has a long red logo band over "Servizi 1" on the reverse. The others resemble *PD2(reverse)* above.

PD - PIKAPPA DEFINITIVE CARDS

First Series. Black controls. Embossed design. Braille.

PD1	*PD1*	L5000	31/12/89	Blue, black, grey, red / white (PAT PEN)	8.00 ▢	5.00 ▢
PD2	*(PD1)*	L10,000	31/12/89	·· ·· ·· ·· ·· ·· ·· (PAT PEN)	10.00 ▢	7.00 ▢

Note. The reverse of PD1 and PD2 is similar to that of PC2 above.

Second Series. Reverse as *PD2(reverse)*. No controls. Embossed with SIP + logo. No Braille.

PD3	*(PD1)*	L5000	31/12/89	Blue, black, grey, red / white	4.00 ▢	2.00 ▢
PD4	*(PD1)*	L10,000	31/12/89	·· ·· ·· ·· ·· ·· ·· ··	8.00 ▢	5.00 ▢

Third Series. Black controls. Embossed. Braille added.

PD5	*(PD1)*	L5000	31/12/89	Blue, black, grey, red / white	6.00 ▢	3.00 ▢
PD6	*(PD1)*	L10,000	31/12/89	·· ·· ·· ·· ·· ·· ·· ··	12.00 ▢	5.00 ▢

Fourth Series. Black controls. Not embossed. Braille added. 'PAT PEN'.

PD7	*(PD1)*	L5000	31/12/89	Blue, black, grey, red / white	15.00 ▢	10.00 ▢
PD8	*(PD1)*	L10,000	31/12/89	·· ·· ·· ·· ·· ·· ·· ··	20.00 ▢	15.00 ▢

Fifth Series. Date changed. No controls. Not embossed. No Braille.

PD9	*(PD1)*	L5000	30/06/90	Blue, black, grey, red / white	10.00 ▢	7.00 ▢
PD10	*(PD1)*	L10,000	30/06/90	·· ·· ·· ·· ·· ·· ·· ··	15.00 ▢	10.00 ▢

Sixth Series. No controls. Embossed. No Braille.

PD11	*(PD1)*	L5000	30/06/90	Blue, black, grey, red / white	5.00 ▢	3.00 ▢
PD12	*(PD1)*	L10,000	30/06/90	·· ·· ·· ·· ·· ·· ·· ··	12.00 ▢	5.00 ▢

Seventh Series. Embossed. Both control and bar code. No Braille.

PD13	*(PD1)*	L5000	31/12/90	Blue, black, grey, red / white	5.00 ▢	3.00 ▢
PD14	*(PD1)*	L10,000	31/12/90	·· ·· ·· ·· ·· ·· ·· ··	12.00 ▢	5.00 ▢

T – Technicard and Polaroid/Technicard Cards.

All are plastic, embossed and have Braille at bottom left. The reverse is similar to
PD3 (reverse) above. The maker's name is again at the extreme right on the reverse.

First Series. Black controls. Maker's name given as Technicard System SpA.

№	Ill.	Units	Valid To	Description	Value	
TD1	*(PD1)*	L5000	30/06/90	Blue, black, grey, red / white	6.00 □	2.50 □
TD2	*(PD1)*	L10,000	30/06/90	·· ·· ·· ·· ·· ·· ·· ··	12.00 □	5.00 □

Second Series. Black controls. Maker's name given as Polaroid / Technicard System SpA.

TD3	*(PD1)*	L5000	30/06/90	Blue, black, grey, red / white	5.00 □	2.00 □
TD4	*(PD1)*	L10,000	30/06/90	·· ·· ·· ·· ·· ·· ·· ··	10.00 □	4.00 □

Third Series. Polaroid / Technicard. Control replaced by bar-code.

TD5	*(PD1)*	L5000	30/06/90	Blue, black, grey, red / white, Bar-code.	5.00 □	2.00 □
TD6	*(PD1)*	L10,000	30/06/90	·· ·· ·· ·· ·· ·· ·· ·· ··	10.00 □	4.00 □

S – SPECIAL CARDS

Following 'forerunner' trial cards with larger illustrations on the reverse (as S1 below), each
of the twenty regional tourist boards of Italy has recently issued a set of three cards, one
complimentary, 5000L and 10,000L, for each of two designs showing scenes or monuments of note in
their areas on the reverse. These have been issued locally in unknown but fairly small numbers
and no complete collection of all of them has, at the time of writing, been formed. It has
therefore, only been possible to list the regions and designs below and illustrate a few
examples.

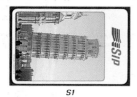

S1   S2   S3

№	Ill.	Units	Valid To	Description	Value	
S1	*S1*	L10,000	31/12/89	Tower of Pisa (T) Trial card.	35.00 □	20.00 □
S2	*(S1)*	L10,000	31/12/89	Leonardo's Last Supper (Detail) (T) Trial.	35.00 □	20.00 □
S3	*(S1)*	L10,000	31/12/89	Palace Interior (T) Trial card.	35.00 □	20.00 □

Note. More of the large picture (S1) type may exist and the numbers S4 to S9 have been left
unallocated to accomodate any more which come to light.

Tourist Authority Issues

Cards are made by Pikappa and Technicard indicated by (P) or (T). It seems that all types were
made by Technicard and that Pikappa made L5000 and L10,000 values, but not complimentaries, of
some types. The fronts are of the standard types. All have a bar-code control. The Pikappa
cards also have a control number in dot-matrix while the Technicard cards have no number. All
reverse designs are multicoloured and that is assumed in the listing below to provide more space
for titles. The numbers of each printed are not known but it is reported that there were around
6,500,000 altogether, that the complimentaries are rare and that the Pikappa cards are less
common than the Technicard cards. A reasonable guess might be 2500 of each complimentary and
8000 of each of the others.

S10	*(S4)*	OMAGGIO	31/12/90	ABRUZZI. PESCARA. La Nave di Cascella. (T)	5.00 □	4.00 □
S11	*(S4)*	L5000	31/12/90	ABRUZZO ·· ·· ·· ·· ·· ·· ·· (T)	5.00 □	4.00 □
S12	*(S4)*	L10,000	31/12/90	·· ·· ·· ·· ·· ·· ·· ·· (T)	10.00 □	8.00 □
S13	*(S4)*	L5000	31/12/90	ABRUZZO ·· ·· ·· ·· ·· ·· ·· (P)	8.00 □	6.00 □
S14	*(S4)*	L10,000	31/12/90	·· ·· ·· ·· ·· ·· ·· ·· (P)	15.00 □	10.00 □
S15	*(S4)*	L5000	31/12/90	ABRUZZI ·· ·· ·· ·· ·· ·· ·· (P)	8.00 □	6.00 □
S16	*(S4)*	L10,000	31/12/90	·· ·· ·· ·· ·· ·· ·· ·· (P)	15.00 □	10.00 □

№	Ill.	Units	Valid To	Description	Value	
S17	–	OMAGGIO	31/12/90	ABRUZZI. PENNE. Cripta del Duomo (T)	5.00 ▢	4.00 ▢
S18	–	L5000	31/12/90	ABRUZZO .. .. (T)	5.00 ▢	4.00 ▢
S19	–	L10,000	31/12/90	.. .. (T)	10.00 ▢	8.00 ▢
S20	–	L5000	31/12/90	ABRUZZO .. .. (P)	8.00 ▢	6.00 ▢
S21	–	L10,000	31/12/90	.. .. (P)	15.00 ▢	10.00 ▢
S22	–	OMAGGIO	31/12/90	BASILICATA. MATERA. Santurio di S. Maria (T)	5.00 ▢	4.00 ▢
S23	–	L5000	31/12/90	.. .. (T)	5.00 ▢	4.00 ▢
S24	–	L10,000	31/12/90	.. .. (T)	10.00 ▢	8.00 ▢
S25	–	OMAGGIO	31/12/90	BOLZANO. APPIANO. Castel Englar (T) (Italian)	10.00 ▢	8.00 ▢
S26	–	OMAGGIO	31/12/90	.. .. (T) (German)	10.00 ▢	8.00 ▢
S27	–	L5000	31/12/90	.. .. (T) (Italian)	10.00 ▢	8.00 ▢
S28	–	L10,000	31/12/90	.. .. (T) (Italian)	20.00 ▢	12.00 ▢
S29	–	L5000	31/12/90	.. .. (T) (German)	10.00 ▢	8.00 ▢
S30	–	L10,000	31/12/90	.. .. (T) (German)	20.00 ▢	12.00 ▢

Note. Only S29 of the German language varieties for use in Alto Adige (the Italian Tyrol) has been reported so far but the other two are assumed to exist.

№	Ill.	Units	Valid To	Description	Value	
S31	(S5)	OMAGGIO	31/12/90	CALABRIA. Bronzi di Riace (T)	5.00 ▢	4.00 ▢
S32	(S5)	L5000	31/12/90	.. .. (T)	5.00 ▢	4.00 ▢
S33	(S5)	L10,000	31/12/90	.. .. (T)	10.00 ▢	8.00 ▢
S34	S2	OMAGGIO	31/12/90	CALABRIA. SERRA DI S.BRUNO. Ch.di S.Biagio (T)	5.00 ▢	4.00 ▢
S35	S2	L5000	31/12/90	.. .. (T)	5.00 ▢	4.00 ▢
S36	S2	L10,000	31/12/90	.. .. (T)	10.00 ▢	8.00 ▢
S37	–	OMAGGIO	31/12/90	CAMPANIA. ERCOLANO. Villa Campolieto (T)	5.00 ▢	4.00 ▢
S38	–	L5000	31/12/90	.. .. (T)	5.00 ▢	4.00 ▢
S39	–	L10,000	31/12/90	.. .. (T)	10.00 ▢	8.00 ▢
S40	–	OMAGGIO	31/12/90	CAMPANIA. SESSA AURUNCA. Duomo di S. Pietro (T)	5.00 ▢	4.00 ▢
S41	–	L5000	31/12/90	.. .. (T)	5.00 ▢	4.00 ▢
S42	–	L10,000	31/12/90	.. .. (T)	10.00 ▢	8.00 ▢
S43	–	OMAGGIO	31/12/90	EMILIA ROMAGNA. BOLOGNA. Le Due Torre (T)	5.00 ▢	4.00 ▢
S44	–	L5000	31/12/90	.. .. (T)	5.00 ▢	4.00 ▢
S45	–	L10,000	31/12/90	.. .. (T)	10.00 ▢	8.00 ▢
S46	–	L5000	31/12/90	.. .. (P)	8.00 ▢	6.00 ▢
S47	–	L10,000	31/12/90	.. .. (P)	15.00 ▢	10.00 ▢
S48	–	OMAGGIO	31/12/90	EMILIA ROMAGNA. FERRARA. Castello Estense (T)	5.00 ▢	4.00 ▢
S49	–	L5000	31/12/90	.. .. (T)	5.00 ▢	4.00 ▢
S50	–	L10,000	31/12/90	.. .. (T)	10.00 ▢	8.00 ▢
S51	–	L5000	31/12/90	.. .. (P)	8.00 ▢	6.00 ▢
S52	–	L10,000	31/12/90	.. .. (P)	15.00 ▢	10.00 ▢
S53	–	OMAGGIO	31/12/90	FRUILI VENEZI GUILIA. PALMANOVA. Il Duomo (T)	5.00 ▢	4.00 ▢
S54	–	L5000	31/12/90	.. .. (T)	5.00 ▢	4.00 ▢
S55	–	L10,000	31/12/90	.. .. (T)	10.00 ▢	8.00 ▢
S56	–	L5000	31/12/90	.. .. (P)	8.00 ▢	6.00 ▢
S57	–	L10,000	31/12/90	.. .. (P)	15.00 ▢	10.00 ▢
S58	(S3)	OMAGGIO	31/12/90	FRUILI VENEZI GUILIA. TRIESTE. Ca.di Duino (T)	5.00 ▢	4.00 ▢
S59	(S3)	L5000	31/12/90	.. .. (T)	5.00 ▢	4.00 ▢
S60	(S3)	L10,000	31/12/90	.. .. (T)	10.00 ▢	8.00 ▢
S61	S3	L5000	31/12/90	.. .. (P)	8.00 ▢	6.00 ▢
S62	(S3)	L10,000	31/12/90	.. .. (P)	15.00 ▢	10.00 ▢
S63	–	OMAGGIO	31/12/90	LAZIO. ROMA. M.Nazionale Villa Giulia (Male)(T)	5.00 ▢	4.00 ▢
S64	–	L5000	31/12/90	.. .. (T)	5.00 ▢	4.00 ▢
S65	–	L10,000	31/12/90	.. .. (T)	10.00 ▢	8.00 ▢
S66	–	OMAGGIO	31/12/90	LAZIO. ROMA. M. Naz. Villa Giulia (Female) (T)	5.00 ▢	4.00 ▢
S67	–	L5000	31/12/90	.. .. (T)	5.00 ▢	4.00 ▢
S68	–	L10,000	31/12/90	.. .. (T)	10.00 ▢	8.00 ▢

№	Ill.	Units	Valid To	Description	Value	
S69	–	OMAGGIO	31/12/90	LIGURIA. RIOMAGGIORE. Panorama (T)	5.00 ☐	4.00 ☐
S70	–	L5000	31/12/90	·· ·· ·· ·· ·· ·· ·· ·· (T)	5.00 ☐	4.00 ☐
S71	–	L10,000	31/12/90	·· ·· ·· ·· ·· ·· ·· ·· (T)	10.00 ☐	8.00 ☐
S72	–	OMAGGIO	31/12/90	LIGURIA. PORTOFINO. Il Porto (T)	5.00 ☐	4.00 ☐
S73	–	L5000	31/12/90	·· ·· ·· ·· ·· ·· ·· (T)	5.00 ☐	4.00 ☐
S74	–	L10,000	31/12/90	·· ·· ·· ·· ·· ·· ·· (T)	10.00 ☐	8.00 ☐
S75	–	OMAGGIO	31/12/90	LOMBARDIA. BERGAMO. Scalone del Broletto (T)	5.00 ☐	4.00 ☐
S76	–	L5000	31/12/90	·· ·· ·· ·· ·· ·· ·· ·· ·· (T)	5.00 ☐	4.00 ☐
S77	–	L10,000	31/12/90	·· ·· ·· ·· ·· ·· ·· ·· ·· (T)	10.00 ☐	8.00 ☐

S4	S5	S6	S7

№	Ill.	Units	Valid To	Description	Value	
S78	–	OMAGGIO	31/12/90	LOMBARDIA. MONTAGNE DELLA VALTELLINA (T)	5.00 ☐	4.00 ☐
S79	–	L5000	31/12/90	·· ·· ·· ·· ·· ·· ·· (T)	5.00 ☐	4.00 ☐
S80	–	L10,000	31/12/90	·· ·· ·· ·· ·· ·· ·· (T)	10.00 ☐	8.00 ☐
S81	–	OMAGGIO	31/12/90	LUCANIA. GRUMENTO NOVA POTENZA. Anfiteatro (T)	5.00 ☐	4.00 ☐
S82	–	L5000	31/12/90	·· ·· ·· ·· ·· ·· ·· ·· (T)	5.00 ☐	4.00 ☐
S83	–	L10,000	31/12/90	·· ·· ·· ·· ·· ·· ·· ·· (T)	10.00 ☐	8.00 ☐
S84	–	OMAGGIO	31/12/90	MARCHE. ASCOLI PICENO. Palazzo dei Capitani (T)	5.00 ☐	4.00 ☐
S85	–	L5000	31/12/90	·· ·· ·· ·· ·· ·· ·· ·· (T)	5.00 ☐	4.00 ☐
S86	–	L10,000	31/12/90	·· ·· ·· ·· ·· ·· ·· ·· (T)	10.00 ☐	8.00 ☐
S87	–	OMAGGIO	31/12/90	MARCHE. ASCOLI PICENO. La Piazza (T)	5.00 ☐	4.00 ☐
S88	–	L5000	31/12/90	·· ·· ·· ·· ·· ·· ·· (T)	5.00 ☐	4.00 ☐
S89	–	L10,000	31/12/90	·· ·· ·· ·· ·· ·· ·· (T)	10.00 ☐	8.00 ☐
S90	–	OMAGGIO	31/12/90	MOLISE. ALTILIA. Zona Archeologica (T)	5.00 ☐	4.00 ☐
S91	–	L5000	31/12/90	·· ·· ·· ·· ·· ·· ·· (T)	75.00 ☐	50.00 ☐
S92	–	L10,000	31/12/90	·· ·· ·· ·· ·· ·· ·· (T)	80.00 ☐	60.00 ☐

Note. S91 and S92 were withdrawn soon after issue and are therefore very rare.

№	Ill.	Units	Valid To	Description	Value	
S93	–	OMAGGIO	31/12/90	MOLISE. CAMPOBASSO. Castel Monforte (T)	5.00 ☐	4.00 ☐
S94	–	L5000	31/12/90	·· ·· ·· ·· ·· ·· ·· (T)	5.00 ☐	4.00 ☐
S95	–	L10,000	31/12/90	·· ·· ·· ·· ·· ·· ·· (T)	10.00 ☐	8.00 ☐
S96	–	L5000	31/12/90	·· ·· ·· ·· ·· ·· ·· (P)	8.00 ☐	6.00 ☐
S97	–	L10,000	31/12/90	·· ·· ·· ·· ·· ·· ·· (P)	15.00 ☐	10.00 ☐
S98	–	OMAGGIO	31/12/90	PIEMONTE. ENOTECA DI GRINZANE CAVOUR (T)	5.00 ☐	4.00 ☐
S99	–	L5000	31/12/90	·· ·· ·· ·· ·· ·· ·· (T)	5.00 ☐	4.00 ☐
S100	–	L10,000	31/12/90	·· ·· ·· ·· ·· ·· ·· (T)	10.00 ☐	8.00 ☐
S101	–	OMAGGIO	31/12/90	PIEMONTE. TORINO. Ponte d. Gran Madre di Dio (T)	5.00 ☐	4.00 ☐
S102	–	L5000	31/12/90	·· ·· ·· ·· ·· ·· ·· ·· (T)	5.00 ☐	4.00 ☐
S103	–	L10,000	31/12/90	·· ·· ·· ·· ·· ·· ·· ·· (T)	10.00 ☐	8.00 ☐
S104	–	L5000	31/12/90	·· ·· ·· ·· ·· ·· ·· ·· (P)	8.00 ☐	6.00 ☐
S105	–	L10,000	31/12/90	·· ·· ·· ·· ·· ·· ·· ·· (P)	15.00 ☐	10.00 ☐
S106	–	OMAGGIO	31/12/90	PUGLIA. ALBEROBELLO. I Trulli (T)	5.00 ☐	4.00 ☐
S107	–	L5000	31/12/90	·· ·· ·· ·· ·· ·· ·· (T)	5.00 ☐	4.00 ☐
S108	–	L10,000	31/12/90	·· ·· ·· ·· ·· ·· (T)	10.00 ☐	8.00 ☐
S109	–	OMAGGIO	31/12/90	PUGLIA. CASTELLANA GROTTE. Le Grotte (T)	5.00 ☐	4.00 ☐
S110	–	L5000	31/12/90	·· ·· ·· ·· ·· ·· ·· (T)	5.00 ☐	4.00 ☐
S111	–	L10,000	31/12/90	·· ·· ·· ·· ·· ·· ·· (T)	10.00 ☐	8.00 ☐

Nº	Ill.	Units	Valid To	Description	Value	
S112	-	OMAGGIO	31/12/90	SARDEGNA. GONI. I Menhir (T)	5.00 ☐	4.00 ☐
S113	-	L5000	31/12/90	·· ·· ·· ·· ·· ·· (T)	5.00 ☐	4.00 ☐
S114	-	L10,000	31/12/90	·· ·· ·· ·· ·· ·· (T)	10.00 ☐	8.00 ☐
S115	-	OMAGGIO	31/12/90	SARDEGNA. ARBATAX. Le Scogliere (T)	5.00 ☐	4.00 ☐
S116	-	L5000	31/12/90	·· ·· ·· ·· ·· ·· (T)	5.00 ☐	4.00 ☐
S117	-	L10,000	31/12/90	·· ·· ·· ·· ·· ·· (T)	10.00 ☐	8.00 ☐
S118	-	OMAGGIO	31/12/90	SICILIA. DUOMO DI MONREALE (T)	5.00 ☐	4.00 ☐
S119	-	L5000	31/12/90	·· ·· ·· ·· ·· ·· (T)	5.00 ☐	4.00 ☐
S120	-	L10,000	31/12/90	·· ·· ·· ·· ·· ·· (T)	10.00 ☐	8.00 ☐
S121	-	L5000	31/12/90	·· ·· ·· ·· ·· ·· (P)	8.00 ☐	6.00 ☐
S122	-	L10,000	31/12/90	·· ·· ·· ·· ·· ·· (P)	15.00 ☐	10.00 ☐
S123	(S6)	OMAGGIO	31/12/90	SICILIA. TRAPANI. Il Giovane di Mozia (T)	5.00 ☐	4.00 ☐
S124	(S6)	L5000	31/12/90	·· ·· ·· ·· ·· ·· ·· ·· (T)	5.00 ☐	4.00 ☐
S125	(S6)	L10,000	31/12/90	·· ·· ·· ·· ·· ·· ·· ·· (T)	10.00 ☐	8.00 ☐
S126	(S6)	L5000	31/12/90	·· ·· ·· ·· ·· ·· ·· ·· (P)	8.00 ☐	6.00 ☐
S127	(S6)	L10,000	31/12/90	·· ·· ·· ·· ·· ·· ·· ·· (P)	15.00 ☐	10.00 ☐
S128	-	OMAGGIO	31/12/90	TOSCANA. MAGLIANO IN TOSCANA. Mon.S.Bruzio (T)	5.00 ☐	4.00 ☐
S129	-	L5000	31/12/90	·· ·· ·· ·· ·· ·· ·· ·· ·· (T)	5.00 ☐	4.00 ☐
S130	-	L10,000	31/12/90	·· ·· ·· ·· ·· ·· ·· ·· ·· (T)	10.00 ☐	8.00 ☐
S131	-	L5000	31/12/90	·· ·· ·· ·· ·· ·· ·· ·· ·· (P)	8.00 ☐	6.00 ☐
S132	-	L10,000	31/12/90	·· ·· ·· ·· ·· ·· ·· ·· ·· (P)	15.00 ☐	10.00 ☐
S133	-	OMAGGIO	31/12/90	TOSCANA. SAN GODENZO. Abbazia Benedettina (T)	5.00 ☐	4.00 ☐
S134	-	L5000	31/12/90	·· ·· ·· ·· ·· ·· ·· ·· (T)	5.00 ☐	4.00 ☐
S135	-	L10,000	31/12/90	·· ·· ·· ·· ·· ·· ·· ·· (T)	10.00 ☐	8.00 ☐
S136	-	L5000	31/12/90	·· ·· ·· ·· ·· ·· ·· ·· (P)	8.00 ☐	6.00 ☐
S137	-	L10,000	31/12/90	·· ·· ·· ·· ·· ·· ·· ·· (P)	15.00 ☐	10.00 ☐
S138	(S7)	OMAGGIO	31/12/90	TRENTO. SEGONZANO. Le Piramid (T)	5.00 ☐	4.00 ☐
S139	(S7)	L5000	31/12/90	·· ·· ·· ·· ·· ·· (T)	5.00 ☐	4.00 ☐
S140	(S7)	L10,000	31/12/90	·· ·· ·· ·· ·· ·· (T)	10.00 ☐	8.00 ☐
S141	-	OMAGGIO	31/12/90	UMBRIA. ASSISI. S.Francesco Basilica Super. (T)	5.00 ☐	4.00 ☐
S142	-	L5000	31/12/90	·· ·· ·· ·· ·· ·· ·· ·· ·· ·· (T)	75.00 ☐	50.00 ☐
S143	-	L10,000	31/12/90	·· ·· ·· ·· ·· ·· ·· ·· ·· ·· (T)	80.00 ☐	60.00 ☐

Note. S142 and S143 were withdrawn soon after issue and are therefore very rare.

Nº	Ill.	Units	Valid To	Description	Value	
S144	-	OMAGGIO	31/12/90	UMBRIA. PERUGIA. Fontana Maggiore (T)	5.00 ☐	4.00 ☐
S145	-	L5000	31/12/90	·· ·· ·· ·· ·· ·· (T)	5.00 ☐	4.00 ☐
S146	-	L10,000	31/12/90	·· ·· ·· ·· ·· ·· (T)	10.00 ☐	8.00 ☐
S147	-	L5000	31/12/90	·· ·· ·· ·· ·· ·· (P)	8.00 ☐	6.00 ☐
S148	-	L10,000	31/12/90	·· ·· ·· ·· ·· ·· (P)	15.00 ☐	10.00 ☐
S149	-	OMAGGIO	31/12/90	VALLE D'AOSTA. SARRIOD DE LA TOUR (T)	5.00 ☐	4.00 ☐
S150	-	L5000	31/12/90	·· ·· ·· ·· ·· ·· (T)	5.00 ☐	4.00 ☐
S151	-	L10,000	31/12/90	·· ·· ·· ·· ·· ·· (T)	10.00 ☐	8.00 ☐
S152	-	L5000	31/12/90	·· ·· ·· ·· ·· ·· (P)	8.00 ☐	6.00 ☐
S153	-	L10,000	31/12/90	·· ·· ·· ·· ·· ·· (P)	15.00 ☐	10.00 ☐
S154	-	OMAGGIO	31/12/90	VALLE D'AOSTA. AYAS. Ch.di S.Martino-Partic. (T)	5.00 ☐	4.00 ☐
S155	-	L5000	31/12/90	·· ·· ·· ·· ·· ·· ·· ·· (T)	5.00 ☐	4.00 ☐
S156	-	L10,000	31/12/90	·· ·· ·· ·· ·· ·· ·· ·· (T)	10.00 ☐	8.00 ☐
S157	-	L5000	31/12/90	·· ·· ·· ·· ·· ·· ·· ·· (P)	8.00 ☐	6.00 ☐
S158	-	L10,000	31/12/90	·· ·· ·· ·· ·· ·· ·· ·· (P)	15.00 ☐	10.00 ☐
S159	-	OMAGGIO	31/12/90	VENETO. GAZZO VERONESE. Ch. di S.Maria Magg. (T)	5.00 ☐	4.00 ☐
S160	-	L5000	31/12/90	·· ·· ·· ·· ·· ·· ·· ·· (T)	5.00 ☐	4.00 ☐
S161	-	L10,000	31/12/90	·· ·· ·· ·· ·· ·· ·· ·· (T)	10.00 ☐	8.00 ☐
S162	-	L5000	31/12/90	·· ·· ·· ·· ·· ·· ·· ·· (P)	8.00 ☐	6.00 ☐
S163	-	L10,000	31/12/90	·· ·· ·· ·· ·· ·· ·· ·· (P)	15.00 ☐	10.00 ☐
S164	-	OMAGGIO	31/12/90	VENETO. PIAZZOLA SUL BRENTA. Villa Contarini (T)	5.00 ☐	4.00 ☐
S165	-	L5000	31/12/90	·· ·· ·· ·· ·· ·· ·· ·· (T)	75.00 ☐	50.00 ☐
S166	-	L10,000	31/12/90	·· ·· ·· ·· ·· ·· ·· ·· (T)	80.00 ☐	60.00 ☐

Note. S165 and S166 were withdrawn soon after issue and are therefore very rare.

A1

G1

G2

ADVERTISING CARD

№	Ill.	Units	Date	Description		Value	
A1	*A1*	L10,000	30/6/90	FESTO AUTOMAZIONE (T)		8.00 ☐	4.00 ☐

CLOSED USER GROUP CARDS

There is uncertainity over the status of the two cards illustrated above. They are of the type produced by Mantegazza but bear no maker's name. One or both may be used on NATO bases in Italy.

№	Ill.	Units	Date	Description		Value	
G1	*G1*	–	1987?	Black, red / pale blue		80.00 ☐	45.00 ☐
G2	*G2*	L1000	1987?	Black, red / white		80.00 ☐	45.00 ☐

Note. G1 would be overprinted with a value for issue as is G2. Any further information on these cards would be welcome.

Parliament Cards

Special vertical format cards, probably made by Pikappa but bearing no name, are issued use in Sida telephones in the Italian Parliament buildings - the Senato or upper house and the Camera or lower house. These have no values on them and the corners do not have to be detached before use. The telephones 'swallow' the cards when they are fully used. They are both rare.

G3

№	Ill.	Units	Valid To	Description		Value	
G3	*G3*	---	–	SENATO DELLA REPUBBLICA, Black / white		80.00 ☐	45.00 ☐
G4	*(G3)*	---	–	CAMERA DELLA REPUBBLICA, Black / white		80.00 ☐	45.00 ☐

OFFICIAL / SERVICE CARDS

Coded service cards for testing telephones have not been reported. There exist plain red, uncoded cards, with "FOURI SERVIZIO" on one side and "IN ALLESTIMENTO" on the other side, the purpose of which appears to be to block the input slot on the telephone when it is out of order or under repair.

IVORY COAST

Magnetic cards are supplied to the Office National des Telecommunications of the Ivory Coast by Autelca of Switzerland.   Control numbers are in black.

D1

№	Ill.	Units	Date	Description					Value
D1	*(D1)*	FCFA 2500	1988	Pale ·blue / white	(160,000)				5.00 ▯
D2	*(D1)*	FCFA 5000	1988	·· ·· ·· ··	(60,000)				10.00 ▯
D3	*D1*	FCFA 9950	1988	·· ·· ·· ··	(40,000)				12.00 ▯

JAPAN

Japanese telephone cards are magnetically encoded and read.   In use a small hole is punched in the card at the end of each call.   Some twenty-five thousand different cards have been issued in Japan where collecting them is already a well established hobby.   A twelve volume catalogue already exists and coverage in this book is both unnecessary and impossible.   NTT, the main Japanese telephone company has, however, issued sets of cards for sale in London, New York and Geneva.   These can only be used in telephones in Japan and are intended for Japanese tourists abroad.   They may be purchased at around £6.50 or equivalent each from Mitsukoshi or Isetan Bond Street (both in London), House of Leman or Les Galeries du Lac (both in Geneva), and Kitano Hotel, Saka Shoji Inc., Takashimaya Shoji, Zen (Tokyo Shoten), Maki International Inc., Sakura Shoji or Tairiku (all in New York).   Cards by other publishers have also been produced ·for sale outside Japan but are not listed here.

LONDON CARDS

DL1

DL2

DL3

DL4

№	Ill.	Units	Date	Description	Value	
DL1	*DL1*	50	1989?	HELLO LONDON, DAY, Multicolour	8.00 ▯	8.00 ▯
DL2	*DL2*	50	1989?	HELLO LONDON, NIGHT, Multicolour	8.00 ▯	8.00 ▯
DL3	*DL3*	50	1989?	GOOD-DAY LONDON, WESTMINSTER, Multicolour	8.00 ▯	8.00 ▯
DL4	*DL4*	50	1989?	GOOD-DAY LONDON, PALACE, Multicolour	8.00 ▯	8.00 ▯

NEW YORK CARDS

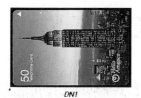

DN1

DN2

DN3

DN4

№	Ill.	Units	Date	Description		Value	
DN1	*DN1*	50	1989?	HELLO AMERICA, EMPIRE STATE BLDG, Multicolour	8.00 ☐	8.00 ☐
DN2	*DN2*	50	1989?	HELLO AMERICA, STATUE OF LIBERTY, Multicolour	8.00 ☐	8.00 ☐
DN3	*DN3*	50	1989?	HELLO AMERICA, MANHATTAN, Multicolour	8.00 ☐	8.00 ☐
DN4	*DN4*	50	1989?	HELLO AMERICA, NEW YORK SKYLINE, Multicolour	8.00 ☐	8.00 ☐
DN5	–	50	1989?	HELLO AMERICA, WASHINGTON, Multicolour	8.00 ☐	8.00 ☐

GENEVA CARDS

DG1

DG2

DG3

DG4

DG5

DG1	*DG1*	50	1989	GENEVE, Multicolour	8.00 ☐	8.00 ☐
DG2	*DG2*	50	1989	JUNGFRAU, Multicolour	8.00 ☐	8.00 ☐
DG3	*DG3*	50	1989	LUZERN, Multicolour	8.00 ☐	8.00 ☐
DG4	*DG4*	50	1989	MATTERHORN, Multicolour	8.00 ☐	8.00 ☐
DG5	*DG5*	50	1989	MONT BLANC, Multicolour	8.00 ☐	8.00 ☐

Jersey Telecoms

PHONECARDS

SERIES 1,2 and 3.

VIEWS

St. Brelades Bay – £1.25
La Rocco Tower – £2.00
Portelet Bay – £4.00

CASTLES

Elizabeth Castle – £2.00
Gorey Castle – £2.00
Grosnez Castle – £4.00

TRAINS

Duke of Normandy at Cheapside – £1.25
La Moye at Millbrook – £2.00
Saddletank at First Tower – £2.00
St. Helier at St. Aubin – £5.00

Information on Jersey Phonecard issues is available from
G. Robbé Ltd., York Street, St. Helier, JE2 3RQ.
Telephone Number (0534) 23084.

JERSEY

Jersey is the largest of the Channel Islands which lie off the French coast between France and England. Like the Isle of Man, the Channel Islands are not members of the European Community. Jersey has formal links with the UK but has its own Government and laws. Its telephone system is independent of British Telecom and the GPT magnetic telephone card system has been adopted. The cost of the first telephone card was reportedly reduced from £2 to £1.25 in June, 1989. The unit is of £0.05. A new set of definitives is about to be issued but only one of these is available for illustration at present. A first 'special' set of four steam engines is also about to appear and a 'wildlife conservation' set is planned. The new cards employ the use-indication technology also used in the more recent cards of Singapore

D - DEFINITIVE CARDS

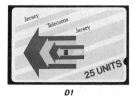
D1

D2

D2 (reverse)

First Issue

№	Ill.	Units	Date	Description	Value
D1	*D1*	25	6/88	Dark and pale blue, yellow / white (10,000)	3.50 ▢

Second Issue

№	Ill.	Units	Date	Description	Value
D2	*D2*	40	3/90	St. BRELADE'S BAY, Multicolour (13,600)	2.50 ▢
D3	--	40	4/90	ROCCO TOWER, Multicolour (10,000)	2.50 ▢
D4	--	40	4/90	ELIZABETH CASTLE, Multicolour (10,000)	2.50 ▢
D5	--	40	4/90	GOREY CASTLE, Multicolour (10,000)	2.50 ▢
D6	--	80	4/90	PORTLET BAY, Multicolour (10,000)	5.00 ▢
D7	--	80	4/90	GROSNEZ CASTLE, Multicolour (10,000)	5.00 ▢

S - SPECIAL CARDS

Steam Locomotive Set

№	Ill.	Units	Date	Description	Value
A1	--	25	4/90	DUKE OF NORMANDY, Multicolour (10,000)	2.00 ▢
A2	--	50	4/90	LA MOYE, Multicolour (10,000)	3.00 ▢
A3	--	50	4/90	SADDLETANK, Multicolour (10,000)	3.00 ▢
A4	--	100	4/90	St HELIER, Multicolour (10,000)	6.00 ▢

Cards may be obtained from G. Robbe Ltd, / York Chambers, / York Street, / St Helier, / Jersey or from Stanley Gibbons.

KENYA

In 1987 Autelca magnetic card operated public telephones were installed.

D1

№	Ill.	Units	Date	Description	Value
D1	*D1*	KSHS 200	1987	Multicoloured (25,000)	10.00 ▢
D2	*(D1)*	KSHS 400	1987	·· ·· ·· (25,000)	15.00 ▢
D3	*(D1)*	KSHS 1000	1987	·· ·· ·· (20,000)	20.00 ▢

Note. The arrows are red on D1, green on D2 and black on D3.

Dual system payphones operated by coins and magnetic cards were supplied to the Korea Telecommunication Authority in 1987 by Autelca of Switzerland. Control numbers are black and vary in size and type as on most Autelca cards.

D - DEFINITIVE CARDS

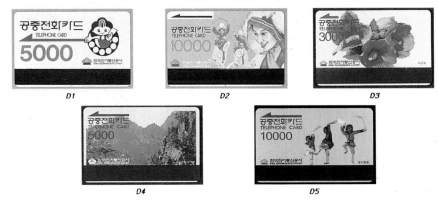

First Issue.

Nº	Ill.	Units	Date	Description	Value
D1	*D1*	W5000	1986	Black, red, blue / white (500,000)	5.00 ◻
D2	*D2*	W10000	1986	Multicoloured (300,000)	8.00 ◻

Second Issue.

Nº	Ill.	Units	Date	Description	Value
D3	*D3*	W3000	1989	Multicoloured (9,600,000) Value in violet.	3.00 ◻
D3(a)	*(D3)*	W3000	1989	Multicoloured (included above) Value in blue.	5.00 ◻
D4	*D4*	W5000	1989	Multicoloured (1,900,000)	7.00 ◻
D5	*D5*	W10000	1989	Multicoloured (1.400,000)	10.00 ◻

Note. D3 to D5 were the first Autelca cards to be manufactured in Korea.

S - SPECIAL CARDS

S1	*S1*	W5000	1988	Multicoloured (400,000) Value in violet	3.00 ◻
S1(a)	*(S1)*	W5000	1988	Multicoloured (incl. above) Value in blue	7.00 ◻
S2	*S2*	W5000	1988	Multicoloured (1,000,000) Value in violet	3.00 ◻
S2(a)	*(S2)*	W5000	1988	Multicoloured (incl. above) Value in blue	7.00 ◻
S3	*S3*	W5000	1988	Multicoloured (1,000,000) Value in violet	3.00 ◻
S3(a)	*(S3)*	W5000	1988	Multicoloured (incl. above) Value in blue	7.00 ◻
S4	*S4*	W10000	1988	Multicoloured (200,000)	5.00 ◻
S5	*S5*	W10000	1988	Multicoloured (300,000)	5.00 ◻
S6	*S6*	W10000	1988	Multicoloured (300,000)	5.00 ◻

KUWAIT

Magnetic cards are supplied to the Ministry of Communications of the State of Kuwait by Autelca. Only definitive cards have been issued, the first series consisting of the 'test card', as used in Nigeria, Sri Lanka, etc., with special controls prefixed with KD (for Kuwaiti Dinar) and the value in dinar. Control numbers are in black.

| | D1 | | D2 |

First Series.

№	Ill.	Units	Date	Description	Value
D1	*D1*	3 KD	1987	Blue / white (5000)	25.00 ☐
D2	*(D1)*	5 KD	1987	·· ·· ·· (5000)	25.00 ☐
D3	*(D1)*	10 KD	1987	·· ·· ·· (10,000)	20.00 ☐

Second Series

№	Ill.	Units	Date	Description	Value
D4	*(D2)*	3 KD	1988	Red, multicoloured, Control number on left (30,000)	10.00 ☐
D4(a)				Control number on right	8.00 ☐
D5	*(D2)*	5 KD	1988	Pale blue, multicoloured, Control on left (25,000)	15.00 ☐
D5(a)				Control number on right	12.00 ☐
D6	*(D2)*	10 KD	1988	Green, multicoloured, Control on left (20,000)	25.00 ☐
D6(a)				Control number on right	20.00 ☐

LIBYA

A single card produced by Gemplus of France for use in Crouzet telephones may have been introduced in 1989 although it has also been reported that the design has been rejected and that this card has not been issued. Copies have, however, appeared on the market in Paris. No further details are available at present and the illustration below is taken from a photocopy.

D - DEFINITIVE CARD

D1

№	Ill.	Units	Date	Description	Value
D1	*D1*	120	1989	Black / shades of green (?000)	50.00 ☐

LUXEMBOURG

P&T Luxembourg is to introduce electronic or 'smart' cards manufactured by Schlumberger Industries, France, in May, 1990. Only definitive cards will be issued initially. There will also be a 'charge transfer' card similar to those used in France and Germany but these are beyond the scope of this book. Illustrations have not, unfortunately, reached me in time to be included in this edition.

D - DEFINITIVE CARDS

№	Ill.	Units	Date	Description	Value
D1	--	50	3/90	NEW TELECOM BUILDING, Multicolour (?000)	5.00 □
D2	--	120	3/90	OLD TELECOM BUILDING, Multicolour (?000)	12.00 □

Note. The numbers of each value are not known yet but it is expected that the first delivery will be of 20,000 cards in all.

MACAU

Magnetic cards supplied by GPT, UK, are to be introduced into Macau, a Portuguese territory at the southern tip of China, in April, 1990. The illustrations below are taken from photocopies of the art-work for the cards and are missing the values. There are two introductory series, one of definitives and one advertising the services of CTM, the Macau telephone company.

D1   D2   D3

D4   D5   D6

D7   A1   A2

A3   A4   A5

CTM 澳門電訊有限公司

Companhia de Telecomunicações de Macau S.A.R.L.

Cards produced: 20,000
Issue date: June 1990
Value: MOP$30

Ruins of St. Paul

Cards produced: 20,000
Issue date: June 1990
Value: MOP$30

Macau-Taipa Bridge

Cards produced: 8,000
Issue date: June 1990
Value: MOP$100

Guia Lighthouse

Cards produced: 10,000
Issue date: June 1990
Value: MOP$200

Hotel Lisboa

Cards produced: 10,000
Issue date: June 1990
Value: MOP$30

Ma Gao Chinese Temple

Cards produced: 16,000
Issue date: June 1990
Value: MOP$100

Jetfoil to Hong Kong

Cards produced: 16,000
Issue date: June 1990
Value: MOP$100

Portuguese style of Architecture in Macau

General Note:
Macau is a Portuguese territory located at the southern tip of China in Asia and has been under Portuguese administration for over 400 years. In addition to the above 7 designs, there are also another 7 designs of cards on CTM's services issued for promotional purposes to commemorate the launch of the cardphone service. Moreover, a series of new cards depicting the annual 'Macau Grand Prix' will also be introduced in November 1990.

All cards shown above are available from:

Stanley Gibbons Publications Ltd.,
Parkside, Ringwood, Hants. BH24 3SH, England.

A6   *A7*

D – DEFINITIVE CARDS (Views of Macau)

№	Ill.	Units	Date	Description		Value
D1	D1	MOP$30	4/90	TEMPLE, Multicolour	(10,000)	4.00 ▢
D2	D2	MOP$30	4/90	DRAGON DANCE, Multicolour	(20,000)	3.00 ▢
D3	D3	MOP$30	4/90	BRIDGE, Multicolour	(?0,000)	3.00 ▢
D4	D4	MOP$100	4/90	JETFOIL, Multicolour	(16,000)	5.00 ▢
D5	D5	MOP$100	4/90	GOVERNMENT HOUSE, Multicolour	(16,000)	5.00 ▢
D6	D6	MOP$100	4/90	LIGHTHOUSE, Multicolour	(8000)	8.00 ▢
D7	D7	MOP$200	4/90	HOTEL LISBOA, Multicolour	(10,000)	15.00 ▢

A – ADVERTISING CARDS

№	Ill.	Units	Date	Description		Value
A1	A1	MOP$10	4/90	CTM: EXTRAFONES, Multicolour	(7000)	3.00 ▢
A2	A2	MOP$10	4/90	CTM: TELEFONE-MEALHEIRO, Multicolour	(7000)	3.00 ▢
A3	A3	MOP$10	4/90	CTM: CHAMADAS, Multicolour	(7000)	3.00 ▢
A4	A4	MOP$10	4/90	CTM: SUPERFAX, Multicolour	(7000)	3.00 ▢
A5	A5	MOP$10	4/90	CTM: TELEMOVEL, Multicolour	(7000)	3.00 ▢
A6	A6	MOP$10	4/90	CTM: TELEFONE, Multicolour	(8000)	3.00 ▢
A7	A7	MOP$10	4/90	CTM: TELEX, Multicolour	(7000)	3.00 ▢

MALDIVES

Two sets of magnetic cards are sold by Dhiraagu for use in the Republic of Maldives, a large group of islands to the south-west of India in the Indian Ocean. The cards of one are in both US dollars and units at a rate of ¢50 per unit while those of the other series are in Rufiyaas, the local currency, at Rf5 to the unit. Both sets of cards are accepted by all cardphones. Only definitive cards of essentially the same design have been issued. Control numbers are in black.

First Series.

D1

№	Ill.	Units	Date	Description		Value
D1	(D1)	$25	9/87	Red, blue / white	(20,000)	10.00 ▢
D2	(D1)	$50	9/87	Green, blue / white	(15,000)	15.00 ▢
D3	D1	$100	9/87	Yellow, blue / White	(10,000)	17.50 ▢

Second Series.

№	Ill.	Units	Date	Description		Value
D4	(D1)	Rf250	9/87	Red, blue / white	(15,000)	15.00 ▢
D5	(D1)	Rf500	9/87	Green, blue / white	(10,000)	17.50 ▢
D6	(D1)	Rf1000	9/87	Yellow, blue / White	(8,000)	25.00 ▢

Optical cards are supplied to O.P.T. & Telemali by Landis and Gyr, Switzerland. Only definitive cards have been issued. It is possible that trial cards were initially used but details are not available.

D1

Nº	Ill.	Units	Date	Description		Value	
D1	*(D1)*	30	1989	Blue?, white / silver	(2000)	10.00 ▢	6.00 ▢
D2	*(D1)*	60	1989	Green, white / silver	(2000)	15.00 ▢	8.00 ▢
D3	*D1*	120	1989	Red, white / silver	(2000)	20.00 ▢	12.00 ▢

MEXICO

A magnetic card operated telephone system by GPT, UK, is to be installed for trials in the near future. The values on the cards are in Pesos.

D1

Nº	Ill.	Units	Date	Description		Value
D1	*D1*	20,000P	1990	Dark blue, blue, pale blue / white (3000)		18.00 ▢
D2	*(D1)*	30,000P	1990	Dark blue, blue, pale blue / white (3000)		20.00 ▢
D3	*(D1)*	50,000P	1990	Dark blue, blue, pale blue / white (4000)		22.00 ▢

MONACO

Electronic smart cards manufactured initially by Solaic and later by Gemplus in France are used. The first special cards have recently been introduced.

D1

D2

D3

| D4 | S1 | S2 |

First Issue. Solaic. Type V contact. Type i. controls. (See under France)

№	Ill.	Units	Date	Description	Value
D1	(D1)	50	24/4/87	Crimson / white (21,500) Control 0285 ↑ & ↓	25.00 ☐
D2	D1	120	24/4/87	Scarlet / white (13,500) Control 0280 ↑ & ↓	30.00 ☐

Second Issue. Solaic. Contact Type VI of France. Type i. controls.

| D3 | (D2) | 50 | 6/10/87 | Crimson / white (6278) Control 4251 | 10.00 ☐ |
| D4 | D2 | 120 | 6/10/87 | Scarlet / white (3311) Control 4094 ↑ & ↓ | 15.00 ☐ |

Third Issue. Solaic. Contact Type VI of France. Type i. controls.

| D5 | (D3) | 50 | 20/4/88 | Crimson / white (13,000+) Controls 0509, 0655, 0575 | 12.00 ☐ |
| D6 | D3 | 120 | 20/4/88 | Scarlet / white (7000+) Controls 0565, 0609, 0711 | 15.00 ☐ |

Fourth Issue. Gemplus. Contact similar to Type VI of France.

D7	(D4)	50	1989	Crimson / white, 2.8mm black control (142C)	7.50 ☐
D7(a)				2.3mm black control (204b)	7.50 ☐
D8	D4	120	1989	Scarlet / white, 2.8mm black control (142A)	12.00 ☐
D8(a)				2.3mm black control (204a)	12.00 ☐

S - SPECIAL CARDS

S1	(S1)	50	8/89	VUE AERIENNE, Multicolour, (SI IV-TI) (10,000)	6.00 ☐
S2	(S1)	120	8/89	VUE AERIENNE, Multicolour, (SI IV-TI) (10,000)	15.00 ☐
S3	(S1)	50	11/89	VUE AERIENNE (Arrow red), Multicolour, (SI III)(10,000)	5.00 ☐
S4	S2	50	12/89	AUDITORIUM MONTE CARLO, Multicolour, (SI IV-TI)(10,000)	6.00 ☐
S5	(S2)	120	12/89	AUDITORIUM MONTE CARLO, Multicolour, (SI IV-TI)(10,000)	12.00 ☐

PRIVATE CARDS

  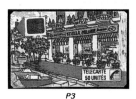

| P1 | P2 | P3 |

P1	P1	50	11/89	BIENNALE DE SCULPTURE (APPEL), Multicolour, (SI) (1000)	12.00 ☐
P2	P2	50	11/89	EXPOSITION UNIVERSELLE DE SAVILLE (KROMY), Multicolour, (SI)(1000)	12.00 ☐
P3	P3	50	12/89	STELLA POLARIS, Multicolour, (SI) (1000)	12.00 ☐

MONTSERRAT

Magnetic cards by GPT (UK) are about to be introduced.

First Issue. Magnetic cards by GPT.

D1

Nº	Ill.	Units	Date	Description		Value
D1	*D1*	EC$5.40	1989	Multicolour	(1000)	20.00 ☐
D2	*(D1)*	EC$10	1989	Multicolour	(10,000)	10.00 ☐
D3	*(D1)*	EC$20	1989	Multicolour	(4000)	15.00 ☐
D4	*(D1)*	EC$40	1989	Multicolour	(2000)	20.00 ☐

Note.   D1 is included in the Cable and Wireless collectors pack of British West Indies cards
(see under Promotional Cards at the end of this book).

MOROCCO

Optical cards were supplied by Landis and Gyr, Switzerland.   Only definitive cards were issued and
these are not common.   The service card with the number '11' in the arrow, listed and illustrated
under Algeria, was also used in Morocco.   The unit equated to 0.5 Dinar.   A single 'smart' card has
recently appeared, apparantly for Morocco, but its status is uncertain.

D1

E1

Nº	Ill.	Units	Date	Description	Value	
D1	*(D1)*	100	8/83	Red / silver (4000)	75.00 ☐	50.00 ☐

2.   ELECTRONIC CARD (Gemplus)

E1	*E1*	?	1989?	MOSQUE – MARRAKESH, Multicolour (?000)	30.00 ☐

Note. The status of this card is uncertain.   It carries no value in the design and may be a
trial card.

NETHERLANDS

Optical cards are manufactured by Landis and Gyr, Switzerland. 1989 has seen the first advertising cards, the advertisements being on the backs of some definitive cards. Those with advertisements have therefore been included with the definitives with appropriate notes. The two upper values carry bonus units like those of Belgium to encourage their purchase. Designs were changed in mid-1989 to accomodate a new PTT logo. The unit is 0.25 G.

C1

C2

D1

D2

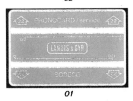

O1

T1

C - COMPLIMENTARY CARDS

Nº	Ill.	Units	Date	Description		Value	
C1	C1	4	2/88	Metallic green, white / silver (100,000)		10.00 D	2,50 D
C2	C2	4	6/89	.. .. (Notched) (100,000)		6.00 D	2.00 D

Note. The white band is 3mm wide on both the above cards. Both have PTT information on the reverse. That on C1 is on a glossy background while C2 has a mainly matt reverse except behind the optical strip where it is polished. C2 has the new logo in the bottom right corner.

D - DEFINITIVE CARDS

First Series. 2mm white band over optical strip.

No	Ill.	Units	Date	Description		Value	
D1	(D1)	20	5/86	Light metallic green, white / silver (51,120)		5.00 D	3.50 D
D2	(D1)	40+5	5/86	Metallic green, white / silver (25,798)		10.00 D	7.00 D
D3	D1	100+15	5/86	Darker metallic green, white / silver (14,866)		50.00 D	40.00 D

Second Series. 4mm white band.

No	Ill.	Units	Date	Description		Value	
D4	(D1)	20	1/87	Light metallic green, white / silver (225,000)		5.00 D	2.50 D
D4(a)				Control inverted		7.00 D	3.50 D
D5	(D1)	40+5	1/87	Metallic green, white / silver (90,000)		10.00 D	3.00 D
D5(a)				Control inverted		14.00 D	4.50 D
D6	(D1)	100+15	1/87	Darker metallic green, white / silver (45,000)		25.00 D	15.00 D

Third Series. 3mm white band. No notch.

No	Ill.	Units	Date	Description		Value	
D7	(D1)	20	2/88	Light metallic green, white / silver (95,000)		5.00 D	1.50 D
D7(a)				Control inverted		6.00 D	2.00 D
D8	(D1)	40+5	2/88	Metallic green, white / silver (122,000)		10.00 D	3.00 D
D9	(D1)	100+15	2/88	Darker metallic green, white / silver (150,000)		25.00 D	10.00 D

Fourth Series. 3mm white band. Notch introduced.

No	Ill.	Units	Date	Description		Value	
D10	(D1)	20	11/88	Light metallic green, white / silver 'CENTRAAL BEHEER' advert. on reverse (430,000)		5.00 D	1.50 D
D11	(D1)	20	1989	Light metallic green, white / silver TELECOM advert. on reverse (10,000)		15.00 D	7.50 D
D12	(D1)	40+5	11/88	Metallic green, white / silver (322,000)		10.00 D	3.00 D
D12(a)				Control inverted		12.00 D	4.00 D
D13	(D1)	100+15	11/88	Darker metallic green, white / silver (286,000)		25.00 D	7.00 D
D13(a)				Control inverted		28.00 D	8.00 D

Fifth Series. Design changed to incorporate new logo. 3mm band and notch as before.

№	Ill.	Units	Date	Description		Value	
D14	(D2)	20	7/89	Light metallic green, white / silver	(211,000)	5.00 ☐	1.50 ☐
D14(a)				Control inverted		6.00 ☐	2.00 ☐
D15	(D2)	20	9/89	Light metallic green, white / silver			
				'CENTRAAL BEHEER' advert. on reverse	(10,000)	15.00 ☐	7.50 ☐
D16	D2	40+5	7/89	Metallic green, white / silver	(20,000)	10.00 ☐	3.00 ☐
D16(a)				Control inverted		12.00 ☐	4.00 ☐
D17	(D2)	40+5	10/89	Metallic green, white / silver, Complimentary.			
				'Telecom - kaart op zak' on reverse	(250)	500.00 ☐	300.00 ☐
D18	(D2)	100+15	7/89	Darker metallic green, white / silver	(20,000)	25.00 ☐	7.00 ☐
D18(a)				Control inverted		28.00 ☐	8.00 ☐

OFFICIAL/SERVICE CARDS and TEST CARDS

The standard blue Landis & Gyr 'Phonecard' service and test cards are used in the Netherlands. These have the number '22' in the arrows.

O1	O1	240	1987	Blue, white / silver, 2mm white band	(5400)	-- ☐	25.00 ☐
O2	(O1)	240	1988	Blue, white / silver, 3mm white band. (incl. above?)		-- ☐	25.00 ☐
T1	T1	---	1987	Blue / silver	(375)	-- ☐	40.00 ☐

NEW ZEALAND

Field trials of a GPT payphone and card system began at two military bases near Christchurch, New Zealand, in May, 1989. The general introduction of cards followed in late 1989.

D - DEFINITIVE CARDS

D1

D2

D3

D4

D5

D6

Trial Issue

№	Ill.	Units	Date	Description	Value
D1	(D1)	$NZ2	4/5/89	Multicolour (6000)	8.00 ☐
D2	(D1)	$NZ5	4/5/89	Multicolour (5707)	4.00 ☐
D3	D1	$NZ10	4/5/89	Multicolour (2339)	30.00 ☐
D4	(D1)	$NZ20	4/5/89	Multicolour (6000)	15.00 ☐
D5	(D1)	$NZ50	4/5/89	Multicolour (5707)	25.00 ☐

First Regular Issue

№	Ill.	Units	Date	Description	Value
D6	D2	$NZ2	12/89	SATELLITE DISH, 1st Issue, Multicolour (100,000)	2.00 ☐
D7	D3	$NZ5	12/89	SATELLITE DISH, 1st Issue, Multicolour (725,000)	4.00 ☐
D8	D4	$NZ10	12/89	SATELLITE DISH, 1st Issue, Multicolour (300,000)	8.00 ☐
D9	D5	$NZ20	12/89	SATELLITE DISH, 1st Issue, Multicolour (125,000)	20.00 ☐

Second Issue. As above but with the "First Issue" motif removed.

№	Ill.	Units	Date	Description		Value
D10	(D2)	$NZ2	1/90	SATELLITE DISH, Multicolour	(450,000)	2.00 ☐
D11	(D3)	$NZ5	1/90	SATELLITE DISH, Multicolour	(975,000)	4.00 ☐
D12	(D4)	$NZ10	1/90	SATELLITE DISH, Multicolour	(550,000)	8.00 ☐
D13	(D5)	$NZ20	1/90	SATELLITE DISH, Multicolour	(125,000)	15.00 ☐
D14	D6	$NZ50	1/90	SATELLITE DISH, Multicolour	(20,000)	25.00 ☐

S - SPECIAL/COMMEMORATIVE CARDS

S1 S2 S3

S4 S5

Commonwealth Games, 1990.

№	Ill.	Units	Date	Description		Value
S1	S1	$NZ2	1990	SWIMMER, Multicolour	(100,000)	2.00 ☐
S2	S2	$NZ5	1990	GYMNAST, Multicolour	(80,000)	4.00 ☐
S3	S3	$NZ10	1990	WEIGHT LIFTER, Multicolour	(47,000)	8.00 ☐
S4	S4	$NZ20	1990	HURDLER, Multicolour	(70,000)	15.00 ☐
S5	S5	$NZ50	1990	CYCLIST, Multicolour	(6000)	25.00 ☐

Collectors may purchase cards from: National Payphone Group, Telecom South, PO Box 1473, Christchurch, New Zealand, Cost: face value plus $NZ2 for postage on orders below $NZ100. Postage free above $NZ100. VISA and MASTERCARD/BANKCARD only at present. Quote Card No., Expiry Date and Name of holder.

NIGER

Optical cards are supplied by Landis and Gyr, Switzerland. Only definitive cards have been issued.

D1

№	Ill.	Units	Date	Description		Value	
D1	(D1)	10	11/89	Yellow / silver	(2000)	15.00 ☐	10.00 ☐
D2	(D1)	20	11/89	Yellow / silver	(2000)	20.00 ☐	10.00 ☐
D3	(D1)	50	11/89	Yellow / silver	(1000)	30.00 ☐	15.00 ☐
D4	D1	100	11/89	Yellow / silver	(1000)	35.00 ☐	20.00 ☐

NIGERIA

Twenty magnetic card operated payphones were installed in Nigeria by Autelca of Switzerland. Standard 'test cards' were used but these are distinguishable by their control numbers which have no prefix. There are two values, 20 and 40 Naira, the values being indicated by the first two numerals of the control. I understand that all cards have been sold and that the system is not in use at present.

D1

№	Ill.	Units	Date	Description		Value
D1	*D1*	N20	1985	Blue / white (15,000)		45.00 ⯀
D2	*(D1)*	N40	1985	·· ·· ·· (4000)		70.00 ⯀

NORWAY

Magnetic cards, manufactured by GPT, UK, have now been adopted following field trials of French smart cards (prefixed 'E' below). Initial deployment has been in high-usage 'closed user group' locations such as hospitals and prisons. Card-operated payphones have also being fitted on Philips Petroleum platforms in the North Sea but it seems that special cards are not being used and that only the normal definitive cards have been issued. It is understood that Schlumberger smart cards are about to be introduced in Norway.

DM1

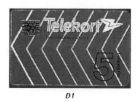

D1

1. MAGNETIC CARDS

DM - DEFINITIVE CARDS

№	Ill.	Units	Date	Description		Value
DM1	*(DM1)*	7 kr	1987	Red, blue / white (1000)		50.00 ⯀
DM2	*DM1*	21 kr	1987	·· ·· ·· ·· (22,500)		6.00 ⯀
DM3	*(DM1)*	70 kr	1987	·· ·· ·· ·· (27,500)		8.00 ⯀

Note: D1 above, although designed as one of the series and listed as such, was used mainly as a complimentary.

2. ELECTRONIC CARDS

Cards manufactured by Schlumberger, France.

№	Ill.	Units	Date	Description	Value
D1	*D1*	5	1984	Red, black / white	50.00 ⯀
D2	*(D1)*	40	1984	Pale blue, black / white	50.00 ⯀
D3	*(D1)*	50	1984	Red, black / white	50.00 ⯀

OMAN

Twenty magnetic card operated pay-phones were supplied by Autelca, Switzerland, to the General Telecommunications Organization of the Sultanate of Oman in 1985 and were phased out after 26 December, 1988. Only definitive cards were issued. Control numbers are in black. Telephones and cards supplied by GPT, UK, are now in use.

1. Autelca Cards

AD1

Nº	Ill.	Units	Date	Description		Value
AD1	*AD1*	R.O 1,500	1985	Red, black / beige	(100,000)	15.00 ☐
AD2	*(AD1)*	R.O 3,000	1985	Black, red / beige	(80,000)	17.00 ☐
AD3	*(AD1)*	R.O 6,000	1985	Black, red / beige	(200,000)	12.00 ☐
AD4	*(AD1)*	R.O 9,000	1985	White, red, black / beige	(80,000)	20.00 ☐

2. GPT cards

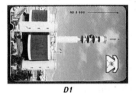
D1

D2

D3

First Issue. Crossed swords, etc, and value in black.

D1	*D1*	RO 3.000	1988	Multicolour	(30,000)	8.00 ☐
D2	*D2*	RO 6.000	1988	Multicolour	(30,000)	10.00 ☐
D3	*(D3)*	RO 6.000	1988	Multicolour	(30,000)	10.00 ☐

Second Issue. Crossed swords, etc, in red and value in white.

D4	*(D1)*	RO 3.000	1989	Multicolour	(160,000)	5.00 ☐
D5	*(D2)*	RO 6.000	1989	Multicolour	(160,000)	8.00 ☐
D6	*D3*	RO 6.000	1989	Multicolour	(160,000)	8.00 ☐

PAPUA NEW GUINEA

Optical cards are supplied by Landis and Gyr, Switzerland. Only a definitive card has been issued so far.

D1

Nº	Ill.	Units	Date	Description		Value	
D1	*(D1)*	20	1988	Blue / silver (13,000)		15.00 ☐	5.00 ☐

PARAGUAY

Optical cards are supplied by Landis and Gyr, Switzerland.

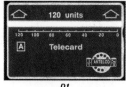

D1

№	Ill.	Units	Date	Description	Value	
D1	(D1)	120	1989	Red / silver (100,000)	20.00 □	4.00 □

PORTUGAL

Optical cards are manufactured by Landis and Gyr, Switzerland. The first series was of 25 and 105 units and the second of 50 and 120 units, both having no white band, while later series have displayed the usual sequence of white bands over the optical strip. The cards bearing the name and logo of Telefones de Lisboa e Porto .(TLP) are apparantly interchangable with the standard CTT cards.The unit equates to 7.5 Esc. Only definitive and service cards exist although one definitive card has a commemorative design on the reverse. As with the Netherlands, this has been listed as a separate card in the definitive series since it has the standard design on the face.

D1

D2

DL1

1. CTT

D - DEFINITIVE CARDS

First Series. No white band.

№	Ill.	Units	Date	Description	Value	
D1	(D1)	25	6/82	Blue / silver (15,000)	20.00 □	10.00 □
D2	D1	105	6/82	·· ·· ·· (11,000)	30.00 □	15.00 □

Second Series. Units changed.

№	Ill.	Units	Date	Description	Value	
D3	(D1)	50	11/83	Blue / silver (20,000)	15.00 □	10.00 □
D4	(D1)	120	11/83	·· ·· ·· (20,000)	25.00 □	15.00 □

Third Series. 1.5mm white band added.

№	Ill.	Units	Date	Description	Value	
D5	(D2)	50	9/84	Dark blue, white / silver (84,100)	10.00 □	4.50 □
D6	(D2)	120	9/84	·· ·· ·· ·· ·· ·· (28,200)	20.00 □	6.00 □

Fourth Series. 2mm white band.

№	Ill.	Units	Date	Description	Value	
D7	(D2)	50	7/85	Dark blue, white / silver (179,000)	8.00 □	4.00 □
D8	(D2)	120	7/85	·· ·· ·· ·· ·· ·· (169,400)	15.00 □	6.00 □

Fifth Series. 4mm white band.

№	Ill.	Units	Date	Description	Value	
D9	(D2)	50	1/87	Dark blue, white / silver (197,500)	3.00 □	1.50 □
D10	(D2)	120	1/87	·· ·· ·· ·· ·· ·· (272,500)	12.50 □	3.50 □

Sixth Series.   3mm white band.   No notch.

Nº	Ill.	Units	Date	Description		Value	
D11	*(D2)*	50	10/87	Dark blue, white / silver (247,000)		5.00 ☐	2.50 ☐
D12	*D2*	120	10/87	`··  ··  ··  ··  ··  ··` (163,000)		14.00 ☐	4.00 ☐

Seventh Series.   3mm white band.   Notched.

D13	*(D2)*	50	1989	Dark blue, white / silver (766,000)		4.00 ☐	1.50 ☐
D14	*(D2)*	120	17/5/89	DIA MUNDIAL DAS TELECOMS. on reverse (30,000)		17.50 ☐	5.00 ☐
D15	*D2*	120	1989	`··  ··  ··  ··  ··  ··` (378,000)		12.50 ☐	3.50 ☐

2. TELEFONES DE LISBOA E PORTO (TLP)

First Series.   3mm white band.   No Notch.

DL1	*(DL1)*	50	1988	Blue, white / silver (205,000)		5.00 ☐	1.50 ☐
DL2	*(DL1)*	120	1988	Blue, white / silver (110,000)		15.00 ☐	3.50 ☐

Second Series.   3mm white band.   Notched.

DL3	*(DL1)*	50	1989	Blue, white / silver (490,000)		4.00 ☐	1.50 ☐
DL4	*DL1*	120	1989	Blue, white / silver (108,000)		12.00 ☐	3.50 ☐

O - OFFICIAL/SERVICE CARDS AND TEST CARDS

O1

T1

OL1

TL1

O1	*O1*	(240)	1982	Blue / silver	--- ☐	20.00 ☐
OL1	*OL1*	(240)	1988	Blue / silver	--- ☐	20.00 ☐
T1	*T1*	–	1982	Blue / silver	--- ☐	20.00 ☐
TL1	*TL1*	–	1988	Blue / silver	--- ☐	20.00 ☐

Note.   Unfortunately no examples of the Service and Test cards of CTT or TLP were available at the time of going to press.   The illustrations are from Landis and Gyr's original artwork.

QATAR

In 1984 fifty magnetic card-operated pay-phones were supplied to Cable and Wireless PLC by Autelca, Switzerland, for use in Qatar. Three series of definitive cards have been issued and these are denominated in the local currency. Recently the Qatar telephone company has become fully independent and has changed its name to Q-TEL. The third issue of cards reflects this change of name but is otherwise similar.

First Series

D1

№	Ill.	Units	Date	Description	Value
D1	*D1*	QR 100	1984	Maroon, black, yellow / white (50,000)	18.00 ☐
D2	*(D1)*	QR 200	1984	Maroon, black, pale blue / white (40,000)	22.00 ☐

Second Series   New values.

| D3 | *(D1)* | QR 20 | 1987 | Maroon, black / white (180,000) | 6.00 ☐ |
| D4 | *(D1)* | QR 50 | 1987 | Maroon, black, pale green / white (150,000) | 10.00 ☐ |

Third Series   'Q-TEL' in place of 'QATAR'.

| D5 | *(D1)* | QR 50 | 1989? | Maroon, black, pale green / white (?,000) | 12.00 ☐ |
| D6 | *(D1)* | QR 100 | 1989? | Maroon, black, yellow / white   (?,000) | 25.00 ☐ |

RUSSIA

Magnetic cards by GPT, UK, were to be introduced in Moscow in January, 1990.

D1

D2

D3

P1

P2

P3

D - DEFINITIVE CARDS

№	Ill.	Units	Date	Description	Value
D1	*D1*	R10	1/90	KOMSTAR, Multicolour (25,000)	4.00 ☐
D2	*D2*	R25	1/90	KOMSTAR, Multicolour (23,000)	10.00 ☐
D3	*D3*	R50	1/90	KOMSTAR, Multicolour (2000)	45.00 ☐

P - PROMOTIONAL CARDS

P1	*P1*	1000	1987	Multicolour (1500)	30.00 ☐
P2	*P2*	R10	4/89	Multicolour (5000)	20.00 ☐
P3	*P3*	R25	4/89	Multicolour (5000)	20.00 ☐

St HELENA

Magnetic cards by GPT (UK) will be introduced and provisional cards are about to be issued.

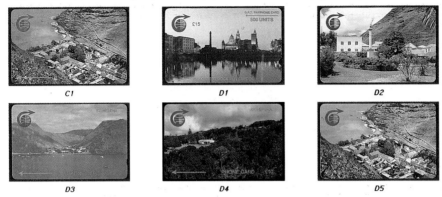

C1   D1   D2

D3   D4   D5

C - COMPLIMENTARY CARD

№	Ill.	Units	Date	Description	Value
C1	*C1*	–	1990	Multicolour (100)	100.00 ☐

D - DEFINITIVE CARDS

First Issue. Provisional Cards.

№	Ill.	Units	Date	Description	Value
D1	*(D1)*	50	1989	Multicolour (1000)	20.00 ☐
D2	*(D1)*	100	1989	Multicolour (2000)	20.00 ☐
D3	*D1*	500	1989	Multicolour (1000)	30.00 ☐

Note. These 'Albert Dock' cards have been used as provisionals in several places. The Cable and Wireless logo and the value are overprinted on the cards.

Second Issue.

№	Ill.	Units	Date	Description	Value
D4	*D2*	£2	1990	Multicolour (2000)	20.00 ☐
D5	*D3*	£5	1990	Multicolour (4000)	25.00 ☐
D6	*D4*	£10	1990	Multicolour (3600)	30.00 ☐
D7	*D5*	£15	1990	Multicolour (400)	75.00 ☐

St KITTS & NEVIS

Magnetic cards were supplied by Autelca, Switzerland, to Cable and Wireless PLC for use on the Caribbean islands of St. Christopher (St. Kitts as it is better known) and Nevis. New cards by GPT (UK) are due to appear shortly. All values of the GPT cards are of the same design.

D1   D2

First Issue. Magnetic cards by Autelca.

№	Ill.	Units	Date	Description	Value
D1	*D1*	15	1986	Red, blue / white (10,000)	20.00 ☐
D2	*(D1)*	25	1986	Pale blue, blue / white (10,000)	10.00 ☐
D3	*(D1)*	50	1986	Green, blue / white (8000)	15.00 ☐

Second Issue. Magnetic cards by GPT.

Nº	Ill.	Units	Date	Description	Value
D4	*D2*	EC$5.40	1989	Multicolour (1000)	20.00 ☐
D5	*(D2)*	EC$10	1989	Multicolour (5000)	10.00 ☐
D6	*(D2)*	EC$20	1989	Multicolour (3000)	17.00 ☐
D7	*(D2)*	EC$40	1989	Multicolour (2000)	22.00 ☐

Note. D4 is included in the Cable and Wireless collectors pack of British West Indies cards (see under Promotional Cards at the end of this book).

St LUCIA

Magnetic cards were previously supplied by Autelca, Switzerland, to Cable and Wireless PLC for use on the Caribbean island of St. Lucia for international direct-dial calls. A magnetic card by GPT (UK) is about to be introduced.

D1   *D2*

First Issue. Magnetic cards by Autelca.

Nº	Ill.	Units	Date	Description	Value
D1	*D1*	EC$ 10	1985	Blue, red / white (50,000)	10.00 ☐
D2	*(D1)*	EC$ 40	1985	Blue, pale blue / white (30,000)	15.00 ☐

Second Issue. Magnetic card by GPT.

Nº	Ill.	Units	Date	Description	Value
D3	*D2*	EC$5.40	1989	Multicolour (1000)	20.00 ☐

Note. D3 is included in the Cable and Wireless collectors pack of British West Indies cards (see under Promotional Cards at the end of this book).

St VINCENT

Magnetic cards were previously supplied by Autelca, Switzerland, to Cable and Wireless PLC for use on the Caribbean island of St. Vincent. Control numbers were prefixed with the letter V. Magnetic cards supplied by GPT, UK, are about to be introduced.

D1   *D2*

First Issue. Magnetic cards by Autelca.

Nº	Ill.	Units	Date	Description	Value
D1	*D1*	5	1984	Green, blue / white (20,000)	15.00 ☐
D2	*(D1)*	10	1984	Pale blue, blue / white (18,000)	7.50 ☐
D3	*(D1)*	20	1984	Red, blue / white (15,000)	10.00 ☐

Second Issue. Magnetic cards by GPT

NO	Ill.	Units	Date	Description		Value	
D4	*D2*	EC$5.40	1989	Multicolour	(1000)	20.00 ☐	
D5	*(D2)*	EC$10	1989	Multicolour	(15,000)	10.00 ☐	
D6	*(D2)*	EC$20	1989	Multicolour	(10,000)	15.00 ☐	
D7	*(D2)*	EC$40	1989	Multicolour	(5000)	20.00 ☐	

Note. D4 is included in the Cable and Wireless collectors pack of British West Indies cards (see under Promotional Cards at the end of this book).

SAUDI ARABIA

Optical pay-phones and cards have been supplied to Saudi Telecom by Landis and Gyr of Switzerland for field trials and a further printing was made. Only definitive cards were issued. The service card used is that with the number '11' in the arrow listed and illustrated under Algeria. The unit equates to 0.2 Riyal. It is understood that an electronic or 'smart' card with a Gemplus-type contact has been introduced very recently but details are still uncertain.

1. OPTICAL CARDS (Landis and Gyr)

First Issue. 1.5mm white band.

D1

NO	Ill.	Units	Date	Description		Value	
D1	*(D1)*	50	10/84	Green / silver	(33,000)	35.00 ☐	20.00 ☐
D2	*(D1)*	100	10/84	·· ·· ·· ··	(21,000)	40.00 ☐	25.00 ☐

Note 1. Cards with 4mm white bands have been reported but do not appear on Landis and Gyr's production records and have not been listed.

Note 2. No card has become available for illustration. The illustration above is the original artwork for the card kindly provided by Landis and Gyr and shows the design rather better than the 'mock-up' shown in the first edition. Areas shown white should be green and black areas should be silver.

SENEGAL

Optical cards were manufactured for SONATEL, Senegal, by Landis and Gyr of Switzerland. The unit equated to 50 FCFA. Only definitive cards were issued. The service card with the number '11' in the arrow, as listed and illustrated under Algeria, were used. A trial card earlier than the D1 listed in the first edition of this book has now come to light and the numbering has been changed to accommodate it. Very recently electronic or 'smart' cards have been supplied by Schlumberger Industries. These have the normal Type IV Schlumberger contact and 2.5mm laser-punched control numbers on the reverse.

OD1   OD2   ED1

1. OPTICAL CARDS (Landis and Gyr)

Nº	Ill.	Units	Date	Description		Value	

First (Trial) Issue. 1.5mm white band.

| OD1 | *(OD1)* | 120 | 10/85 | Red / silver | (5000) | 30.00 ☐ | 15.00 ☐ |

Note. No specimen of OD1 is available and the illustration is from a photocopy.

Second Issue. 2mm white band.

| OD2 | *(OD2)* | 40 | 1/86 | Blue / silver | (5000) | 15.00 ☐ | 8.00 ☐ |
| OD3 | *(OD2)* | 120 | 1/86 | ·· ·· ·· ·· | (45,000) | 25.00 ☐ | 10.00 ☐ |

Third Issue. 3mm white band. No notch.

| OD4 | *(OD2)* | 40 | 11/87 | Blue / silver | (10,000) | 12.00 ☐ | 6.00 ☐ |

Fourth Issue. 3mm white band. Notched.

| OD5 | *OD2* | 40 | 5/88 | Blue / silver | (50,000) | 8.00 ☐ | 3.50 ☐ |

2. ELECTRONIC CARDS (Schlumberger Industries)

| ED1 | *ED1* | 50 | 1989 | Blue, olive, black / white | (1350) | 35.00 ☐ |
| ED2 | *(ED1)* | 120 | 1989 | Blue, olive, black / white | (650) | 50.00 ☐ |

Note. The above illustration is of a punched sample card.

SEYCHELLES

Seychelles Telephones, a Cable and Wireless plc company, introduced Landis and Gyr telephones and cards around May, 1989. A new, six-colour definitive series was introduced at the end of 1989.

First Series. 3mm white band. Notched.

D1

D2

Nº	Ill.	Units	Date	Description		Value	
D1	*D1*	120	5/89	Green, red / white	(4000)	15.00 ☐	5.00 ☐
D2	*(D2)*	240	5/89	Green, red / white	(4000)	25.00 ☐	8.00 ☐

Second Issue. 3mm white band. Notched.

| D3 | *(D1)* | 120 | 12/89 | Six colours | (8000) | 15.00 ☐ | 5.00 ☐ |
| D4 | *D2* | 240 | 12/89 | Six colours | (4000) | 25.00 ☐ | 8.00 ☐ |

Note. The face values of these cards are SR (Seychelles Rupees) 100 (about £11) and SR 200 (about £21) from which it is evident that they are intended mainly for international calls.

Singapore Telecom, unfortunately omitted in the first edition of this book, introduced Japanese cards by Anritsu in 1985. Cards and telephones supplied by GPT were introduced in January, 1989.

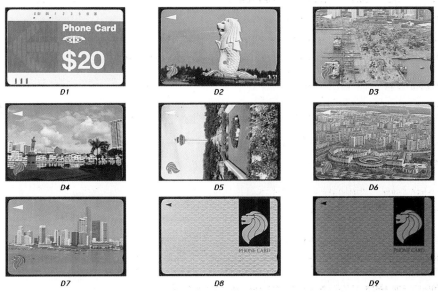

D1	D2	D3
D4	D5	D6
D7	D8	D9

First (Anritsu) Issue. No notch.

№	Ill.	Units	Date	Description		Value
D1	(D1)	$2	9/85	Red, black / white (???)		15.00 □
D2	(D1)	$5	9/85	·· ·· ·· ·· ·· (???)		10.00 □
D3	(D1)	$10	9/85	·· ·· ·· ·· ·· (???)		15.00 □
D4	(D1)	$20	9/85	·· ·· ·· ·· ·· (???)		20.00 □
D5	(D1)	$50	9/85	·· ·· ·· ·· ·· (???)		25.00 □

Second Issue. As above but with notch.

№	Ill.	Units	Date	Description		Value
D6	(D1)	$5	1987?	·· ·· ·· ·· ·· (???)		4.00 □
D7	(D1)	$10	1987?	·· ·· ·· ·· ·· (???)		4.00 □
D8	D1	$20	1987?	·· ·· ·· ·· ·· (???)		8.00 □
D9	(D1)	$50	1987?	·· ·· ·· ·· ·· (???)		15.00 □

Third (GPT) Issue.

№	Ill.	Units	Date	Description			
D10	D2	$10	1/89	MERLION, Multicolour	(50,000)	7.00 □	5.00 □
D11	D3	$10	1/89	CONTAINER TERMINAL, Multicolour	(50,000)	7.00 □	5.00 □
D12	D4	$10	1/89	RAFFLES STATUE, Multicolour	(50,000)	7.00 □	5.00 □
D13	D5	$10	1/89	CHANGI AIRPORT, Multicolour	(50,000)	7.00 □	5.00 □
D14	D6	$10	1/89	HOUSING ESTATE, Multicolour	(50,000)	7.00 □	5.00 □
D15	D7	$10	1/89	SKYLINE, Multicolour	(50,000)	7.00 □	5.00 □
D16	D8	$20	4/89	Silver	(150,000)	22.00 □	15.00 □
D17	D9	$50	4/89	Gold	(50,000)	35.00 □	25.00 □

Fourth Issue. As above but wording on reverse altered. (See Note 1 below.)

№	Ill.	Units	Date	Description			
D18	D2	$10	?/89	MERLION, Multicolour	(385,000)	4.00 □	3.00 □
D19	D3	$10	?/89	CONTAINER TERMINAL, Multicolour	(325,000)	4.00 □	3.00 □
D20	D4	$10	?/89	RAFFLES STATUE, Multicolour	(335,000)	4.00 □	3.00 □
D21	D5	$10	?/89	CHANGI AIRPORT, Multicolour	(335,000)	4.00 □	3.00 □
D22	D6	$10	?/89	HOUSING ESTATE, Multicolour	(335,000)	4.00 □	3.00 □
D23	D7	$10	?/89	SKYLINE, Multicolour	(385,000)	4.00 □	3.00 □
D24	D8	$20	?/89	Silver	(300,000)	12.00 □	10.00 □
D25	D9	$50	?/89	Gold	(100,000)	25.00 □	20.00 □

Note 1. D18 to D25 have the same words as D10 to D17 on the reverse but on D18 to D25 the word "approximate" falls completely onto the fifth line while on D10 to D17 it is hyphenated and split between the fourth and fifth lines.

Note 2. D10 to D25 incorporate a new technology for indicating the degree to which cards have been used. There is a scale on the back into which a small hole, not penitrating the front, is drilled or punched at the end of each call. It does, however, produce a small bump on the front. There are two types - one with a outline scale (with numbers in silver) and long wedge below it and the other with these in solid silver with the numbers in black. The outline type seems to have come first and is called type 1 and the other type 2. My copy of D6 is type 1 and the others type 2. It appears that the change from type one to type two took place at the same time as that from the first to second type of wording on the reverse. If, however, the two changes came at different times there may be a third series of the D10 to D17 cards. There are also two types of control numbers - 3.5mm and 3.0mm - and these are found on otherwise similar cards providing further opportunities for specialisation.

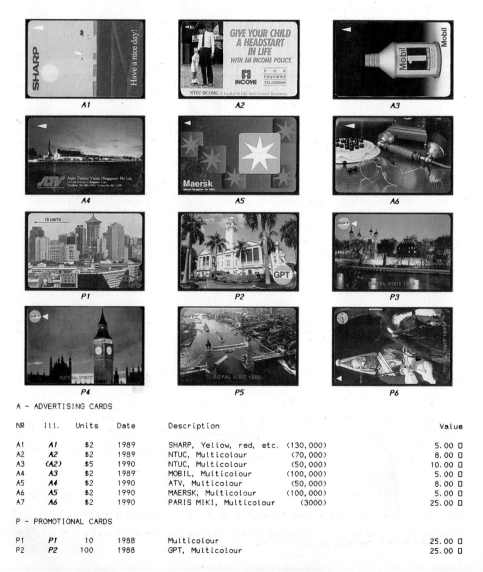

A - ADVERTISING CARDS

№	Ill.	Units	Date	Description		Value
A1	*A1*	$2	1989	SHARP, Yellow, red, etc.	(130,000)	5.00 ☐
A2	*A2*	$2	1989	NTUC, Multicolour	(70,000)	8.00 ☐
A3	*(A2)*	$5	1990	NTUC, Multicolour	(50,000)	10.00 ☐
A4	*A3*	$2	1989	MOBIL, Multicolour	(100,000)	5.00 ☐
A5	*A4*	$2	1990	ATV, Multicolour	(50,000)	8.00 ☐
A6	*A5*	$2	1990	MAERSK, Multicolour	(100,000)	5.00 ☐
A7	*A6*	$2	1990	PARIS MIKI, Multicolour	(3000)	25.00 ☐

P - PROMOTIONAL CARDS

P1	*P1*	10	1988	Multicolour	25.00 ☐
P2	*P2*	100	1988	GPT, Multicolour	25.00 ☐

Note. The status of P1 and P2 is not clear but their control numbers seem to place them before D1 to D8 above in line.

Queen's Visit, 1989.

№	Ill.	Units	Date	Description					Value	
P3	*P3*	$2	9/89	Multicolour,	TOWER OF LONDON	(6,000)	10.00 □	7.00 □
P4	*P4*	$2	9/89	·· ·· ··	BIG BEN	(6,000)	10.00 □	7.00 □
P5	*P5*	$5	9/89	·· ·· ··	TOWER BRIDGE	(6,000)	10.00 □	7.00 □
P6	*P6*	$5	9/89	·· ·· ··	HORSE GUARD	(6,000)	10.00 □	7.00 □

Note. P3 to P6 have usage indication while P1 and P2 do not. P3 to P6 have 4.2mm controls.

Albert Dock Promotional Cards.

P7	--	$2	1990	Multicolour with silver text (75,000)	8.00 □
P8	--	$5	1990	Multicolour with gold text (25,000)	15.00 □

Note. P7 and P8 are similar to those illustrated as provisional cards under St Helena. New versions of these cards (P9 and P10) with GPT holograms in the upper left corners were issued in Singapore in March, 1990, but were too late to be included in this book.

SOUTH AFRICA

South Africa began trials of of Telkor (South Africa) GEC cards and telephones between March and October, 1988, in Pretoria, Johannesburg, Cape Town and Durban. It is not known whether a decision to adopt a nation-wide system has yet been reached. Both values of the trial cards carry a bonus value over the face value.

D1

S1

First Trial Issue. No Notch.

№	Ill.	Units	Date	Description		Value
D1	*(D1)*	R5+40c	3/88	Grey, blue, orange, green / black	(60,000)	10.00 □
D2	*(D1)*	R10+R1	3/88	Brown, blue, white / black	(40,000)	15.00 □

Second Trial Issue. Notched.

D3	*(D1)*	R5+40c	11/88?	Grey, blue, orange, green / black	(60,000)	3.00 □
D4	*D1*	R10+R1	11/88?	Brown, blue, white / black	(40,000)	7.00 □

Third Trial Issue. White edge. Notched.

D5	*(D1)*	R5+40c	11/88?	Grey, blue, orange, green, black, white	(,000)	3.00 □
D6	*(D1)*	R10+R1	11/88?	Brown, blue, white, black, white	(,000)	7.00 □

Note. D1 to D4 were printed on black plastic giving the white areas a slight tone. D5 and D6 were printed on a white plastic surface resulting in purer whites.

S - SPECIAL CARD

S1	*S1*	120	9/9/85	Pale blue / silver	150.00 □	100.00 □

Note. This card, by Landis and Gyr, was issued at an exhibition in Johannesburg in September, 1985.

Cards may be ordered from: The Postmaster General, Buying and Supplies Division (213), PO Box 447, PRETORIA 0001, Republic of South Africa.

SPAIN

Earlier optical card, manufactured by Landis and Gyr in Switzerland, were used in two separate tests in Madrid from 1981 onwards. The later series of optical cards were introduced in Alicante and Las Palmas starting in February, 1986. Those with including IVA on the reverse were for use in Spain and those without for use in the Canary Islands. Only definitive and service cards were issued. The Alicante trials finished in October, 1988 and those in Las Palmas will end in 1990. Recently smart cards, manufactured in Spain by a company in which Bull CP8 of France has a minority holding, were introduced on in Murcia province in May, 1989. These cards have the standard Bull CP8 contact design previously used in France but it is set rather lower on the card as on the German cards.

1 OPTICAL CARDS (Landis and Gyr)

OD1   OD2   OD3

OD - DEFINITIVE CARDS

First Trial Issue.

Nº	Ill.	Units	Date	Description		Value	
OD1	*OD1*	120¹	9/81	Green / silver	(200)	70.00 ☐	70.00 ☐
OD2	*(OD1)*	120¹	9/81	Blue-green / silver	(415)	50.00 ☐	50.00 ☐

Note 1. While both OD1 and OD2 are denominated 120 units, OD1 has "1 unidad = 5 ptas." at bottom left and OD2 has "1 unidad = 25 ptas.". Thus the first Spanish cards provided two values by changing the value of the unit rather than by changing the number of units as is usual.

Second Field Trial Issue.

OD3	*(OD2)*	120	1/84	Green / silver	(6000)	30.00 ☐	20.00 ☐
OD4	*OD2*	240	1/84	·· ·· ·· ··	(2000)	40.00 ☐	30.00 ☐

Note. The value of the card was in this case proportional to the number of units in the usual way.

Third (First Regular) Issue. 2mm white band.

OD5	*(OD3)*	600	2/86	Blue, black, white/silver. Compliments (1500)		50.00 ☐	30.00 ☐
OD6	*(OD3)*	600	6/86	Blue, black, white/silver. With IVA (52,000)		15.00 ☐	4.00 ☐
OD7	*OD3*	1200	6/86	·· ·· ·· ·· ·· ·· ·· ·· (50,000)		20.00 ☐	8.00 ☐

Note. The unit now equals 5 pesetas but the scale is in pesitas rather than units.

Fourth Issue. 2mm white band. Without IVA on reverse. (Canary Islands)

OD8	*(OD3)*	600	11/86	Blue, black, white/silver. No IVA (97,500)		10.00 ☐	4.00 ☐
OD9	*(OD3)*	1200	11/86	·· ·· ·· ·· ·· ·· ·· ·· (50,000)		20.00 ☐	8.00 ☐

Fifth Issue. 4mm white band (COMPLIMENTARY).

OD10	*(OD3)*	200	1/87	Blue, black, white/silver (4000)	15.00 ☐	10.00 ☐

Sixth Issue. 3mm white band. (Mainland Spain)

OD11	*(OD3)*	600	10/87	Blue, black, white/silver. With IVA (100,000)		4.00 ☐	1.50 ☐
OD12	*(OD3)*	1200	10/87	·· ·· ·· ·· ·· ·· ··	(76,000)	10.00 ☐	3.50 ☐

Seventh Issue. 3mm white band. (Canary Islands)

OD13	*(OD3)*	600	1988	Blue, black, white / silver. No IVA (52,000)		5.00 ☐	2.50 ☐
OD14	*(OD3)*	1200	1988	·· ·· ·· ·· ·· ·· ·· ·· ·· (16,000)		10.00 ☐	4.50 ☐

OO and OT - OFFICIAL/SERVICE and TEST CARDS

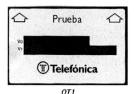

001

OT1

Nº	Ill.	Units	Date	Description		Value	
001	*(001)*	(1200)	1986	Green, black, white / silver (5200)	--- ☐	25.00 ☐
OT1	*(OT1)*	--	1986	Green, black, white / silver (70)	--- ☐	75.00 ☐

Note. No cards are available so illustrations are from artwork kindly supplied by Landis and Gyr. Areas shown as white should be green and black areas are silver.

2 ELECTRONIC (SMART) CARDS

D1

D1	*D1*	500ptas	9/89	Multicolour	2.50 ☐
D2	*D1*	1000ptas	9/89	Multicolour	5.00 ☐
D3	*D1*	2000ptas	9/89	Multicolour	7.00 ☐
D4	*D1*	2100ptas	9/89	Multicolour	25.00 ☐

Note. D4 is a promotional card which gives an extra 100 ptas of free value.

P - PROMOTIONAL CARDS

The magnetic cards illustrated below were used at exhibitions and other special occasions initially in Spain and later elsewhere. They were exhibited by GPT, UK.

P1

P2

P3

P4

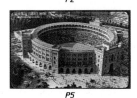

P5

P6

P1	*P1*	1000	1987	F. C. Barcelona (1500)	30.00 ☐
P2	*P2*	1000	1987	(F. C.) R. Madrid (1500)	30.00 ☐
P3	*P3*	1000	1987	Weeping Madonna (1500)	30.00 ☐
P4	*P4*	1000	1987	Expo 92 - Sevilla (1500)	30.00 ☐
P5	*P5*	1000	1987	Bull ring (1500)	30.00 ☐
P6	*P6*	1000	1987	Port scene (1500)	30.00 ☐

SRI LANKA (CEYLON)

Magnetic cards by Autelca were field tested in Sri Lanka (formally Ceylon) in 1986. The standard test card (as used in Kuwait, Nigeria, Thailand and Yugoslavia) was employed with the prefix R (for Rupies) before the black control number. Only one value was issued and the illustration is essentially the same as that shown for Nigeria or Kuwait.

№	Ill.	Units	Date	Description	Value
D1	–	Rs200	1986	Blue / white (5000)	40.00 ▢

SWEDEN

Swedish Telecom is currently conducting field trials of three different systems in different cities. It is expected that the use of smart cards will begin nationally in the summer of 1990. Optical cards are supplied by Landis and Gyr, Switzerland, for trials in 70 telephones in **Uppsala** (prefixed 'U' below). In **Stockholm** GPT cards are being tested in two military bases and a hospital ('ST' below). Japanese cards by Tamura are being tested in 15 telephones in a hospital in **Linköping** ('L' below). Swedish Telecom is not currently able to supply cards to collectors. In addition to the Swedish Telecom cards there are cards issued by the Swedish Railways (SJ) for use on their trains. These are bought in the buffet cars when the train is moving and no source for collectors outside Sweden has yet been discovered.

1 – UPPSALA (OPTICAL CARDS, Landis and Gyr)

Initially the cost was 10 Swedish Krona (SKr) for a 25 unit card and 30 SKr for a 90 unit card. These have now changed to 15 SKr and 40 SKr respectively. The minimum cost is one unit.

First Series.

№	Ill.	Units	Date	Description		Value	
U1	(U1)	25	11/81	Blue / silver (135,000)		20.00 ▢	7.50 ▢
U2	U1	90	11/81	·· ·· ·· (85,000)		35.00 ▢	10.00 ▢

Second Issue. Notched.

U3	(U1)	90	1989	Blue / silver (10,000)		20.00 ▢	4.50 ▢

UO – OFFICIAL/SERVICE CARDS

UO1	UO1	90	1981	Blue / silver (4256)		--- ▢	30.00 ▢

Note. No test cards have been produced especially for Sweden . Presumably the standard Landis and Gyr test cards are used.

2 – STOCKHOLM (MAGNETIC CARDS, GPT, UK)

Military cards

ST1	ST1	30	11/87	Multicolour (5000)		20.00 ▢
ST2	ST2	100	11/87	Multicolour (5000)		25.00 ▢

Hospital cards

№	Ill.	Units	Date	Description	Value
ST3	*ST3*	30	11/87	Multicolour (9000)	15.00 ☐
ST4	*ST4*	100	11/87	Multicolour (5000)	25.00 ☐

Note. The 30 and 100 unit cards cost 17 SKr and 50 SKr respectively and an initial fee of two units is charged making the minimum cost three units. There is no special service card.

L1

L2

3 - LINKÖPING (MAGNETIC CARDS, Tamura)

L1	*L1*	30	3/89	Multicolour (?000)	8.00 ☐
L2	*L2*	100	3/89	Multicolour (?000)	20.00 ☐

Note. Charges are as for Stockholm above.

RAILWAY TELEPHONE CARDS

Information on these interesting cards is far from complete. Their use apparantly began some time in 1985 and at least two different printers seem to have been involved in their manufacture. The listing below must be regarded as provisional and any further information would be welcomed.

SJ1

SJ2

SJ3 (reverse)

SJ4 (reverse)

SJ5 (reverse)

SJ01

First (?) Issue.

№	Ill.	Units	Date	Description	Value
SJ1	*(SJ1)*	SKr10	1985	Not known.	20.00 ☐
SJ2	*SJ1*	SKr20	1985	Brown, orange / cream. Reverse: Multiple 'InterCity'	25.00 ☐
SJ3	*(SJ1)*	SKr100	1985	Not known	20.00 ☐

Note. The existence of SJ1 and SJ3 is assumed from SJ2. The reverse of SJ2 is entirely covered with 'InterCity' as in the area above the magnetic strip on the front.

Second (?) Issue.

№	Ill.	Units	Date	Description	Value
SJ4	*(SJ2)*	SKr10	1987?	Pink, turquoise. Brown strip. Reverse as *SJ3*	15.00 ☐
SJ5	*(SJ2)*	SKr20	1987?	Not known. Reverse not known	20.00 ☐
SJ6	*SJ2*	SKr100	1987?	Green, blue. Brown strip. Reverse as *SJ4*	25.00 ☐

SWEDEN - SWITZERLAND

Third (?) Issue.

№	Ill.	Units	Date	Description	Value
SJ7	*(SJ2)*	SKr10	1988?	Pink, turquoise. Black strip. Reverse as *SJ5*	6.00 □
SJ8	*(SJ2)*	SKr20	1988?	Not known. Reverse not known	15.00 □
SJ9	*(SJ2)*	SKr100	1988?	(?) Green, blue. Black strip. Reverse not known	25.00 □

Note. SJ5, SJ8 and SJ9 are again assumed on the basis of cards known to exist. SJ7 to SJ9 were printed by Nässjö Tryckiert ab and the earlier cards by one or more other printers.

SJO - OFFICIAL CARD

SJO1	*SJO1*	SKr100	1985?	Black / white. Reverse: Multiple 'TJÄNSTE' at an angle	25.00 □

SWITZERLAND

Optical cards are manufactured by Landis and Gyr in Switzerland. The unit is 0.10 SFr.

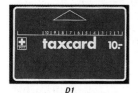
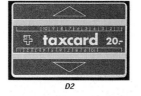

D1	D2	P1

D - DEFINITIVE CARDS

First Issue.

№	Ill.	Units	Date	Description	Value	
D1	*D1*	10 SFr	1/82	Red / silver (257,000)	20.00 □	15.00 □

Second Issue. 1.5mm white band. 20 SFr (200 units) card introduced to replace 100 unit card.

D2	*(D2)*	10 SFr	9/84	Red, white / silver (5000)	75.00 □	40.00 □
D3	*(D2)*	20 SFr	9/84	Red, white / silver (2000)	120.00 □	80.00 □

Note. D3 were special cards for internal field trials by the PTT and were not generally issued.

Third Issue. 2mm white band.

D4	*(D2)*	20 SFr	11/85	Red, white / silver (1,010,000)	20.00 □	4.00 □

Note. It is possible that 3.2mm and 4.5mm gap varieties analogous to those of France, Belgium and Austria exist but these have not been reported. 10,000 of the above were numbered C... in the old style and the rest were numbered as today - 6, two numbers, letter, five numbers.

Fourth Issue. 4mm white band.

D5	*D2*	20 SFr	8/86	Red, white / silver (????)	15.00 □	3.00 □

Fifth Issue. 3mm white band. Notched.

D6	*(D2)*	20 SFr	1988	Red, white / silver (37,000)	25.00 □	15.00 □

Note. D6 cards were thinner with grooves on the reverse and were for a field-trial.

Sixth Issue. 3mm white band. Notched.

D7	*(D2)*	10 SFr	1989	Red, white / silver (500,000)	25.00 □	5.00 □
D8	*(D2)*	20 SFr	1989	Red, white / silver (600,000)	10.00 □	2.00 □

Note. D7 and D8 have "PTT : Ihr Partner Tag für Tag" in four languages in the center section on the reverse.

Seventh Issue. 3mm white band. Notched.

D9   *(D2)*   20 SFr   1989?   Red, white / silver (?000)   25.00 ☐   5.00 ☐

Note.   D9 has text at top, center and bottom on the reverse: "Aufgebrauchte taxcard ..." ,
Prière de rendre ...." and "Consegnare p.f. le taxcard ...." respectively.

Eighth Issue. 3mm white band. Notched.

D10   *(D2)*   10 SFr   1988   Red, white / silver (100,000)   5.00 ☐   2.00 ☐

P – PRIVATE CARDS

This section includes those limited advertising issues which were not on general sale to the
public.

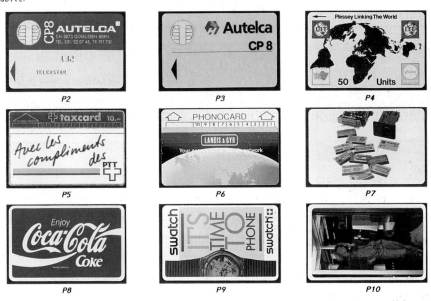

№	Ill.	Units	Date	Description		Value	
P1	*P1*	120	10/83	TELECOM '83, Blue / silver (?00) (L&G)	60.00 ☐	40.00 ☐	
P2	*P2*	Note 1	1984	BULL/AUTELCA CARD '84, Blue, gold / white (2000)		35.00 ☐	
P3	*P3*	Note 1	1985	BULL/AUTELCA CARD '85, Black, red / white (3000)		30.00 ☐	
P4	*P4*	50	10/87	PLESSEY LINKING THE WORLD, Multicoloured (?000)		40.00 ☐	
P5	*(P4)*	100	10/87	PLESSEY LINKING THE WORLD, Multicoloured (?000)		40.00 ☐	
P6	*(P4)*	500	10/87	PLESSEY LINKING THE WORLD, Multicoloured (?000)		40.00 ☐	
P7	*P5*	100	10/87	COMPLIMENTS des PTT 1, Multicolour (400,000)	15.00 ☐	6.00 ☐	
P8	*P6*	100	10/87	TELECOM '87, Multicolour (10,000)	20.00 ☐	15.00 ☐	

Note 1.   P2 and P3 above and also the Closed User Group Bull CP8/Autelca cards (G2 – G7) below,
had no fixed value. · Customers paid for as many units as they wanted and the cards were then
encoded at the place of sale. Customers could also, if they wished, buy further units on the
same card when the first lot had been used up.

Note 2.   P4-P6 have the Telecom '87 logo and dates (20-27.10.'87) on the reverse.

Note 3.   4000 each of two multicoloured 'cards' by Landis and Gyr advertising Sunways and Landis
and Gyr were issued in September, 1987, for promotional purposes but no optical strips were
incorporated so these have not been listed.

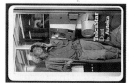
P11

P12

P13

P14

P15

P16

P17

P18

P19

P20

P21

P22

P23

P24

P25

№	Ill.	Date		Value	№	Ill.	Date		Value
P9	P7	(1987)	(1000)	35.00 □	P10	P8	(1987)	(1500)	30.00 □
P11	P9	(1987)	(1000)	35.00 □	P12	P10	(1987)	(1000)	35.00 □
P13	P11	(1987)	(800)	40.00 □	P14	P12	(1987)	(1000)	35.00 □
P15	P13	(1987)	(800)	40.00 □	P16	P14	(1987)	(1800)	30.00 □

Note. The eight magnetic cards (P9 - P16) by Autelca, Switzerland, were also used at TELECOM 87 in Geneva. They have also been used for demonstration purposes elsewhere.

№	Ill.		Date					Value
P17	P15	100	10/87	100 JAHRE TELEFON, Multicolour	(600)	100.00 □	75.00 □
P18	P16	100	9/88	NESTLÉ, Multicolour	(2000)	30.00 □	25.00 □
P19	P17	100	9/88	SANDOZ, Blue, yellow, silver	(500)	100.00 □	75.00 □
P20	P18	100	10/88	ALCATEL - STR, Black,red, white	(1500)	30.00 □	25.00 □
P21	P19	100	10/88	SARASIN BANK, Blue / white	(1000)	45.00 □	35.00 □
P22	P20	100	11/88	SODECO, Multicolour	(2000)	35.00 □	25.00 □
P23	P21	100	1/89	ASCOM, Black, white, red	(1000)	45.00 □	35.00 □
P24	P22	100	3/89	L&G - 100,000,000th	(3000)	30.00 □	25.00 □
P25	P23	100	4/89	EUROVISION '89, Black / silver	(1500)	50.00 □	40.00 □
P26	P24	100	4/89	FRANKE, Red, black, white	(3000)	30.00 □	25.00 □

Note. 1000 of P15 were delivered in 10/88 and a further 500 in 7/89. It may be possible to distinguish the two printings from the control numbers.

P26

P27

P28

P29

P30

P31

P32

P33

P34

P35

G1

G2

Nº	Ill.	Units	Date	Description	Value	
P27	*P25*	100	5/89	TELIC 1600 - STR, Multicolour (2000)	40.00 ☐	30.00 ☐
P28	*P26*	100	7/89	FRIBOURG, Multicolour (5000)	25.00 ☐	15.00 ☐
P29	*P27*	100	7/89	COMPLIMENTS PTT 2, Blue, white (6000)	20.00 ☐	15.00 ☐
P30	*P28*	100	8/89	METO-BAU, Blue, black, white (1500)	45.00 ☐	35.00 ☐
P31	*P29*	50	8/89	AEG, Black, white, red (2000)	35.00 ☐	25.00 ☐
P32	*P30*	50	9/89	L&G ENERGY MANAGEMENT, Blue, grey, white (3000)	25.00 ☐	20.00 ☐

Note. No cards were available to illustrate P17 and P21 above and Landis and Gyr's original artwork has been used.

Nº	Ill.	Units	Date	Description	Value	
P33	*P31*	10	9/89	COHEN-DUMANI, Black, white (10,000)	15.00 ☐	10.00 ☐
P34	*P32*	100	9/89	100 JAHRE - CHUR, Yellow, dark brown (1000)	50.00 ☐	40.00 ☐
P35	*P33*	100	9/89	IDEAL JOB, Green, black, white (2000)	35.00 ☐	25.00 ☐
P36	*P34*	20	10/89	MANPOWER, Black, red, white (5000)	20.00 ☐	15.00 ☐
P37	*P35*	100	10/89	TVIII, Black, white (100)	150.00 ☐	145.00 ☐
P38	-	100	11/89	TRIMEDIA, ????? (1200)	50.00 ☐	45.00 ☐

G - CLOSED USER GROUP CARDS

The electronic cards below were manufactured by Bull CP8 in France for Autelca, Switzerland. G2 - 6 were used at the last five annual meetings of the World Economic Forum at Davos.

G1	--	100	1981	PALAIS FEDERAL, ??????, (4255)	100.00 ☐
G2	*(G1)*	Note 2	1985	WORLD ECONOMIC FORUM, Blue / white (950)	60.00 ☐
G3	*(G1)*	··	1986	·· ·· ·· ·· ·· ·· ·· ·· ·· ·· (1100)	50.00 ☐
G4	*(G1)*	··	1987	·· ·· ·· ·· ·· ·· ·· ·· ·· ·· (1100)	50.00 ☐
G5	*G1*	··	1988	·· ·· ·· ·· ·· ·· ·· ·· ·· ·· (1100)	40.00 ☐
G6	*(G1)*	··	1989	·· ·· ·· ·· ·· ·· ·· ·· ·· ·· (1100?)	50.00 ☐

Crans Montana, (Downhill Skiing Event) Card for VIPs. 1987.

Nº	Ill.	Units	Date	Description	Value
G7	*G2*	Note 2	1987	CRANS MONTANA, Red, black, gold / white (1100)	700 ◻

Note 1.   G1 was for use in the Federal Government building.   No other details are known.

Note 2.   See Note 1 on page 161.

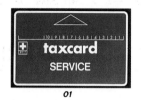
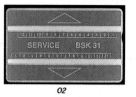
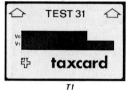

O1	*O2*	*T1*

O - OFFICIAL/SERVICE CARDS

O1	*O1*	(100)	1982	Red / silver	(4700)	--- ◻	45. 00 ◻
O2	*(O2)*	(240)	1985	Red, white / silver, 1.5mm white band (2009)		--- ◻	65. 00 ◻
O3	*(O2)*	(240)	1985	Red, white / silver, 2mm white band (15,000)		--- ◻	30. 00 ◻
O4	*(O2)*	(240)	1985	Red, white / silver, 4mm white band	(4000)	--- ◻	50. 00 ◻
O5	*(O2)*	(240)	1985	Red, white / silver, 3mm white band (12,000)		--- ◻	25. 00 ◻
O6	*(O2)*	(240)	1989	Grey, white / silver, 3mm white band (2088)		--- ◻	40. 00 ◻

T - TEST CARDS

T1	--	-	1982	Red / silver	(607)	--- ◻	100. 00 ◻
T2	*(T1)*	-	1986	Red / matt silver (800)		--- ◻	75. 00 ◻

Note.   The existance of T1, probably similar to T1 of Belgium, is assumed from the printing records.   No card being available, the illustration of T2 is taken from Landis and Gyr artwork.

TAIWAN

Optical cards were originally manufactured by Landis and Gyr in Switzerland but are now produced in Taiwan.   Over fifteen million cards have now been supplied.

D - DEFINITIVE CARDS

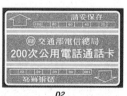
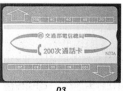

D1	*D2*	*D3*

First Issue

Nº	Ill.	Units	Date	Description	Value
D1	*D1*	100	6/84	Red / silver (175,000)	15. 00 ◻ 10. 00 ◻
D2	*(D1)*	200	6/84	Red / silver (5000)	40. 00 ◻ 25. 00 ◻

Second Issue.   2mm white band over optical strip.

D3	*(D2)*	100	3/86	Red, white / silver (3,601,750)	5. 00 ◻ 3. 00 ◻
D4	*D2*	200	3/86	Blue, white / silver (125,900)	20. 00 ◻ 8. 00 ◻

Third Issue.   4mm white band.

D5	*(D2)*	100	1/87	Red, white / silver (100,000)	4. 00 ◻ 2. 00 ◻

Fourth Issue.   3mm white band. No notch.

№	Ill.	Units	Date	Description	Value	
D6	*(D2)*	100	10/87	Red, white / silver (100,000)	4.00 ▯	2.00 ▯

Fifth Issue.   3mm white band. Notched.

| D7 | *(D2)* | 100 | 1988 | Red, white / silver (11,038,957) | 4.00 ▯ | 2.00 ▯ |
| D8 | *(D2)* | 200 | 10/87 | Blue, white / silver   (70,000) | 10.00 ▯ | 4.00 ▯ |

Note.   Of D7 some 4 million were made in Taiwan.   It is not known whether these can be distinguished from those made in Switzerland.

Sixth Issue.   New design.

D9	*D3*	200	7/88	Blue, white / silver, NTTA, (50,000)	12.00 ▯	5.00 ▯
D10	*(D3)*	200	7/88	Blue, white / silver, CTTA, (50,000)	12.00 ▯	5.00 ▯
D11	*(D3)*	200	9/89	Blue, white / silver, (70,000)	10.00 ▯	3.00 ▯

S - SPECIAL / COMMEMORATIVE CARDS

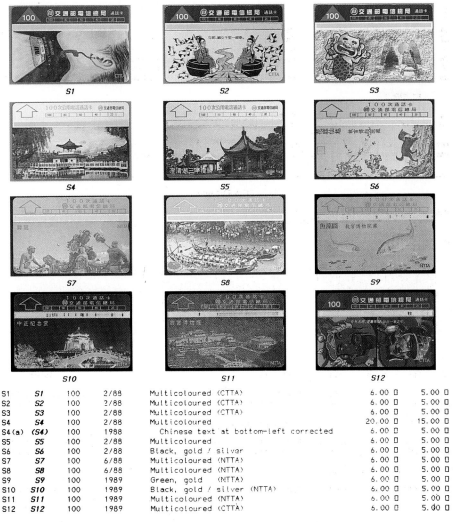

S1 S2 S3 S4 S5 S6 S7 S8 S9 S10 S11 S12

S1	*S1*	100	2/88	Multicoloured (CTTA)	6.00 ▯	5.00 ▯
S2	*S2*	100	2/88	Multicoloured (CTTA)	6.00 ▯	5.00 ▯
S3	*S3*	100	2/88	Multicoloured (CTTA)	6.00 ▯	5.00 ▯
S4	*S4*	100	2/88	Multicoloured	20.00 ▯	15.00 ▯
S4(a)	*(S4)*	100	1988	Chinese text at bottom-left corrected	6.00 ▯	5.00 ▯
S5	*S5*	100	2/88	Multicoloured	6.00 ▯	5.00 ▯
S6	*S6*	100	2/88	Black, gold / silver	6.00 ▯	5.00 ▯
S7	*S7*	100	6/88	Multicoloured (NTTA)	6.00 ▯	5.00 ▯
S8	*S8*	100	6/88	Multicoloured (NTTA)	6.00 ▯	5.00 ▯
S9	*S9*	100	1989	Green, gold (NTTA)	6.00 ▯	5.00 ▯
S10	*S10*	100	1989	Black, gold / silver (NTTA)	6.00 ▯	5.00 ▯
S11	*S11*	100	1989	Multicoloured (NTTA)	6.00 ▯	5.00 ▯
S12	*S12*	100	1989	Multicoloured (CTTA)	6.00 ▯	5.00 ▯

S13

№	Ill.	Units	Date	Description	Value	
S13	*S13*	100	1989	Multicoloured	6.00 ☐	5.00 ☐

Note. It was originally intended that there should be sixteen of this series but only the 13 above have been issued.

The Chinese Year Series

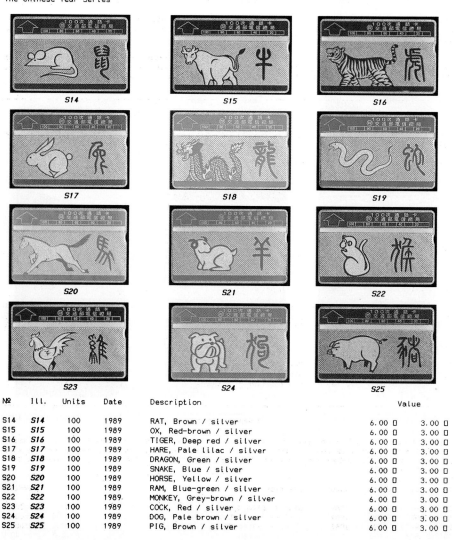

№	Ill.	Units	Date	Description	Value	
S14	*S14*	100	1989	RAT, Brown / silver	6.00 ☐	3.00 ☐
S15	*S15*	100	1989	OX, Red-brown / silver	6.00 ☐	3.00 ☐
S16	*S16*	100	1989	TIGER, Deep red / silver	6.00 ☐	3.00 ☐
S17	*S17*	100	1989	HARE, Pale lilac / silver	6.00 ☐	3.00 ☐
S18	*S18*	100	1989	DRAGON, Green / silver	6.00 ☐	3.00 ☐
S19	*S19*	100	1989	SNAKE, Blue / silver	6.00 ☐	3.00 ☐
S20	*S20*	100	1989	HORSE, Yellow / silver	6.00 ☐	3.00 ☐
S21	*S21*	100	1989	RAM, Blue-green / silver	6.00 ☐	3.00 ☐
S22	*S22*	100	1989	MONKEY, Grey-brown / silver	6.00 ☐	3.00 ☐
S23	*S23*	100	1989	COCK, Red / silver	6.00 ☐	3.00 ☐
S24	*S24*	100	1989	DOG, Pale brown / silver	6.00 ☐	3.00 ☐
S25	*S25*	100	1989	PIG, Brown / silver	6.00 ☐	3.00 ☐

O - OFFICIAL/SERVICE and T - TEST CARD

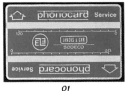

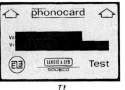

O1   T1

N°	Ill.	Units	Date	Description		Value	
O1	(O1)	240	1986	Blue, white / silver, 2mm white band	--- ☐	35.00 ☐	
O2	O1	240	1987	Blue, white / silver, 4mm white band	--- ☐	30.00 ☐	
O3	(O1)	240	1988	Blue, white / silver, 3mm white band	--- ☐	25.00 ☐	
T1	(T1)	-	1986	Blue / silver, (4575)	--- ☐	35.00 ☐	

Note. The illustration for T1 is taken from artwork kindly supplied by Landis and Gyr. Printings took place each year from 1986 to 1990 and it is not known whether all were of the same type.

The cards of Taiwan can be purchased at face value directly from: N.T.T.A. Pay Station Service Center, / 3F, No. 52, Sec 2, Jin Shan S. Rd. / Taipei, / TAIWAN, / R.O.C. 100 unit cards cost NT$100 which roughly equals US$3.70. Postage should be added.

TCHAD

Optical cards are supplied by Landis and Gyr, Switzerland. Only definitive cards have been issued.

First Series. 3mm white band. No notch.

D1

N°	Ill.	Units	Date	Description		Value	
D1	(D1)	30	5/88	Green / silver (6000)	8.00 ☐	5.00 ☐	
D2	(D1)	60	5/88	Blue / silver (5000)	12.00 ☐	8.00 ☐	
D3	D1	120	5/88	Red / silver (3000)	20.00 ☐	12.00 ☐	

Second Series. 3mm white band. Notched.

D4	(D1)	30	10/88	Green / silver (11,000)	5.00 ☐	4.00 ☐	
D5	(D1)	60	10/88	Blue / silver (26,000)	8.00 ☐	6.00 ☐	
D6	(D1)	120	10/88	Red / silver (10,000)	15.00 ☐	10.00 ☐	

THAILAND

Payphones using magnetic cards supplied by Autelca, Switzerland, were introduced in 1987. The cards are of the test card type used in Kuwait, Nigeria, Sri Lanka and Yugoslavia and can be distinguished only by their serial numbers which are of the type '0001-150' where the '150' is the value in Thai currency - the Baht.

N°	Ill.	Units	Date	Description	*	Value
D1	-	150	1987	Blue / white (1000)		50.00 ☐
D2	-	300	1987	.. .. .. (500)		75.00 ☐
D3	-	500	1987	.. .. .. (500)		75.00 ☐

TRINIDAD AND TOBAGO

Magnetic cards were originally supplied by Autelca, Switzerland, and were intended for international calls. Magnetic cards supplied by GPT (UK) are now being introduced.

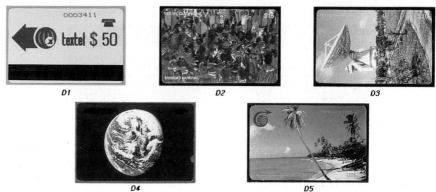

D1   D2   D3

D4   D5

First Issue. Magnetic cards by Autelca.

Nº	Ill.	Units	Date	Description	Value
D1	(D1)	$ 30	1987	Dark blue / pale blue (10,000 of which 2009 issued)	20.00 ☐
D2	D1	$ 50	1987	·· ·· ·· ·· ·· (7000 of which 3289 issued)	30.00 ☐

Second Issue. Magnetic Cards (Autelca)

| D3 | D2 | $15 | 1989 | CARNIVAL, Multicoloured (1450 issued) | 20.00 ☐ |
| D4 | D3 | $30 | 1989 | TEXTEL EARTH STATION, Multicoloured (1650 issued) | 30.00 ☐ |

Third Issue. Magnetic Card (GPT)

| D5 | D4 | $50 | 1989 | GLOBE, Multicolour (970 issued) | 35.00 ☐ |
| D6 | D5 | $2 | 1990 | Multicoloured (1000) | 20.00 ☐ |

Note. D6 is included in the Cable and Wireless collectors pack of British West Indies cards (see under Promotional Cards at the end of this book).

TUNISIA

Optical cards, manufactured by Landis and Gyr, Switzerland, were field tested in Tunisia. Only definitive and service cards exist. Service cards identical to that listed and illustrated for Algeria have also been used.

D - DEFINITIVE CARDS

D1   O1

Nº	Ill.	Units	Date	Description	Value	
D1	(D1)	10	1986	Red / silver (1000)	75.00 ☐	50.00 ☐
D2	D1	20	3/83	·· ·· ·· (179,200)	20.00 ☐	15.00 ☐
D3	(D1)	50	1984	·· ·· ·· (90,600)	25.00 ☐	15.00 ☐

O - OFFICIAL / SERVICE CARD

| O1 | (O1) | 120 | 1983 | Red, white / silver (400) | --- ☐ | 25.00 ☐ |

Note. The illustration above is of a sample and lacks the white strip.

Optical cards are manufactured by Landis and Gyr in Switzerland. Only definitive cards have been issued although some have advertising on the reverse. The unit equates to 75 TL.

D - DEFINITIVE CARDS

D1   D2

First Issue.   2mm white band.   No notch.

№	Ill.	Units	Date	Description		Value	
D1	(D1)	120	1986	Metallic yellow, white / silver (600,000)		25.00 ☐	12.00 ☐

Second Issue.   4mm white band.   No notch.

| D2 | D1 | 120 | 1/87 | Metallic yellow, white / silver (600,000) | | 15.00 ☐ | 8.00 ☐ |

Third Issue.   3mm white band.   No notch.

| D3 | (D1) | 20 | 1988 | Metallic yellow, white / silver (500,000) | | 5.00 ☐ | 2.00 ☐ |
| D4 | (D1) | 30 | 1988 | .. .. (768,000) | | 6.00 ☐ | 3.00 ☐ |

Note. Both D3 and D4 have an advertisement for "T.C.ZIRAAT BANKASI" in pale green on the reverse.

Fourth Issue.   3mm white band.   Notched.

D5	(D1)	30	1988	Metallic yellow, white / silver		6.00 ☐	4.00 ☐
D6	(D1)	30	1988	.. Advert. as for D3-4 but on matt reverse		6.00 ☐	4.00 ☐
D7	(D1)	30	1988	Metallic yellow, white / silver		6.00 ☐	4.00 ☐

Fifth Issue.   Design changed to omit 'KONTÖR ATIŞI'.   3mm white band.   Notched.

D8	D2	30	1989	Metallic green, white / silver (782,000)		3.00 ☐	1.00 ☐
D8(a)				r. TC. ZIRAAT BANKASI in yellow (300,000)		4.00 ☐	2.00 ☐
D9	(D2)	60	1989	Metallic blue, white / silver (1,250,000)		4.00 ☐	2.00 ☐
D9(a)				r. TC. ZIRAAT BANKASI in yellow (200,000)		5.00 ☐	2.00 ☐
D10	(D2)	120	1989	Metallic yellow, white / silver (750,000)		10.00 ☐	4.00 ☐

Note. The advertising for TC.ZIRAAT BANKASI on the reverse of D8(a) and D9(a) is in yellow and differs from that on D3, 4 and 6 in that it has "ZIRAAT'siz bir Türkiye düsünülemez." across the top.

O - OFFICIAL/SERVICE CARDS

The general Landis and Gyr types of service and test cards with the number '12' in the arrows are in use.

TURKS AND CAICOS ISLANDS

Magnetic cards are supplied by Autelca, Switzerland, to Cable and Wireless for use on the Turks and Caicos Islands in the West Indies. The upper values are intended primarily for international calls. The 50c card (not 5c as in the 1988-9 edition) was used mainly as a complimentary and is no longer available. Control numbers are in black.

D1

№	Ill.	Units	Date	Description	Value
D1	(D1)	50c	1987	Gold, blue / white (12,000)	20.00 ☐
D2	D1	$10	1987	Red, blue / white (15,000)	20.00 ☐
D3	(D1)	$20	1987	Green, blue / white (20,000)	20.00 ☐

UNITED ARAB EMIRATES

Over 5,000,000 magnetic cards have been supplied to ETISALAT by Tamura of Japan. There would seem to have been only one series so far but each value exists in four varieties.

D1

D2

D3

D4

№	Ill.	Units	Date	Description	Value	
D1	D1	30	1988?	Green, black, orange / white (wording "News....")	4.00 ☐	3.00 ☐
D2	D2	30	1988?	·· ·· ·· ·· ·· ·· (wording "Phone home....")	4.00 ☐	3.00 ☐
D3	(D3)	30	1988?	·· ·· ·· ·· ·· ·· (wording "No matter....")	4.00 ☐	3.00 ☐
D4	(D4)	30	1988?	·· ·· ·· ·· ·· .. (wording "Now you can...")	4.00 ☐	3.00 ☐
D5	(D1)	60	1988?	Green, black, pink / white (wording "News....")	6.00 ☐	4.00 ☐
D6	(D2)	60	1988?	·· ·· ·· ·· ·· (wording "Phone home....")	6.00 ☐	4.00 ☐
D7	D3	60	1988?	·· ·· ·· ·· ·· (wording "No matter....")	6.00 ☐	4.00 ☐
D8	(D4)	60	1988?	·· ·· ·· ·· ·· (wording "Now you can....")	6.00 ☐	4.00 ☐
D9	(D1)	90	1988?	Green, black, blue? / white (wording "News....")	9.00 ☐	6.00 ☐
D10	(D2)	90	1988?	·· ·· ·· ·· ·· ··(wording "Phone home....")	9.00 ☐	6.00 ☐
D11	(D3)	90	1988?	·· ·· ·· ·· ·· ·· (wording "No matter....")	9.00 ☐	6.00 ☐
D12	(D4)	90	1988?	·· ·· ·· ·· ·· .. (wording "Now you can...")	9.00 ☐	6.00 ☐
D13	(D1)	120	1988?	Green, black, pale green/white (wording "News...")	12.00 ☐	8.00 ☐
D14	(D2)	120	1988?	·· ·· ·· ·· ·· ·· (wording "Phone home....")	12.00 ☐	8.00 ☐
D15	(D3)	120	1988?	·· ·· ·· ·· ·· (wording "No matter....")	12.00 ☐	8.00 ☐
D16	D4	120	1988?	·· ·· ·· ·· ·· ·· (wording "Now you can....")	12.00 ☐	8.00 ☐

Note. All cards have the ETISALAT logo in pale green in the center of the lower part of the design.

The general use of prepaid telephone cards has not yet been adopted in the USA but optical cards manufactured by Landis and Gyr in Switzerland have been used for long distance service on some military bases in the USA and optical cards have also been supplied to Michigan Bell, a regional US telephone company, and for use in a prison in North Carolina. A Landis and Gyr card was also issued for an exhibition in Washington, D.C., in 1985 and for another in Michigan in 1988. Trials of the GPT magnetic card system are planned for federal prisons and GPT promotional cards have been used at exhibitions in the USA. Also listed under the USA are the Communications Satellite Corporation (COMSAT) cards for use on ships through Inmarsat since the head offices of COMSAT are in Washington, DC, although the cards may, of course, be bought wherever the ships using the system happen to be.

1 MICHIGAN BELL CARDS

Optical cards supplied by Landis and Gyr, Switzerland. Only definitive cards were issued for use on on the State University campus. Use of these cards has now ceased. The unit is 5 cents on the lower (blue) values for local use and 20 cents on the yellow, high value, international call cards.

D1   D2

№	Ill.	Units	Date	Description						Value		
D1	(D1)	$0.40	1987	Blue, white/silver, 4mm band. Not notched					(10,000)	50.00 ▢	40.00 ▢
D1(a)	(D1)	$0.40	1988	·· ·· ·· ·· ·· 3mm band. Notched					(20,000)	25.00 ▢	25.00 ▢
D2	(D1)	$2	1987	·· ·· ·· ·· ·· 4mm band. Not notched					(5000)	20.00 ▢	15.00 ▢
D2(a)	(D1)	$2	1987	·· ·· ·· ·· ·· 3mm band. Not notched					(500)	75.00 ▢	50.00 ▢
D3	D1	$5	1987	·· ·· ·· ·· ·· 4mm band. Not notched					(10,000)	25.00 ▢	15.00 ▢
D4	(D2)	$10	1987	·· ·· ·· ·· ·· 4mm band. Not notched					(10,000)	30.00 ▢	20.00 ▢
D5	(D1)	$20	1987	Yellow, white/silver, 3mm band. Not notched					(2500)	40.00 ▢	30.00 ▢
D6	D2	$40	1987	·· ·· ·· ·· ·· ·· ·· ·· ·· ·· ··					(2500)	50.00 ▢	35.00 ▢

Note. The standard general L&G service card with the number '5' in the arrows was used.

2 MILITARY COMMUNICATIONS CENTER CARDS

These optical cards are produced by Landis and Gyr, Switzerland. They are 200 unit cards.

M1   M2

M1	M1	$20	9/86	Blue, white / silver. 2mm band. (5000)	35.00 ▢	30.00 ▢
M2	(M1)	$20	4/88	Blue, white / silver. 3mm band. (135,000)	25.00 ▢	20.00 ▢
M3	M2	$20	7/88	Blue, white / silver. 3mm band. Notched.	20.00 ▢	15.00 ▢

Note. There were 135,000 of M2 and M3 together. It is not known how many of each were issued.

3. PRISON CARDS

These cards are manufactured by Landis and Gyr, Switzerland, for use in the canteen at Manning Prison in Columbia, South Carolina.

J1

First Issue. 3mm white band. Notched.

№	Ill.	Units	Date	Description	Value	
J1	*(J1)*	$5	4/89	Carmine / silver (20,000)	10.00 ☐	6.00 ☐

Second Issue. 3mm white band. Notched.

№	Ill.	Units	Date	Description	Value	
J2	*(J1)*	$5	1989	Green / silver (30,000)	10.00 ☐	5.00 ☐
J3	*J1*	$10	1989	Carmine / silver (10,000)	20.00 ☐	12.00 ☐

4. COMSAT CARDS

These cards are for use on ships by way of INMARSAT. Coverage currently includes the Atlantic and Pacific areas although it is hoped to provide world-wide coverage before long. The electronic or smart cards, manufactured by Schlumberger Industries at Chesapeake in the USA, are denominated in both units and in minutes of satellite time. The unit is six seconds and each minute costs $10. A new three minute card has been introduced and the 5 minute card is being phased out to be replaced by a 6 minute card.

First Issue (0189 on reverse)

COM1

COM1	*(COM1)*	5 min.	1/89	Green, gold, silver, dk.brown, white / blue (?000)	33.00 ☐
COM2	*(COM1)*	10 min.	1/89	Green, gold, silver, dk.brown, white / blue (?000)	65.00 ☐
COM3	*(COM1)*	15 min.	1/89	Green, gold, silver, dk.brown, white / blue (?000)	100.00 ☐

Second Issue (0989 on reverse - Schlumberger contact type IVd with white rim)

COM4	*(COM1)*	3 min.	9/89	Green, gold, silver, dk.brown, white / blue (?000)	20.00 ☐
COM5	*(COM1)*	6 min.	9/89	Green, gold, silver, dk.brown, white / blue (?000)	40.00 ☐
COM6	*(COM1)*	10 min.	9/89	Green, gold, silver, dk.brown, white / blue (?000)	65.00 ☐
COM7	*COM1*	15 min.	9/89	Green, gold, silver, dk.brown, white / blue (?000)	100.00 ☐

Note. The first issue has Schlumberger type VI contacts on a uniform dark background with the (slightly darker) blue of the cards right up to the contact. The second issue has the contact against a dark hatched background (called TI for Texas Instruments in France) and is inset to give a thin white line round it. The above values are those of unused cards. No used cards are known to have come onto the market so far but prices of a little less than half of these might be reasonable.

5 PROMOTIONAL AND EXHIBITION CARDS

P1

P2

P3

P4	P5	P6

P7	P8

Landis and Gyr, Switzerland.

№	Ill.	Units	Date	Description	Value	
P1	*P1*	120	15/4/85	INTELEXPO 85. Pale blue / silver	50.00 ☐	30.00 ☐
P2	*P2*	$10	2/87	LANDIS & GYR. Pale blue / silver	50.00 ☐	30.00 ☐

GPT, UK.

P3	*P3*	1000	6/87	Multicolour (1500)		35.00 ☐
P4	*P4*	1000	6/87	Multicolour (1500)		35.00 ☐
P5	*P5*	1000	6/87	Red, grey / white (1500)		35.00 ☐
P6	*P6*	$5	7/87	PLANET EARTH, Multicolour (750)		50.00 ☐
P7	*(P6)*	$10	7/87	PLANET EARTH, Multicolour (1000)		45.00 ☐
P8	*(P6)*	$20	7/87	PLANET EARTH, Multicolour (2000)		35.00 ☐
P9	*(P6)*	$25	7/87	PLANET EARTH, Multicolour (750)		50.00 ☐
P10	*(P6)*	$50	7/87	PLANET EARTH, Multicolour (500)		60.00 ☐
P11	*P7*	$10	20/6/88	STROMBERG CARLSON, Multicolour (9900)		20.00 ☐
P12	*(P7)*	$10	20/6/88	As P11 with Stouffer Waverley Hotel on reverse (1000)		75.00 ☐

Note. The magnetic cards, P3 to P5, were issued by GPT, UK, and were first used in Atlanta in the USA. They have been used for demonstration purposes in other countries since then. The Planet Earth cards were used for general promotional purposes in the USA in July, 1987 and the two Stromberg Carlson cards were used at PACE '88 in Atlanta, Georgia, 20-23 June, 1988.

Landis and Gyr, Switzerland.

P13	*P8*	$2	1988?	STRATEGIC DIRECTIONS. Blue, black, white	50.00 ☐	40.00 ☐

URUGUAY

Magnetic cards are supplied to the Administracion Nacinal de Telecomunicaciones (ANTEL) by Tamura, Japan. There appears to have been only one series.

First Issue.

D1	D2

D3

D4

Nº	Ill.	Units	Date	Description	Value
D1	*D1*	100	2/88	ESTACION TERRENA MANGA, Multicoloured	4.00 ☐
D2	*D2*	200	2/88	MONUMENTO LA CARRETA, Multicoloured	7.00 ☐
D3	*D3*	300	2/88	FORTALEZA - MONTEVIDEO, Multicoloured	10.00 ☐
D4	*D4*	500	2/88	BALNEARIO PUNTA DEL ESTE, Multicoloured	15.00 ☐

VENEZEULA

Some 4,000,000 cards have been supplied by Tamura, Japan, for use in Venezuela. It is understood that the two lower values have been devalued by inflation and are no longer on sale. Other reports suggest that only the top value is available or that no cards are on sale any longer. There appears to have been only one set issued.

D1

D2

D3

D4

D5

Nº	Ill.	Units	Date	Description	Value
D1	*D1*	20	1987	PICO BOLIVAR, Multicoloured	10.00 ☐
D2	*D2*	50	1987	PARQUE CENTRAL, CARACAS, Multicoloured	10.00 ☐
D3	*D3*	100	1987	SALTO ANGEL, Multicoloured	12.00 ☐
D4	*D4*	200	1987	LAGUNA DE SINAMAICA, Multicoloured	12.00 ☐
D5	*D5*	400	1987	PLAYA CHORONI, Multicoloured	15.00 ☐

YEMEN ARAB REPUBLIC

Magnetic cards are supplied by Autelca of Switzerland to Cable and Wireless PLC for use in the Yemen Arab Republic. Only definitive cards exist. Control numbers are in black.

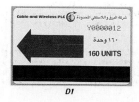
D1